ON BEING AND HAVING A MOTHER

ON BEING AND HAVING A MOTHER

ERNA FURMAN

INTERNATIONAL UNIVERSITIES PRESS
Madison   Connecticut

Copyright © 2001, International Universities Press, Inc.

INTERNATIONAL UNIVERSITIES PRESS ® and IUP (& design) ® are registered trademarks of International Universities Press, Inc.

All rights reserved. No part of this book may be printed or reproduced or utilized in any form or by any electronic, mechanical or other means, now known or hereafter invented, including photocopying and recording, or in any information storage or retrieval system, without permission in writing from the publisher.

Library of Congress Cataloging-in-Publication Data

Furman, Erna.
   On being and having a mother / Erna Furman.
     p. cm.
   Includes bibliographical references and index.
   ISBN 0-8236-3732-8
     1. Motherhood—Psychological aspects. 2. Mothers—Psychology. 3. Mother and child. 4. Developmental psychology. I. Title

HQ759.F86 2001
306.874'3—dc21

2001039895

Manufactured in the United States of America

Contents

Introduction	vii
Acknowledgments	xiii
1. *Anna Karenina:* A Book on Mothers	1
2. Parenthood as a Developmental Phase	21
3. The Death of a Newborn: Assistance to Parents	29
4. Mothers Have to Be There to Be Left	39
5. Self-Care and the Mother–Child Relationship	51
6. Early Aspects of Mothering: What Makes It So Hard to Be There to Be Left	67
7. Helen, Andy, and Their Mothers	83
8. Early Steps in the Development of Gender	89
9. Mothers, Toddlers, and Care	99
10. On Trauma: When Is the Death of a Parent Traumatic?	123
11. Parenting the Hospitalized Child: Consulting with Child Life Workers	141

12. Children of Divorce 155

13. Some Effects of the One-Parent Family on
    Personality Development 173
        Erna Furman and Robert A. Furman, M.D.

14. On Motherhood 201

Afterword 219
References 221
Name Index 231
Subject Index 233

Introduction

Colleagues, friends, and parents I have worked with have often asked me to bring together my various papers on parenting, and especially on mothers and mothering, because some that were published are not readily available and a number never appeared in print. Their requests were one reason for the present volume on this topic. Another reason was my own need to integrate my thinking and feeling by reaching back to its professional beginning, almost forty years ago, by following in my own footsteps, and assessing how far I have been able to come in my understanding. Grandmothering has given it an added perspective, a time for taking stock along the path of motherhood with its ever-changing tasks, its satisfactions, and its hardships.

The idea that parenthood is not something that automatically happens when we have children but, like other phases in life, presents us with specific developmental tasks to engage in and master more or less successfully, has, no doubt, long since come to the minds of many a father or mother. Artists too have known and used it as a creative theme, which is why Tolstoy's *Anna Karenina* became the subject of chapter 1 of this book. But for me, the concept of parenthood as a developmental phase (chapter 2) was a milestone in my thinking, a new level of awareness and understanding. It first appeared in print included in the chapter on "Treatment via the Mother" in *The Therapeutic Nursery School* (R. A. Furman and A. Katan, 1969) and became the indispensable basis for my later explorations of the many facets of parenting, mothering, and fathering (E. Furman, 1969a). It still serves me well, although I have come to understand it more deeply and clearly over the years, and refined it in later expositions. It therefore seemed appropriate to include some pertinent excerpts from the original chapter.

The professional context in which this work took shape was important then and throughout all the subsequent years. It served as the base for most of my clinical data with children and families from the most varied backgrounds, and afforded me the opportunity to discuss and compare my experiences with highly skilled colleagues at regular twice weekly staff meetings year in and year out. This unique setting is the Hanna Perkins Center in Cleveland, Ohio. It encompasses three parts: the first is the Hanna Perkins Therapeutic School, in operation since 1951, for children aged 15 months to 7 years; the second is the Cleveland Center for Research in Child Development (CCRCD) which administers the child analytic treatment clinic for children up to 18 years as well as a training course in child analysis, ongoing research studies, internships, and postdoctoral fellowships. The third is the Extension Service for teaching and consulting with educators, childcare workers, and mental health professionals.

In the School's Toddler Group, Nursery School, and Kindergarten the parents are essential participants in helping their children's growth. When treatment via the parents is the chosen form of intervention they are part of a close-knit team with the child's teacher and a child analyst whom they see in weekly consultation hours. When a child needs an analysis, he is seen five times weekly by a child analyst who also meets with his parents on a weekly basis, at least to start with. Among our school-aged and adolescent patients there are also many who are treated in once or twice weekly psychotherapies.

A special advantage of our Center is that all these services are provided on such a liberal sliding fee scale that no form of treatment or consultation or teaching has ever been refused or terminated for monetary reasons. This makes long-term work and follow-up possible with children and their families as well as with the centers and professional groups with whom we consult. Many of the latter have worked with us for almost fifty years, even as new ones start all the time.

Introduction

The chapters in this book have drawn on all I have learned with and through the work of the Hanna Perkins Center. They combine data, insight, and understanding gained from the experiences in the School, from the treatment of patients in the analytic clinic, and from consultations with professionals, just as happens in daily work. I am deeply thankful to my colleagues, coworkers, students, child patients, and their families for all they have helped me learn.

Although I had formulated, at the very start, the ways in which a father's and mother's investment of their child are alike and how they differ, it was not until I worked closely with mothers who had lost a newborn that I came to appreciate fully the specific *bodily* maternal investment, the fact that the baby really *is* experienced as a part of her own body and its loss represents an amputation. Helping these mothers cope with their distress (chapter 3, "The Death of a Newborn: Assistance to Parents") enabled me, in time, better to understand mothers' responses to the developmental losses of their child, the growing up and away steps he takes, which she needs to support and facilitate. This ongoing and never ending process is, so to speak, the daily bread and butter of mothering, earned over and over the hard way, balancing gains and losses in a bittersweet mixture. "Mothers Have to Be There to Be Left" (chapter 4), "Self-Care and the Mother–Child Relationship" (chapter 5), and "Early Aspects of Mothering" (chapter 6) address the nature and origins of these maternal experiences, the ways in which mothers cope and how it affects their children. The special focus in these chapters is on the mutually crucial process in the mother–child relationship during the child's earliest developmentally self-initiated steps toward becoming a person in his own right, including weaning and other areas of acquiring bodily self-care. However, there are also examples from much later, and more subtle milestones in the mother–child relationship and this theme is taken up again in chapter 7, "Helen, Andy and Their Mothers." There, a young girl's and boy's commonplace pieces of behavior during their kindergarten year describe the nonverbal communication between mothers and children and the ways in which they, like many of us, hark back to earlier levels of relating during which the self–other boundaries were still fluid.

Problems other than ordinary developmental ones are also a part of parenting. They afflicted many of the families I worked with and were often the topic of discussion with caregivers and other professionals. Separations between mother and child, especially those caused by the increasing use of day-care facilities for the very young, were of widespread concern. It was important to realize that it was the concern that was new rather than the practice of separation. Mothers, by which I mean the person who has invested the child in a maternal way and not necessarily the biological parent, have always had periods of separation from their children, either because they went to work outside the home, or because they attended to family or social duties, or were ill, or perhaps could not tolerate the enormous stress of continuous childcare. After all, even "at home" mothers are not always available to their child, physically or emotionally. The effects of these separations and of substitute care by family members, servants, or professional caregivers became an area of close study for us. We were able to single out some of the stresses and hazards as well as ways to mitigate them ("Mothers, Toddlers and Care," chapter 9).

The death of a parent poses a permanent and devastating change in the parent–child relationship, leaving the surviving parent or parent substitute to deal with much more than the trials of ordinary parenting as he or she takes on the additional role of primary helper of the bereaved child's wounded psyche. Working with the bereaved helped us to understand the process of mourning and to pinpoint helpful interventions and educational measures at a time when the emotional impact of parental bereavement was not yet appreciated (E. Furman, 1974). But later, when it was often singled out as *the* trauma of childhood, we could share our findings that even these tragedies are not always overwhelming and ways can be found to mitigate the stress ("On Trauma: When Is the Death of a Parent Traumatic?" chapter 10), just as there are ways of helping bereaved parents, as was mentioned above in describing chapter 3, "The Death of a Newborn: Assistance to Parents."

Illness, even if not fatal but requiring hospitalization, is a common cause of parent–child separation at a time when the children need their parents more than ever. Yet well-meaning professionals tend to keep mothers from actively caring for their children and parents acquiesce and stand by helplessly. Helping the parents and staff to cooperate effectively in the child's care is the province of the Child Life workers with whom I have consulted for many years. It is an area where helping professionals to help the parents can make a big difference (chapter 11, "Parenting the Hospitalized Child: Consulting with Child Life Workers").

Separation through divorce is another frequent cause of upheaval and concern, all the harder because the parents themselves bring it about. Individual parents' and children's experiences vary enormously but always have an impact on the child, the parents, and the parent–child relationships. Our work with many such stricken families has ultimately yielded positive results. The road is not easy, but there are specific ways in which parents can help their children and even themselves to come to terms with the situation and make the best of it (chapter 12, "Children of Divorce").

It has been our experience that single parents and their children, be it through bereavement, divorce, or by choice, contend with a variety of special hardships, although this does not imply that families with both parents are free of troubles. Chapter 13, "Some Effects of the One-Parent Family on Personality Development," describes the clinical experiences which alerted us to the inherent long-term risks for the child and the special problems for the single parent in keeping in tune with the child. Their relationship can be optimally positive and satisfying when the real voids and stresses are acknowledged and discussed truthfully. All difficulties, big and small and caused by separations or otherwise, are always better managed when they are recognized and faced, and when the pained feelings can be shared by parent and child, even though we cannot take away the feelings or change the realities that cause them.

Much of my work as a child psychoanalyst consists of feeling with others and participating in their struggle to understand themselves and master the inner and outer hurdles in their lives. I have grown myself as I have helped them to find ways of coping. I have become able to reach and conceptualize earlier levels of experience, which constitute the primitive basis of motherhood, the female body ego with its vulnerable, flexible, and penetrable boundaries. Chapter 8, "Early Steps in the Development of Gender" and the final chapter, "On Motherhood" describe these aspects of motherhood. They are gratifying and threatening to the mother as well as to others. They also have a profound impact on the growing boy's and girl's attempts to differentiate themselves from the mother in bodily terms and to delineate their own sex-specific ego. The nature and outcome of this difficult process has a significant effect on women's and men's attitudes to motherhood, which often remain conflicted and defensive throughout life. There is much left to study and understand in this field.

Erna Furman

Acknowledgements

Chapter 2. "Parenthood as a Developmental Phase" contains several sections from "Treatment via the Mother" by Erna Furman, in *The Therapeutic Nursery School*, editors R. A. Furman and A. Katan. New York: International Universities Press, 1969, pp. 64–123. The pages reproduced here with the permission of International Universities Press are 66, 67–70, 71–72, 74, 76.

Chapter 3. "The Death of a Newborn: Assistance to Parents" was previously published in *The Child in His Family: Preventive Child Psychiatry in an Age of Transitions*, edited by E. J. Anthony, C. Koupernik, and C. Chiland, Vol. 6, 1980, pp. 497–506. New York: John Wiley & Sons, copyright 1980, John Wiley & Sons, Inc. It is reprinted here by permission of John Wiley & Sons.

Chapter 4. "Mothers Have to Be There to Be Left" was originally published in *The Psychoanalytic Study of the Child*, 37:15–28. New Haven, CT: Yale University Press, 1982, and is reprinted here with the permission of Yale University Press.

Chapter 5. "Self-Care and the Mother–Child Relationship" was originally published in *Toddlers and Their Mothers* by Erna Furman. Madison, CT: International Universities Press, 1992, pp. 111–130. It was also published in *Toddlers and Their Mothers: Abridged Version for Parents and Educators* by Erna Furman. Madison, CT: International Universities Press, 1993, pp. 51–67, and is included here by permission of International Universities Press.

Chapter 6. "Early Aspects of Mothering: What Makes It So Hard to Be There to Be Left" was previously published in *Journal of Child Psychotherapy,* 20(2):149–164, 1994, and is included here by permission of the publishers.

Chapter 9. "Mothers, Toddlers, and Care" was most recently published in *Preschoolers: Questions and Answers,* by Erna Furman. Madison, CT: International Universities Press, 1995, pp. 85–105. It is included here by permission of International Universities Press.

Chapter 10. "On Trauma: When Is the Death of a Parent Traumatic?" was originally published in *The Psychoanalytic Study of the Child,* 41:191–208. New Haven, CT: Yale University Press, 1986. It is included here with the permission of Yale University Press.

Chapter 11. "Parenting the Hospitalized Child: Consulting with Child Life Workers" was originally published in *Child Analysis,* 7:88–112, 1996. Pages 94–112 are reprinted here by agreement with the editors of *Child Analysis,* 2084, Cornell Road, Cleveland, OH 44106.

Chapter 12. "Children of Divorce" was originally published in *Child Analysis,* 2:43–60, 1991, and is reprinted here by agreement with the editors of *Child Analysis,* 2084, Cornell Road, Cleveland, OH 44106.

Chapter 13. "Some Effects of the One-Parent Family on Personality Development" by Erna Furman and Robert A. Furman was originally published in *The Problem of Loss and Mourning: Psychoanalytic Perspectives,* edited by D. R. Dietrich and P. C. Shabad. Madison, CT: International Universities Press, 1989, pp. 129–157. It is included here by permission of International Universities Press.

Chapter 14. "On Motherhood" was originally published in the *Journal of the American Psychoanalytic Association, Supplement, The Psychology of Women*, 44:429–447, edited by A. D. Richards and P. Tyson. Madison, CT: International Universities Press, 1996. It is included here by permission of International Universities Press.

1

Anna Karenina: A Book on Mothers

A work of art may be judged great for many reasons. One of these is its ability to reveal many aspects of humanity in such a way that its readers can accept them, understand them, and understand themselves better through them. The more aspects a work of art offers us, the more opportunity we have to select what we can respond to. *Anna Karenina* is such a great work of art. In choosing to focus on its deeply revealing portrayal of mothers and mothering, I meet it with my own interest. It is perhaps not the topic most frequently selected by readers, but I am sure that many share my predilection, not least because the artist emphasizes it so strongly and reveals so much.

We get to know three mothers: Anna Karenina herself, Dolly Oblonsky, Anna's sister-in-law, and Kitty, younger sister of Dolly. Dolly and Kitty, especially, maintain close relationships with their parents. Anna is described as "brought up by an aunt" (Tolstoy, 1876, p. 791)[1] of whom she thinks only once as a potential but immediately dismissed haven, just prior to suiciding; there is no mention of her mother or father.

Leo (Lev Nikolayevich) Tolstoy first published *Anna Karenina* in 1876. The translation used here is by Joel Carmichael, published by Bantam Books, New York, 1960.

ANNA'S RELATIONSHIP WITH HER SON

Tolstoy introduces Anna as she arrives in Moscow by train where her elderly travel companion, Countess Vronsky, introduces Anna to her own son in these words, "Anna has a little son, eight years old, I think.... She's never been separated from him and keeps worrying about having left him" (p. 66). Anna's mission in Moscow is to save her brother's family life by persuading her sister-in-law Dolly to forgive him his philandering, which had recently produced a crisis in the form of a no longer deniable affair with their children's governess. Anna is welcomed by all, but especially by the Oblonsky children who rush to her like bees to honey and in whose affection she basks. Tanya, her favorite, is about the age of her son Seryozha—the diminutive she always uses in lieu of his given name Sergei—but, Anna notes, is somewhat more advanced in her studies and skills. However, Anna's success in patching up Dolly's marriage and the children's adoration did not fill her empty inner space. In the midst of an evening family get-together, "taking advantage of the first pretext that came up," she went to get her photo album for them. "Toward ten o'clock, when she usually said good night to her son and often tucked him in bed herself before going to a ball, she had grown sad at being so far away from him; and no matter what was being talked about her thoughts kept returning to her curly-headed Seryozha. She longed to look at his picture and talk about him" (p. 79). At that moment, strangely late in the evening, Count Vronsky called briefly, also on a pretext. Kitty thought his real purpose was herself, in keeping with their developing relationship, which she anticipated soon would culminate in a marriage proposal. Anna, however, sensed that Vronsky was calling on her, continuing their initial, brief encounter at the railway station.

The link is now clearly made between Anna's unmet need for physical closeness with her child during their separation and her barely preconscious attracting of a potential lover's admiring attention. The stage is set for exploring Anna's narcissistic needs and her efforts to meet them via her relationships with her children and with men. In this way, we can begin to understand the depth of depletion she experiences when these external supplies fail her, and that her reserves of love and self-love ultimately prove inadequate to taming the overwhelming tide of her own aggression.

By the time she concludes her visit in Moscow, she has guiltily but irresistibly enthralled Vronsky and permanently disrupted his relationship with Kitty. Perceptively, the children "were completely unconcerned by her departure," perhaps feeling "that Anna was not the same that day as she had been when they had fallen so much in love with her, and that she no longer took an interest in them" (p. 102).

Returning to Petersburg, her home, Anna is newly aware of finding her welcoming husband unattractive and her relationship with him cold and hypocritical. She greets him with "How is Seryozha?" a snub he later avenges with the knowingly "wounding" remark that the boy had not missed her at all. Seryozha's boisterously loving greeting gives this the lie. But it is Anna who finds her son disappointing, not as wonderful as in her imagination, and at one point she even tells him of little Tanya's superior achievements. She soon adapts her expectations to reality, however, especially as she "experienced an almost physical enjoyment in feeling his closeness and his caresses," and finds again the charm of his "fair curls, blue eyes, and plump shapely legs" (p. 113).

Anna's preference for son over husband is obvious, but what of her difficulty in reuniting with her son? She overcomes the initial inner barrier by focusing on the sensuous bodily aspects of their relationship, perceiving and feeling him more like a 4- to 5-year-old than as a schoolboy of 8 years. Could it be that as an 8-year-old latency boy he not only shines less than his cousin Tanya but also fails to meet his mother's need for the kind of bodily closeness more age-appropriately maintained with a younger child? Could Anna's missing of him, feeling depleted without him, and having to attract the phallic–narcissistic admiration and bodily closeness of others, first of other children, then of a lover, could they all have stemmed not only from her current actual separation from her son but from the underlying context of her developmental loss of him? Such loss may have been denied until the occasion arose to see him "anew," just as the depth of her lack of marital fulfillment became more conscious when the perceived loss of her son occasioned a tempting encounter with a more gratifying partner. In a later, much more painful and poignant reunion with her son, her need for early bodily closeness with him is more strongly underlined, as is the impact of her loss of it.

During the ensuing months of Anna's developing affair with Vronsky, her conflict of choosing between son and lover continues to plague her. At the passionate height of their relationship, with Anna already pregnant, Vronsky begs her to leave with him, regardless of Karenin's reaction. They knew, of course, that in Russia, at the time, "only the innocent party could obtain a divorce, and then with difficulty. The guilty party could not remarry, and lost custody of any children" (p. 200), but they did not discuss these realities. It never occurred to Vronsky that Anna's adamant refusal to "run away" or even talk about it related to her feelings about losing her son. *Her* inner dilemma was highlighted by the fact that she could never mention the word *son* to him, much less share her guilty conflict of loyalty. She even, unjustly, attributed to him first the idea that he "would take her pregnancy lightly" and then that "something had to be done about it" (p. 199). Assuming that he does not care about children, Anna opts for hiding her conflict and misgivings from herself, even as her behavior increasingly alerts the world to her affair.

Following the finally unavoidable confrontation with Karenin, she becomes terrified: She will be disgraced, and rejected because of her disgrace, and she is so sure that even Vronsky will reject her that she cannot any longer love him or believe in his love for her. At that moment of desperate loss of inner and outer supplies of love, the maid comes in and reminds her that Seryozha and the governess are waiting for her. With that, "She remembered her son's existence" (p. 308) and:

> Suddenly the thought of her son pulled Anna out of her hopelessness. She recalled the partially sincere though largely exaggerated role of a mother living for her son that she had taken on during the past few years, and she joyfully felt that in her situation she had one prop that was independent of her relation to her husband and to Vronsky. That prop was her son [p. 309].

Instead of addressing the matter of her son's little naughtiness that awaited her disposition, she could really only ask him, "Do you love me?" (p. 310). Feeling that her son's love would reconstitute her, she resolved to run away with him, leaving husband, lover, and society.

But she soon abandons her plan in response to her husband's letter which offers her a carry-on-as-usual way out to maintain appearances and reminds her that a divorce would involve her losing her son. "He knows I won't abandon my child, that without my child there won't be any life for me even with the man I love, but that if I abandon my child and run away from him I would be behaving like the most shameful, the most contemptible of women—he knows I won't have the strength to do that" (p. 313). Yet, within hours, when Vronsky again urges her to leave her husband and counters her protestation with "which is better? To leave your son or to continue in this humiliating position?" (p. 338), she cries out, "There's only one thing left for me, just one thing—your love. If I have that I feel myself so exalted, so proud of my position" (p. 338). She senses herself to be on shaky ground, dreading disgraced rejection so much that she exalts her lover's love as a bolster now, as much as she had exalted her son's a while ago, with reality set aside.

DOLLY'S RELATIONSHIP WiTH HER CHILDREN

By way of contrast to Anna's need of her son, an interposed chapter describes the role of her children for Dolly. She spends the summer with her six young children on their impoverished country estate, lacking in amenities and domestic help, her unloving, self-centered husband having departed to enjoy himself in the city. She finds her happiness as well as distraction from thoughts about her lack of conjugal love by absorbing herself in the care of her children and in her worries about their well-being, education, and character development, with never a moment's rest. Yet her investment in her children is such that she can gain sufficient self-love and gratification from the small joys they provide. "These joys were so small they were imperceptible, like grains of gold in sand" (p. 279). Although small and rare, they nevertheless made her feel that "she had charming children, all six of them, each one in a different way but all of them rarities—and she was happy in them and proud of them" (p. 280). What a different maternal investment! When Levin, just a neighbor and family friend at the time, comes by, "she was particularly glad because [surrounded by all her children] he was seeing her in all her glory. No one could understand her splendor better than Levin . . . 'you are just like a hen with her brood, Dolly!' " (p. 284).

ANNA'S PREGNANCY AND INVESTMENT IN HER NEWBORN DAUGHTER

As Anna's pregnancy progresses she becomes increasingly convinced that she will die in childbirth. She views it as a good solution to all her troubles and longs for death, even as she flaunts her affair, enrages her husband by not maintaining the agreed upon appearances, and sparks even Vronsky's doubts about his commitment to her. Yet she is afraid, too. She shares her sinister foreboding with Vronsky as confirmed by the recurrence of an old repetitive nightmare. When Karenin leaves her, threatening to divorce her and take away her son, she begs him, "Leave me Seryozha until my—I'm going to have a baby soon, let me have him!" (p. 391). She does not want to face death alone. Following the delivery of a baby girl, Anna nearly does die of puerperal fever. For days she alternates between states of strange lucidity, dissociation, and coma, and brings about a quasiresolution as all three parties acknowledge their guilt and forgive each other in the face of Anna's impending death. But their atonement is for naught and their respective death wishes go unfulfilled. Anna survives and so, inevitably, do all the conflicts and tensions.

How did Anna invest her baby daughter during this troubled period? Early on she suspected Vronsky of not wanting the child and, after delivery, she suspected Karenin of not wanting the child, but she herself did nothing to interfere with the pregnancy and, in fact, felt calmed when she tuned into "the new life" and its movements inside her. This suggests that she had invested the "inside baby" as a part of herself, at least to an extent. Yet when she anticipated and longed for her own death, she did not give a thought to how the newborn, the baby outside her body, would fare as a motherless orphan, and she did not plan for the care of either of her children after her demise. She also never implied that the baby would die with her. It seems that she could only imagine the catastrophic moment of childbirth, when the inside baby would leave her. She could not imagine that she would survive this loss or that the baby, after parturition, would have a life of its own. During her feverish musings she did, at some points, give directions as to where Seryozha should sleep and about his dinner, and she also voiced a plan of going away into a wilderness near Rome, taking both children with her. Poignantly, however, she worried that if she drank water it would be bad for her little girl and, just before Karenin's arrival, she added, "Very well then, give her to a nurse" (p. 440).

During the weeks and months of her subsequent recuperation Anna appears to have paid no heed to the baby, little Anna, first perhaps due to her illness but later certainly due to disinterest. She was even unaware of the strange development in Karenin's attitude to the infant:

> For the newly born little girl he experienced a sort of special feeling not only of pity but also of tenderness. At first it had been a feeling of compassion alone that had made him take care of the newborn feeble little girl, who was not his daughter and had been neglected during her mother's illness, and would certainly have died if he hadn't taken care of her. He himself did not notice how fond of her he had grown [pp. 447–448].

He spent long periods quietly sitting by her and watching her, "completely serene and at peace with himself" (p. 448), and he closely supervised the nanny's and wet-nurse's care. One morning, when little Anna was just a couple of months old, he noticed she was somewhat ill and sent for the doctor before going to his office. On his return in the afternoon he stopped in the nursery first, heard that the doctor had prescribed baths and apparently judged the illness of minor import. Karenin, however, was distressed by the baby's crying and her refusal to nurse, and quickly picked up on the governess's and nanny's suspicion that the wet-nurse did not have enough milk.

Anna, by contrast, had been unaware of her infant's discomfort, had absorbed herself in talking with her visiting friend about seeing or not seeing Vronsky for a good-bye, and, when Karenin told her he had sent for the doctor, she at first thought the patient was herself. However, on learning about the wet-nurse's supposedly insufficient milk, she had an outburst, "Then why didn't you allow me to nurse her myself when I begged you to? Anyway"—Karenin understood what "anyway" meant—"She's an infant and they're going to kill her." (It is the first mention of what Anna foresaw for her infant.) She ordered the baby brought in. "I asked to nurse it, I wasn't allowed, and now I'm reproached for it." "I'm not reproaching you for—" "Yes, you are! Oh my God, why didn't I die!" (pp. 453–454).

Had Karenin really forbidden Anna to nurse her baby? Would it have helped her to invest little Anna positively enough to want both of them to live? Or would even nursing not have been sufficient to override the initial "I am bad for her" and the later "They are going to kill her" and "Why didn't I die?" It was not the first or last time when Karenin tried to be the mother, the better mother, but it was the only time when he succeeded, when it really helped the child, and when he felt truly comfortable with his parenting. In Winnicott's (1971) sense, he had found and used the ability "to be." Would it have made that crucial difference if he had been able to enjoy and support Anna's mothering instead of usurping it for himself? Or was he too deprived of love, her love, himself?

This book is, of course, almost as much about fathers as it is about mothers, but especially about the part of men that wants to be the mother and how they deal with it.

LOVER V. SON

Vronsky, as befitted his character and class, had earlier expected to receive Karenin's challenge to a duel. Later, in the aftermath of their reconciliation at Anna's deathbed, he had shot himself and nearly died. He had also purged himself of feelings in the process and was about to accept an advantageous position in far away Tashkent. But on seeing Anna during their leave taking, he once again succumbed to her attraction and changed plans: They would live together, in Italy at first, sustained by their love alone. When she worried, "Only I still don't know what he's going to decide about Seryozha" (p. 464), Vronsky "was quite incapable of understanding how at this moment of reunion she could remember and think about her son.... Could any of that matter?" (p. 464). And again Anna responded, "Oh, why didn't I die, that would have been the best" (p. 464).

On arrival in Italy, Anna soon managed to isolate herself from the disaster she had left behind. At first she had thought she would atone for the suffering she had caused by suffering herself, "I've deprived myself of what I treasured most—my good name and my son" (p. 495), but soon she felt no shame at all, was not tormented by the separation from her son, and seldom thought about him. She absorbed herself in her idealizing love of Vronsky and especially in his love of her. Yet, even during this time out of life, the fragility of her love and self-love readily surfaced. She was forever fearful that he would cease to love her if he found out about her "consciousness of her own worthlessness compared with him" (p. 456). When he once had supper on his own "with some acquaintances, [it] had put Anna in a state of unexpected and disproportionate depression" (p. 497). And she could not stave off "her only secret sorrow" (p. 499), namely her quite unwarranted jealousy of little Annie's beautiful wet-nurse whom Vronsky had painted in one of his pictures.

Anna's desperate, sole dependence on Vronsky's supplies of love excluded even little Annie. She had at first hoped to put her love of "his child" (p. 495) in place of that for her son. She sometimes played with Annie in an adoring way, as if with a beautiful doll, and she "spoiled her" (p. 499) to cover up her jealousy of the wet-nurse. Not one word, however, speaks to Anna's maternal investment in the sense of the child as representing so loved a part of herself that the infant's well-being would make the mother feel worthwhile. Nor is there the sense that she could forego her own satisfactions for the sake of the child without experiencing it as a self-diminishment; in other words, she was in no way a mother like Dolly.

KITTY BECOMES A MOTHER

At this point, however, Tolstoy does not ask us to compare Anna with Dolly, whose only love—self-love, love of other, being loved—resided in her relationships with her children. Instead, he describes the way a healthy and fortunate young woman enters the phase of motherhood. Not surprisingly, birth and death are once again intertwined. The woman is Kitty. She had matured beyond her early infatuation with and rejection by Vronsky and was now married to her long-time devoted suitor, Konstantin Levin. He not only loved her as a woman but as a potential mother—he was the family man who had complimented Dolly on her "brood." All along also, Kitty had maintained a fond relationship with her mother and could count on her support in all matters, especially motherhood.

When Levin is called in an emergency to go to his seriously ill and now probably dying brother, Kitty is so bound and determined to accompany her husband that she prevails over his intense misgivings. Levin had not only wanted to spare Kitty the stress and discomfort of travel and inadequate accommodation, but had also wanted to shield her from the obvious manifestations of Nicholas's poverty, dissolute way of life, and companion Masha, a woman of low rank and questionable history. Much to Levin's amazement, Kitty took it all in stride, immediately transformed Nicholas's quarters into a milieu rich with care and love, tended to Nicholas's bodily pains as well as feelings with such empathy and skill as to bring out the best in him and in Masha, and actually made him feel comfortable, loved, and loving. Yet she also sensed when not to be active and was able just to be with him when death came. She had mothered him to the end. She had also mitigated Levin's long-standing horror of death. At that very moment, "This one mystery of death, that remained an enigma, had not had time to be consummated before his [Levin's] eyes before a second one, just as enigmatic, had emerged, summoning him to love and life. The doctor confirmed his surmise about Kitty. Her illness [actually a minor indisposition] had been pregnancy" (p. 540).

Even before Kitty had a chance fully to invest her inside baby she was already able to invest an outside baby—a needy someone—unconcerned about the transition between the two. We can follow the successful unfolding and integration of her pregnancy, delivery, and dedicated care of her baby over many pages, to the very end of the book. No clinical case study can match the richly detailed account of her maternal functioning, embedded in the context of her other relationships, enabling her to struggle through and master the inevitable worries and upsets and to grow in the process. Tolstoy's deeply empathic ability to portray the "ordinary good enough mother" (Winnicott, 1949) serves us as a guide to understanding its variations—Dolly at one extreme and Anna at the other.

ANNA LOSES HER SON

Driven, in large part, by her reawakened longing for her son, Anna and entourage returned to Petersburg a couple of days before Seryozha's ninth birthday. Her written request to visit him was rejected, wounding her deeply, and she was enraged to learn he had been told she had died because she had been bad. She determined all the more to see him, and laden with presents, made her way into his bedroom in the early morning, partly protected by the loyal old servants. Seryozha had never believed she was dead, had longingly looked for her everywhere, and then having inadvertently heard from their old nanny that his mother was indeed alive, he made her reappearance his secret big birthday wish. That morning, after some time of just embracing and reexperiencing their physical closeness, he greeted her with "I knew you'd come!" (p. 571).

Once again Anna was surprised by his appearance. "During the time they had been separated, and with the gush of love she had been feeling all this last time, she had imagined him as a four-year-old child, which was how she had loved him best" (p. 570). In tears, she at first tried to preserve that memory by fondling and addressing him as of old. But toward the hurried end of her visit she realized that not only her son's body had grown but that his mind too now pondered and understood much of what had transpired, so, quite briefly, she portrayed his father as worthy of love and herself as having wronged him. On leaving she sensed that she had lost her son forever, lost him in different ways. She could never come to terms.

In the immediate aftermath of the visit, as she was looking through her photographs of Seryozha, she realized that she never had and never would love baby Annie as she had loved her son. Certain that Vronsky would never empathize with her sorrow, she turned her rage on him as its cause, provoked society's open rejection of her by attending the opera in an ostentatious manner, and reproached him unjustly of no longer loving her. They made up in the nick of time and, once again escaping the external sources of their troubles, left to live at his country estate. We meet Anna there through Dolly's eyes.

WHAT IT MEANS TO HAVE CHILDREN

Dolly and her brood had by now been rescued from their dilapidated rural dwelling and were charitably ensconced at the estate of Levin and Kitty, her sister and brother-in-law. Despite her hosts' misgivings about Vronsky, who had quickly carved out a niche for himself among the area's land- and serf-owning gentry, Dolly determined it was "her duty to visit Anna and show her that her own feelings could not change regardless of any change in Anna's position" (p. 646). The trip, short in distance and time spent, would be Dolly's only time away from her children. It was also her first time without a baby—her seventh, the youngest, having died of croup not too long before.

Traveling by horse drawn carriage, this unique opportunity to be on her own and reflect on her life brought out her unhappiest thoughts. She could not reconcile within herself her deepest, most heartrending sorrow at her infant son's death on the one hand, and a young peasant woman who had shared her relief at being free after the death of her own little daughter. Having children was a mixed blessing. Dolly bemoaned the constant worry and work that not only kept her busy with her children but had, through the wear and tear of pregnancies, childbirths, and nursing, disfigured and aged her prematurely, perhaps causing her husband to turn away from her. Realizing that her own chances of a romantic and fulfilling love life had passed her by, she empathized with Anna who, Dolly thought, had chosen that path for herself.

Nothing could have thrown Dolly's threadbare, worn, and downtrodden appearance into sharper relief than coming face to face with Anna and her surroundings. It was not just that Anna's beauty was more radiant than ever, that she wore expensively tailored clothes, but everything around her reeked of money-no-object, ostentatious opulence. There were the thoroughbred riding horses and a stud farm; well-trained servants; the luxurious mansion and adjacent buildings, the furnishings, guest rooms, and meals. It was a showplace for everything, including planned hospital facilities for the peasants to gratify Vronsky's self-aggrandizing aspirations among his new peers. Little Annie's nursery, too, dazzled with all the latest equipment as well as an English nanny in addition to the Italian wet-nurse and Russian nursemaid. This showplace nursery, alas, quickly turned into a sad showdown in Dolly's view.

Although Dolly admired the little girl's looks and ability to crawl, she took an instant dislike to the "general atmosphere of the nursery" (p. 660) and to the Englishwoman in particular.

> Aside from this Dolly realized at once, from a few remarks that Anna, the wet-nurse, the nanny, and the child were strangers to one another, and that a visit from the child's mother was something exceptional. Anna had wanted to get the little girl some toy and she couldn't find it. And what was most astonishing of all was that in answering a question about how many teeth the little girl had Anna made a mistake; she knew nothing at all about the two latest teeth. "It's hard for me sometimes

to realize how superfluous I am around here," Anna said on leaving [p. 661].

Dolly's anticipation of Anna's love-filled life, confirmed initially by Anna's self-professed "unbelievable" happiness, receives another blow when Vronsky confidentially solicits her help. Would Dolly persuade Anna to ask for a divorce? As it is, not only Annie but all as yet unborn children of their union would bear Karenin's name. "And if a son is born tomorrow, *my* son, in law he'll be—Karenin's; he won't be heir either to my name, or to my property." He concludes with, "The main thing is that in carrying on my work I must be sure that what I'm doing isn't going to die with me, that I'm going to have heirs" (p. 669). In taking up this issue with Anna later on, Dolly called Vronsky's wish for children "egotism, but what legitimate, what noble egotism!" (p. 679). She is not fooled, but can empathize better with his attitude than with what she now learns from Anna.

"I'm not going to have more children" (p. 679). "Why? And is it moral?" Anna relates that with the help of her doctor's advice, she will not allow a pregnancy to disfigure her lest she risk losing Vronsky's love; and she would not want to bear children who would be ashamed of her and therefore have unhappy lives. She also will not ask for a divorce which would humiliate her without solving her dilemma. "You must understand that I love only two beings, I think equally, but both of them more than myself—Seryozha and Alexis [Vronsky]. . . . I love these two beings alone, and one excludes the other. I can't unite them, and that's the only thing I want. And if I can't have that then nothing else matters" (p. 683). Anna is so sure that she can't regain her son and so unsure of keeping Vronsky's love, that she cannot consider the possibility of being granted a divorce and of then pursuing some of the special remarriage and adoption dispensations Vronsky looks to with hope. She, whose self-love has always depended on external supplies, cannot imagine that remarriage would, at least to an extent, reconstitute her "good name" in the eyes of society. She cannot *think* about any of these issues; she can only *feel* desperate and undone, so much so that on leaving Dolly she took a "wineglass and poured into it several drops of a medicine principally made up of morphia" (p. 684) to help her regain a "reassured and cheerful mood" (p. 684)

One cannot help but wonder whether the causes of Anna's hopelessness and resort to drugs lie more within her than in the external circumstances, difficult though they are. She could never invest herself in son and lover, could never unite them in her own heart.

Already, earlier in the day, after her conversation with Vronsky and watching Anna's somewhat flirtatious play with young Veslovsky, one of their guests, Dolly thought she would not stay for as long as the intended two days. "Those painful maternal worries she had detested so much on the way, by now appeared to her in a different light, after a day spent without them, and were drawing her back" (p. 677). After talking with Anna, any remaining doubt was gone. She could not imagine that it would have been better for her own beloved son Grisha not to have been born.

> She had been sorry for Anna with all her heart while she had been talking to her, but now she could not make herself think about her. Thoughts of home and children rose up in her imagination with a special, novel charm, a sort of fresh radiance. This world of hers seemed to her so precious and charming now that on no account did she wish to spend another day away from it; she made up her mind she would leave the following day without fail [p. 683].

As Anna unwittingly helps Dolly to find the love of her life again in her children, Anna herself edges closer to her abyss.

HOSTILITY TAKES OVER

The more desperately Anna feels herself to need Vronsky's love, the less does she trust it. His every interest feels to her like an abandonment. She uses her charms to hold him, she even agrees to ask for a divorce in the hope that remarriage might tie him to her. Above all, she cannot bear his physical absence. During a few days of his needing to be away she sustains herself with increasing doses of morphine and finally summons him back on the pretext of Annie's illness—a ruse he figures out at once, not only because Annie's indisposition was minimal but because Anna so obviously cannot love Annie. When he again plans a trip, this time to Moscow, she insists on going with him, and so, in November, they move to their mansion in that city to spend the winter. And winter sets in in their relationship too, which cannot absorb the stress and strain of Anna's loveless internal terror.

In desperate attempts to assure herself of external supplies of love, Anna "adopts" a needy adolescent girl and her family, deserted by their father and husband, lavishing the kind of care on them, and especially on the girl, that prompts her brother Oblonsky to say, "It'll all end by your loving her more than your own" (p. 744). And at a later point Vronsky calls her "infatuation with that little girl unnatural" (p. 787), wounding her by exposing the defensive nature of her investment and contrasting it with her lack of love for their own child.

Another means of filling the void was Anna's increasing seductiveness. One evening she managed to enthrall even her guest Levin, much to his wife Kitty's chagrin, which led to a night's upset between them before they made up. The meaning of this conquest for Anna was quite different:

> After seeing her visitors out Anna did not sit down, but began pacing back and forth in the room. Unconsciously she had been doing everything in her power all evening to kindle in Levin a feeling of love for her (which she had been doing lately with respect to all young men), and she knew she had achieved this as far as it was possible to in a single evening ... the moment he left the room she stopped thinking about him. There was one thought and one thought only that in different forms pursued her implacably. If I have this effect on others ... why is it that *he's* so cold toward me? [p. 749].

She is unaware that her own ability to love has ebbed away and regressed to a level where Vronsky, at one point, rightly describes it as torturing herself and him. Sometimes this manifests itself in hurting each other's feelings, sometimes in coldness or power struggles. There is no forgiving, and less and less chances for making up.

When Vronsky returns home, just after Levin's visit, Anna engages him in yet another of these interactions. She savored her triumph on this occasion but quickly realized that he had not

> [F]orgiven her for her victory . . . was colder to her than before, as though regretting his submission. And recalling the words that had assured her victory—"I'm close to a catastrophe and I'm afraid of myself"—she realized this was a dangerous weapon, which she wouldn't be able to use again. And she felt that together with the love that bound them together some evil spirit of strife had grown up between them that she could not cast out of his heart, and still less out of her own [pp. 751–752].

The downward spiral accelerated, with intensified provocations of hurting and feeling hurt as she needed to misinterpret and misunderstand his every word and move and saw even his reiterated wish for children as a rejection of herself. "And death, as the only means of reviving love for her in his heart, of punishing him, and of winning a victory in the struggle the evil spirit in her heart was carrying on against him, came to her mind clearly and vividly" (p. 798). After taking her usual daily morphia—and thinking of drinking the whole phial—she spent the night wallowing in fantasies of Vronsky's suffering and regrets after her death.

> But toward morning her repetitive nightmare came to her again and woke her up. The little old man with the matted beard was leaning over an iron bar doing something, muttering senseless words in French, while she, as usual in this nightmare (this was what made it so horrible) felt that the little old man was paying no attention to her but was doing something dreadful to her with the iron bar [p. 799].

This nightmare long predates her acquaintance with Vronsky, recurred when she anticipated her death in childbirth, and became interwoven with a reality at the very start of the book. Then, their first meeting at the railway station was overshadowed by the fatal accident of a railway worker killed by a train while fixing something on the track with an iron bar. Railways, railway stations, train accidents, and little old men forever adjusting things with iron bars on the wheels of carriages and behind trains were a common experience and focal point of all traffic which enhanced their ready symbolic value, individually and in the society at large. They encompassed not only comings and goings, separation and reunion, but human traffic in the sense of sexuality and death.

Convincing herself that Vronsky had turned to another woman to marry, Anna announced she would leave him, but then panicked when he left on an out-of-town errand. Partly depersonalized, she now starts to experience everything and everybody solely in terms of hatred and deceit, unable to turn to or trust anyone. Frantic telegrams to and from Vronsky miss the recipient or are misunderstood, symbolizing the failure of their communication, and finally, as Anna tries to reach him by train, she recognizes, in terror, the misshapen old railway worker of her dream passing by her carriage. At the first stop, Anna gets out to walk along the platform. The "evil spirit," her defused aggression, leads her to throw herself under a moving train.

ON BIRTH AND DEATH AND LOVING ONE'S CHILDREN

The phallic–narcissistic woman who conquers and subdues men, refuses to become a mother, and dies by suicide preoccupied Tolstoy long before he wrote *Anna Karenina*. She is a prominent character, the beautiful Helene, in *War and Peace*. But it is only in *Anna Karenina* that she is sympathetically understood in the context of mothering, its early investment levels of self and other, and related primitive love and hate conflicts.

Tolstoy underlines the childbirth–death connection by interrupting his account of Anna's deterioration at the point where she first verbalizes her suicidal intent, and interpolating Levin's experience of Kitty's delivery, the birth of his first child. Bewildered and stricken by her agony:

> [A]ll he [Levin] knew and felt was that what was happening was similar to what had happened the year before . . . on his

brother Nicholas's deathbed. But that had been grief—this was joy. But both that grief and this joy alike were outside all the usual circumstances of life; in this ordinary life they were like an opening through which something sublime could be seen [p. 759].

At the worst moments he indeed thought she was dying and when she emerged alive he was ecstatic. "But the child? Where did it come from? Why? . . . and it took him a long time to get used to it" (pp. 762–763).

Anna's death did not bring a solution to these dilemmas; they are carried on by Kitty and Levin. She is the one who integrates childbearing and rearing with devotion, equanimity, and loving concern in the face of hardship. He is the one torn apart, lost in what feels like a new world, struggling to subdue his inner demons, even though in the external world all is essentially good fortune. "He was in the position of someone looking for food in a toyshop or a gunshop" (p. 835). What a poignant metaphor! Consciously he grappled with the existential question of "knowing what I am and why I'm here" (p. 837), agonizing over the falsehood of beliefs. He experienced himself to be in the power of a terrible evil from which he had to free himself, that it was impossible to submit to, and, like Anna, he saw but one means of escape—death. "And Levin, a happy, healthy family man, was so close to suicide a number of times that he hid a rope, in order not to hang himself, and walked about without a gun for fear of shooting himself" (p. 838). But as he went on living he found it impossible not to attend to the many aspects of taking care of his farm and peasants and dependents, "just as it would be impossible to abandon a baby you were already holding in your arms" (p. 839). "He was living (without being aware of it) in accordance with the spiritual truths he had drunk in with his mother's milk, but he was thinking not only without acknowledging these truths but taking pains to evade them" (p. 846).

Two events ultimately helped him to reach inner peace, to love his child: On a hot day Kitty had taken little Mitya to rest in the shade of a big tree in the nearby woods. A storm blew up and sent Levin in hurried search of them only to witness lightning strike just where they were. He found them unharmed, for him seemingly returned from the dead. On bathing Mitya on their return home came the second revelation as Kitty joyfully called him to demonstrate that their son now knew her and preferred her to anyone else. He was a person and his father was thrilled. " 'Well, I'm glad you're beginning to like him,' " said Kitty to her husband, after she had settled herself placidly in her usual place with the child at her breast. " 'I'm very glad. I was beginning to get upset about it' " (p. 865).

Levin resolved his philosophical problem by recognizing that love has to outweigh and tame anger, the evil power, within himself and toward his child. Kitty understood his struggle all along at the feeling level and in his trouble with parenting. When they both understood and felt understood by each other, their bond as a couple included the new rich dimension of being their child's parents.

This triadic investment was beyond Anna's reach. It is hard to avoid the feeling that the early loss of her mother had caused insurmountable obstacles (Furman, 1974). Some of these would have included a severe narcissistic depletion and insecure boundaries, resulting in inadequate self-love and inconstancy in her love of others. Another aftermath would be a toddlerlike inability to tame anger and a prevalence of sadomasochistic trends, so that death would be linked to the primal scene and to childbirth and even an unwanted sibling—regardless of whether these inner experiences and connections were confirmed by the actual reality of events.

Tolstoy, himself maternally bereaved at a very early age and, not much later, paternally bereaved as well, would fathom these disconcerting primitive feelings. How fortunate for us that he could draw on them to create his art.

2
Parenthood as a Developmental Phase

> The concept of parenthood as a developmental phase[1] was stimulated by clinical work with parents of children in all age groups, including work with pregnant mothers. It derived, however, primarily from the observations of and experiences with mothers and young children in the Hanna Perkins Nursery School. It has been applied mainly in the work with parents of under-fives. Theory and practice thus are intimately linked and influence each other [E. Furman, 1969a, p. 66].

The particular form of therapeutic intervention, namely treatment of underfives by way of their parents (E. Furman, 1957), had been developed in the setting of the Hanna Perkins Nursery School and my colleagues and I had early on been able to pinpoint which childhood disturbances responded to it best, assessed by diagnostic categories (Daunton, 1969).

The assessment of suitable parents for this form of treatment was much harder to categorize. We had, of course, learned that some mothers were much better able to utilize this approach in working with us to help their children. Earlier we had focused on delineating specific difficulties in the mother–child relationship, which seemed to limit the chances

---

"T. Benedek's [1959] article came to my attention only some time after I had completed this paper. We concur with her concept of parenthood as a developmental phase but, since my concept is based on different clinical material, I note different manifestions and mechanisms in describing it" (E. Furman, 1969a, p. 66).

of successful intervention or might even jeopardize the work altogether. Among these apparent obstacles were such manifestations as mother and child sharing symptoms or unconscious defenses (E. Furman, 1957). Extended clinical experience, however, taught us that the previously pinpointed obstacles were not always insurmountable. It was, indeed, not specific pathologies of the mother–child relationship or of the maternal handling that were the deciding factors. What then was?

My coworkers and I were still struggling with the question in the early sixties, when we were writing *The Therapeutic Nursery School* (R. A. Furman and A. Katan, 1969), the follow-up study of our first hundred cases treated at the Hanna Perkins School.

One aspect of the treatment work with all these cases was especially striking:

> [We were not working with] the parent's total personality but only with the aspect that functions as a parent and manifests itself in the parent–child relationship. We ourselves were puzzled at first by this differentiation and apparently arbitrary division within a personality. But experience repeatedly showed us that the overall functioning of a person's personality did not necessarily affect his functioning as a parent in all respects. Some well-adjusted adults proved to have severe difficulties as parents, while others with considerable personality disorders were able to progress and develop as parents, and often could keep their neurotic traits or symptoms out of their relationship with their child. This became more understandable when parenthood was viewed as a maturational phase [E. Furman, 1969a, p. 67].

PARENTHOOD AS A DEVELOPMENTAL PHASE

As in other developmental phases, marked inner changes occur and bring new elements to bear on the individual's intrapsychic balance and adaptation. As adolescence particularly shapes the person's adult sexuality, so the experiences of conception, pregnancy, birth, and care for the young child shape the adult's role as a parent. It is a period of great flux and mental flexibility. The parent's early experiences of being mothered and fathered come closer to consciousness, frequently stimulated by, and interacting with, the daily experiences with his own child. Similarly, early infantile fantasies of being a mother or father are reactivated and brought in line with the current realities. A new aspect of identification occurs with his own parents, and additional new figures are sought to supplement, and coordinate with, these more basic identifications. In integrating these various factors many trial adaptations are made, and eventually a flexible equilibrium is established.

In parenthood as a developmental phase, similar principles apply as in other periods of maturational change. Previously existing personality makeup strongly influences the course of development but does not solely determine it. The maturational forces of the phase itself, and the individual reality experiences during the phase, play an important and usually unpredictable part. The preparenthood personality may inhibit the maturational forces so that no phase-adequate manifestations can occur. The difficulty is similar to that of the disturbed latency child who does not reach the maturational phase of adolescence. Such an individual cannot truly function as a parent. In other cases, the preparental personality may be of such a pathology that the maturational phase can only extend the old conflicts instead of influencing and rearranging existing attitudes. Again, there is the parallel of the teenager whose adolescent urges become an inextricable part of his previously established neurosis. Similarly, with some disturbed adults, the new experiences of parenthood are only drawn into the orbit of their neuroses so that their functioning as parents and their relationship with their child is patterned solely on their pathology and cannot be influenced by new urges and realities.

In the population at large, such instances of pathology are not too common. For the most part, adults are able to enter the developmental phase of parenthood and come to terms with the new inner and outer demands. To these adults, the reactivation of their own early experiences and infantile fantasies serves as an essential and helpful background toward achieving a new inner equilibrium.

The phase of parenthood is probably never quite completed, but its strongest urges and most intense inner struggles occur in its earliest years, when the child is an infant and

> under 5. While the child's transition into latency and later into adolescence always creates the need for new inner readjustments, it is in the earliest years of the parent–child relationship that the parent's inner flexibility is at its peak and the attempts at a new realignment of inner forces are most intense. It is therefore not only the time when early experiences of and fantasies about mothering and fathering gain a new importance, but also it is the time when real experiences with the child himself, or with outsiders concerned with the child, are most influential. The first five years of life, the period of greatest emotional growth for the child, is also the most important one for the parent's development. The child changes rapidly and presents the parent almost daily with new demands and reactions. All of these affect the inner life of the parent and usually require an immediate reaction on his or her part. It is to be expected that during these years the parent sometimes veers either to the extreme of drawing solely (even inappropriately) on his own earlier experiences and conflicts or to the other extreme of only acting upon the advice (again often inappropriate) of hastily sought new models of identification. Most of these trial adaptations to parenthood are soon discarded in favor of a more reality-adapted selection and integration of parental attitudes. It is during this period of rapid shifts that a parent's capacity to establish himself as a parent can be most fruitfully influenced—and most readily jeopardized.
>
> The maturational forces as well as the actual experiences of parenthood are different for men and women. The mother, through her bodily closeness to the fetus, baby, and young child, and through her constant exposure to the child's behavior, is much more intimately affected by all the internal and external forces. Fathers receive much less immediate bodily and psychological stimulation during the earliest years with the child [E. Furman, 1969a, pp. 67–70].

This formulation helped us to focus on the positive factor which fueled a mother's dedication to doing her best by her child, instead of looking for the negatives that interfered.

Our primary task in assessing a mother's ability to pursue the aims of working with her child is to assess whether she has entered the developmental phase of motherhood at all, and if so, whether her flexibility is grossly and rigidly impaired by her previously established character structure.

> From initial contacts it is difficult enough to establish whether the mother is functioning in her maternal role. It is much more difficult to assess how grossly and inflexibly her functioning is impaired. In the case studies, the overt pathology of the child and of the maternal handling told us little about that, in fact they were often misleading [E. Furman, 1969a, p. 70–71].

Other areas of motherhood proved to be much more helpful as diagnostic signs. In time, we came to view them as the hallmarks of parental functioning—a sense of responsibility with healthy guilt, the specific nature of the investment in the child, and the flexibility of the concept of motherhood (parenthood).

A SENSE OF RESPONSIBILITY—HEALTHY GUILT

> One hallmark of self-acceptance as a mother is the feeling of responsibility for the child's bodily and mental welfare. A mother feels badly when her child's development is impaired. Even in cases where unavoidable reality produced the pathology and where the mother bears little or no blame, she feels responsible for mitigating the difficulty. In cases of emotional disturbances the healthy mother always feels guilty. This guilt provides a stimulus for her to work toward the child's improvement even at the cost of considerable inconvenience. The availability and motivational force of a mother's guilt is one of the most important diagnostic clues to assessing whether a mother is succeeding in her adjustment as a mother and whether she is sufficiently motivated to work on the child's difficulties consistently and for a long period.
> While the mother without feelings of guilt and personal responsibility is developing neither as a mother nor sufficiently motivated for the arduous work ahead, it is equally true that not all types of guilt are of positive value for the work. Various forms of unconscious guilt are very severe taskmasters to the mother's ego but are either unavailable to her as motivators for work or actually strive to undo any success; for example, unconscious guilt which forbids the mother to function as a

mother, or guilt which forces her to fail with her child. Similarly, appropriate guilt and responsibility differ from feelings of narcissistic injury, though this may be difficult to distinguish. A mother may feel most concerned about her child's trouble and the part she played in its etiology, but if her concern is predominantly one of hurt self-esteem it will not enable her to seek help and to work effectively; for example, she may need to hide all or some of the child's symptomatology or history to avoid exposing herself unfavorably, or she may vociferously and repeatedly lament her "sins" without changing the situation, or she may be unable to bear improvements through the work because they would only prove to her how much she had done wrong in the past.

Thus the important point to assess is the presence of available motivating guilt and its relative prevalence over other forms of pathological guilt or narcissistic injury [E. Furman, 1969a, pp. 71–72].

THE NATURE OF THE INVESTMENT IN THE CHILD

The feelings of narcissistic injury, however, are not altogether pathological or unhelpful to a mother. A certain measure stems in part from the mother's ties to her child—a blend of narcissistic and object libidinal cathexes. In the course of the phase of motherhood the child is invested with varying degrees of narcissistic and object-libidinal ties. In general, the younger the child, the greater is the narcissistic investment, which is at its height during the pregnancy and the first weeks of the baby's life. The importance of this for the care of the baby is well known. Only the extension of the mother's narcissism onto her baby makes it possible for her to bear the hardships of the child's round-the-clock demands and to enjoy responding to them. As the child grows, the mother's relationship to him changes in that he is increasingly regarded as a love object in his own right. The under-five's physical and emotional dependency requires the mother to keep considerable amounts of narcissistic libidinal cathexes in her relationship with her child during these years, yet she needs to have invested sufficient object libidinal ties in him to be able to interact with him as with a love object when his developing personality needs it. In her development as a mother she makes continuous adjustments in the distribution of object and narcissistic libido in her relationship with her child. This distribution needs to be not only age-adequately adapted to the child's growth, but also needs to be flexible enough that immediate changes can occur in response to the child's day-to-day status. For example, when the 4-year-old becomes physically ill, when he is unusually tired, or when he is otherwise under stress, the mother's cathexis of him has to readjust itself at once in favor of an increased balance of narcissistic ties so that she can meet his needs adequately on his currently regressed level.

In the mother–child relationship, both the distribution and flexibility of the mother's libidinal ties are of great importance in assessing her development as a mother. They furnish valuable motivation for her wish to seek help for her child and to work effectively toward his improvement. From her narcissistic cathexis comes the wish to help that part of herself which is invested in the child and to persist even if her efforts entail much inconvenience; his suffering is hers, and in helping him she truly helps herself. From her object libidinal ties come her feelings of sympathy and empathy for him and her altruistic wish to do well by him; in helping him she helps a most beloved person.

In one sense, the intensity, balance, and flexibility of libidinal cathexes determine the extent to which the mother has achieved equilibrium in her maternal development. The complexities and interdependencies of the narcissistic and libidinal ties to the child are so great that minor transitory disharmonies occur frequently during the child's early years. It is only in cases of considerable pathology, though, that the cathexes are either of themselves insufficiently strong or are rigidly maintained in an inappropriate balance, leading to extremes in either direction [E. Furman, 1969a, pp. 72–73].

A FLEXIBLE CONCEPT OF MOTHERHOOD

In the above brief discussion of motherhood as a developmental phase, it was mentioned that one of its most important aspects is for the woman to achieve a newly integrated concept of herself as a mother. This is based in part on the experiences of being mothered, the infantile fantasies of being a mother, current new aspects of identification with her own mother as a mother, real present experiences with her own child's behavior and personality, and events specifically connected with him (e.g., type of delivery, nursing experience, pattern of motility, times of illness, individual physique). In addition, a mother makes new partial identifications with persons who affect her attitude to her child (friends, neighbors, other mothers, books, magazines, nurses, pediatricians, therapists, and teachers). If the mother is sufficiently flexible, she will be able to integrate such supplementary identifications in her total image and ideal of herself as a mother. If she has not entered the phase of maternal development, she can usually use therapists, teachers, and others, only as substitute mothers for her child; that is, people who take over her role. If she has entered the developmental phase, but it has become a sole field for the play of her earlier conflicts, then she would again be unable to make the necessary integrated selective partial identifications. Instead, the work and the staff would be used as a further area for extending her neurosis. This can lead either to an inability to identify with the means and aims of the work or, by contrast, to a total, unselective identification, which would be employed defensively against inner conflicts and therefore could not serve the healthier purposes [E. Furman, 1969a, p. 74].

MATURING AS A MOTHER

Whenever the hallmarks of entry into the phase of motherhood are evident, this, more often than not, presages ongoing growth.

> Mothers in this group are generally not only able to work successfully toward helping their child but experience the additional gratification of maturing as mothers in the process of the work. The latter factor is not among our primary aims but becomes in time an important incentive for the mother to carry on the work and greatly benefits her children. It enables her to continue her work with the particular child in the future and to apply her new maturity to the upbringing of his siblings [E. Furman, 1969a, p. 76].

3

The Death of a Newborn: Assistance to Parents

Since 1960, medical research has made significant strides in the treatment of prematurely born babies. As a result, many have survived with the help of weeks or months of intricate hospital care. For many parents this has meant happy fulfillment in rearing an infant where previously there would have been loss and despair. However, these improvements in medical management have not resulted in unqualified success. Many infants still die, sometimes after a long period of anxious hope, and with those who survive it has been found that a significantly high percentage return to the hospital within their first two years of life as battered or failure-to-thrive infants, while many others experience less severe but still marked impairment in their development (Klaus and Kennell, 1976).

Investigation of the causative factors has pointed to interferences in mothering. Specifically, research showed that the prolonged lack of postnatal contact between mother and child made it difficult and, in some instances, impossible for mothers to establish with their infants the kind of relationship that facilitates the optimal parenting so essential to the baby's bodily and mental growth. At Cleveland's Rainbow Babies and

---

This chapter was previously published in *The Child in His Family: Preventive Child Psychiatry in an Age of Transitions*, edited by E. J. Anthony, C. Koupernik, and C. Chiland, Vol. 6, 1980, pp. 497–506. New York: John Wiley & Sons, copyright 1980 John Wiley & Sons, Inc. It is reprinted here by permission of John Wiley & Sons.

Children's Hospital, effective corrective steps have been taken. Since the 1970s, mothers have had full access to their prematurely born babies and have learned how to handle them in the incubators and care for their needs. Follow-up studies suggest that this approach not only helped the initial relationship but has beneficial effects on parent, child, and their interactions in later years (Klause and Kennell, 1976).

This new focus on the earliest stages of parenting, however, has pointed the way also in another area, namely, how to help parents when their baby dies. Until the 1970s, the parents not only lacked contact with their hospitalized newborn while he lived, but were frequently quite uninvolved when he died. They did not see, much less touch, the dead baby, consented to have the body disposed of by the hospital without service or grave, glossed over the loss with their surviving children, and sometimes even within themselves and with each other. It seemed as though their physical distance from the baby sometimes led to their emotional distance—a nonbaby and a nondeath. The hospital took exclusive charge of it from beginning to end. The unhappy outcomes of this approach would show up later in parental psychiatric disturbances, in difficulties encountered in parenting the next born child, or in maladjustments of the siblings who had not been helped to understand and master the disappearance of a baby whom they had, consciously or unconsciously, expected to join the family.

With the changed emphasis on the importance of the immediate and continued parental care of the newborn, mothers' and fathers' reactions to the loss of their child were better recognized and understood. Helpful measures could be taken to assist the bereaved family. The initial personal contact with the child proved as important for the parents in coping with his death as in rearing him to live.

Drs. Klaus and Kennell have cooperated closely with specialists from several disciplines in the context of their work. My own contribution (Furman, 1969a, 1974), as a child analyst, has been only sporadic. It has been based on the areas of my earlier research, namely the mother–infant relationship and bereavement, and has focused on understanding and helping with the parents' experience of the death of a newborn.

THE NATURE OF THE PARENT–CHILD RELATIONSHIP

During the many months while the baby lives inside his mother he is a part of her, bodily and mentally. She knows him as a real, separate person only from his movements and hiccups, and insofar as she invests him with other attributes, these represent her fantasies, hopes, and fears; that is, they too are an extension of herself. Birth brings about a big step in perceiving the child as a person in his own right, and from then on it becomes possible to get to know him and love him as an individual. But, at the same time, birth constitutes only a small step for the mother in differentiating him from herself. Under normal circumstances the child remains a part of her mentally, and, when she holds her baby and nurses him, their bodily unity is also restored. The only difference is that before birth the baby was an inside part of her whereas after birth he is an outside part of her. This feeling of physical and emotional oneness is essential to the mother's own well-being as well as to her capacity for effective mothering.

As the infant grows, develops his own characteristics, and contributes his share to their interactions and experiences, the mother increasingly regards him as a separate, loved person, but her self-investment of him diminishes only very gradually, and to an extent, always remains a part of her relationship with him. What happens to him, even years later and when he is fully grown, continues to affect her in a way that is very different from all her other relationships, however close and meaningful they may be. This holds equally true for the child. For him, too, she is initially indistinguishable from the self, for a long time functions as part of him, and remains both a loved person and a part of the self.

The father–child relationship develops along somewhat different lines. The baby is never an integral part of his body and, owing to the fact that he normally spends less time in caring for the child in the earliest weeks and months, it also takes the father longer to get to know and love his child as an individual in his own right. Mentally and emotionally, however, the infant is very much a part of him and, in this respect, his earliest, even prenatal relationship with the baby parallels the mother–child relationship. Moreover, as Winnicott (1965) has stressed, the father empathizes with the mother and relates to the mother–child unit as a whole. This enables him to feel with mother and baby, to protect and support them, and to be active on their behalf with respect to the environment at the time of their greatest vulnerability. In this way the father's role for the mother–child unit is akin to the mother's role with the infant. In caring for them he cares for himself. When the father is prevented from assuming this part, for internal or external reasons, his development as a father is jeopardized, as happens with the mother when she is deprived of contact with her baby. But, beyond that, the father's special investment in the mother–child unit is essential to the mother, who builds her relationship of devotion to the child with the help of his devotion to them. In this complex and mutually dependent interaction, each represents to the other both a loved person and a part of his or her self.

This double investment makes the parent–child relationship unique. When the partners are lost to one another, their experience of the separation is unique because it represents both the loss of a loved one and the loss of a part of the self. When a child dies, the parent is faced with two mental tasks, mourning a loved one and adapting to the loss of a part of the self. Let us first look at these processes separately, then apply them to the death of a newborn, and, finally, discuss some practical ways in which bereaved parents can be assisted in coping with their distress.

MOURNING

Recent research has clarified the components of mourning, by which I mean the mental task of coping with the death of a loved person (E. Furman, 1974). In each instance it depends first on individual circumstances, the personality and current mental state of the bereaved and the form of death; for example, whether it was sudden and what caused it. No two deaths are alike, and each bereaved person is different from all others. Second, the bereaved person has an opportunity to know and accept the realities of the death. It has been found to be extremely important that the bereaved learn the exact cause of death, that he have a chance to be present at the death, or to perceive the dead body, that he participate in arranging and attending the funeral services, and have access to the grave or urn containing the bodily remains of the deceased. This awareness and understanding of the concrete aspects of the death favors its realistic acceptance and paves the way for the ensuing mental adjustment through the mourning process.

After the initial extreme stress, which is sometimes cushioned with the help of temporary defenses, such as denial, mourning proper consists of two apparently contradictory processes. On the one hand, there is detachment, the loosening of the ties with the dead loved one; on the other hand, there is identification, the taking into oneself of some aspects of the dead person, and thereby keeping him forever by making him a part of one's own personality. Detachment entails the reliving of each and every memory of one's experiences with the deceased, longing for him, enduring the intense accompanying feelings of pain, anger, guilt, and helplessness, and then, gradually, withdrawing one's emotional investment. Identification proceeds at the same time. It softens and diminishes the stressful task of detachment, but how much it can be used and how well it benefits the bereaved, depends in each instance on the personality of the survivor and the personality of the deceased. In some cases, such as with the death of a spouse or aged parent, identification may play a large role in the mourning process, and the taking on of the deceased person's interests, hobbies, or values may enrich the personality of the bereaved; in other instances, for example, with the death of a young child, identification can assume only a minor role or may interfere with the bereaved person's adaptation if he takes on attributes that ill fit his adult personality, such as the child's need to be cared for.

Mourning is not necessarily observable by outsiders. Contrary to common assumption, it may not be accompanied by overt expression of feelings or withdrawal from the tasks of daily life. It is an internal mental process, and, to a considerable extent, even the mourner may not be aware of it. There is no time limit to mark its end; in fact, it may never end completely. But we know that a major part of mourning has been accomplished when the bereaved resumes age-appropriate functioning and continues his personal growth.

When parents have to cope with the death of a newborn their mourning has to adapt itself to the requirements of this particular bereavement. Identification becomes impossible because an adult can in no way become like a baby without serious jeopardy to his adjustment. The entire loss has to be dealt with by mental detachment. Others sometimes minimize this task saying, "Oh, they hardly knew him, they'll soon get over it." It is true that the brief life did not allow for many memories to be formed, but it tends to be forgotten how highly invested the few existing memories are, how utterly acute the parent's pain and unhappiness is, and how strong the guilt feelings are in most instances because the death is so untimely. This makes the mourning process acutely difficult to bear, but, even so, it deals with only the part of the relationship that viewed the baby as a separate person. Since he was still primarily regarded as a part of the parent's self, we have to examine now how people cope with that aspect of the loss.

COPING WITH THE LOSS OF A PART OF THE SELF

Losing a part of oneself usually takes the form either of an amputation, for example the loss of a limb, or of a function, such as paralysis or blindness. As with the death of a loved one, a person's manner of coping depends on his individual personality and current emotional state, on the circumstances in which the loss occurred, and on his opportunity to know and acknowledge the concrete realities of the loss—to understand why and how it happened. As with a death, the afflicted tends to shield himself during the initial period of extreme stress by employing defensive measures, such as denial.

The subsequent mental processes, however, differ from mourning, as do some of the accompanying feelings and sensations. The psychological task of dealing with the loss of a part of oneself consists of detaching one's mental investment from the lost part and adjusting one's self-image to the new objective reality. Detachment in this case is characterized not only by pain, anger, helplessness, and guilt, but by a marked loss of self-esteem and feeling low. Adjusting one's self-image involves giving up the accustomed view of oneself as complete, accepting oneself as imperfect and damaged, and relinquishing the wished-for and expected future which the new limitation renders unrealizable. To some extent we are all familiar with this process, as we have to experience it repeatedly throughout life under ordinary circumstances. For example, aging forces us to relinquish our image of ourselves as youthfully attractive and vigorous, but under stress of extreme change and diminishment the task becomes incomparably more arduous and unavoidable.

This exceptionally painful and frustrating inner task awaits the parents, especially mothers, when their newborn dies. The experience of emptiness may take many forms: a bodily lack of well-being, a concern about being ill, the feeling that there is a big hole in one's body, or the sensation of aching arms—the arms that expected to cradle the baby and to draw him back into the mother's body-unity. Since mothers usually do not understand the reasons for these sensations, they feel even stranger, and lead the mothers to worrying about being crazy, about something being utterly wrong with them, or about dying themselves. The loss of self-esteem, often shared by the fathers, may show in feeling hopeless, drained, angry, or incompetent, withdrawing from people and activities, feeling incapable of accomplishing the tasks of daily living, or becoming very sensitive to real or suspected criticism as not liking oneself spreads to feeling unloved, unlovable, as well as unloving. The adjustment of the self-image involves coming to terms with the bodily and mental inadequacy in the present as well as giving up the hopes of a lifelong future with the child. It makes parents feel bad and guilty in themselves and often ashamed in facing the world.

How do outsiders respond? Usually they consciously underestimate the experiences of the stricken and unconsciously fear the perception of their damage as a potential threat to themselves. Amputees are shunned and implicitly expected to hide their affliction and distress from the view of the healthy lest they shatter the latters' defenses and kindle their fears of what might happen to *them*. Thus, where the experience of the death of a loved one draws the support and sympathy of many, both privately and in the societal form of the funeral rites and services, the amputee, the paralyzed, and the parent of a dead newborn often find themselves isolated, their experience belittled or glossed over, without empathy or sympathy even from family members; nor is there an accepted rite or service to acknowledge the event, rally support, or express a sense of shared fate.

It is not surprising that many parents flounder under such stress, fail in accomplishing the necessary mental work, and suffer as the ill-healed wounds subsequently interfere in their personal adjustment, marital relationship, or ability to parent their living children.

ASSISTANCE TO PARENTS

As noted earlier, both parents are helped in developing their relationship with the baby when the mother is not sedated and the father can be present and actively involved at the time of the birth, and when they are encouraged to participate in the baby's subsequent care even, or perhaps especially, if the infant is premature or sick and requires special handling in the hospital. This opportunity to make the step from the "inside" baby to the "outside" baby, and to get to know him as a real, separate individual, also paves the way for the parents' ability to cope with his death. It is easier to deal with the loss of something that is known than of something that is realistically unknown.

When the baby dies, it helps the parents if they understand the exact causes and circumstances of the death and to have a chance to get their many questions answered and misunderstandings clarified. Far from being ultimately relieved by the hospital assuming responsibility for the baby's body, most parents benefit from the opportunity to see and hold their dead child. Doctors and nurses can also encourage the parents to arrange a proper funeral with services that suit their customs and beliefs. When first confronted with the death it may seem easier to parents to forgo these steps, but in the long run it may be reassuring to have access to a grave or urn that provides a concrete memento of the child that was and of the experiences with him. It may also prove helpful to their other offspring in conceptualizing what happened to their deceased brother or sister. Moreover, by sharing in the care of their infant's body in life and in death the parents can feel that they have fulfilled the full measure of their responsibilities as parents and can jointly embark on the mental task that now faces them.

It is very important that both parents be helped to know and understand the double nature of this mental task—the mourning of the infant as a separate person and the coping with the loss of him as a part of the self. The intellectual grasp of these processes helps them to tolerate within themselves the intense pain, guilt, and anger, gain some perspective on their sensations and emotional experiences, empathize with one another, and deal with the responses of outsiders.

Perhaps the most crucial aspect of coping with this special loss is the need to master one's utter helplessness and repair one's self-esteem. Many parents fail in this by withdrawing into inactivity or by busying themselves frantically with random tasks. It helps them to know that channeled activity can provide them with a better remedy. Specifically, they can be active and find satisfaction in supporting one another and, for some, in helping others in similar circumstances, either among their acquaintances or in the framework of organized groups for bereaved parents.

Most of all, however, they can help themselves and reaffirm their self-esteem as parents by assisting their surviving children in understanding and dealing with the death of their sibling. For both parents and children this is by far the most essential and rewarding undertaking, but, unfortunately, also one of the most taxing and therefore most often neglected. It is so tempting for parents to preserve their own denial by glossing over the experience with their children and to protect themselves from working through it by assuming that it has not affected their youngsters. The most valuable diagnostic indication of whether and to what extent parents have truly addressed themselves to the necessary mental tasks in themselves lies in their attempts and success in helping all their children with it, even the youngest.

What makes this task so especially difficult is the fact that, for the surviving children, the newborn was neither a known and loved person nor a part of themselves, but a potential rival whose arrival was expected, at best, with mixed feelings. The baby's sickness and death then further increased the children's anger because they preoccupied the parents mentally and in terms of time. This great difference between the nature of the parents' and children's feelings can create a barrier. It makes it all the more important that the parents respect and tolerate the children's emotions and responses, assist them in understanding the facts of the death and its circumstances, and help them with their main concerns, "Can it happen to me or to you?" and "Is it your fault or is it my fault?"

Parents may find that they require some professional assistance in this difficult undertaking. This does not mean that they have, once again, failed as parents, but on the contrary, that they have responsibly recognized their children's needs and are taking appropriate steps to meet them. With or without professional help, the parents' understanding of the children's concerns will implicitly encourage reciprocal empathy so that the tragedy which can so easily leave family members at odds with themselves and with one another comes to represent, instead, an individual mastery and forges a bond of mutual trust and appreciation.

4

Mothers Have to Be There to Be Left

The title of this chapter is not a new dictum. It is well known to most people, but its full meaning often reveals itself only gradually through personal and professional experiences. I heard it for the first time from my teacher, Anna Freud, when I stood on the threshold of a new, more independent phase of my life and bid her good-bye. I was struck by her response, a simple quiet aside, "A mother's job is to be there to be left." I did not understand it, but it touched me deeply and remained with me, ready to resurface on many occasions and to be integrated in time. I know now that my surprise was not due to the fact that I had not yet experienced the maternal responsibility and feeling of being left; rather, I had not yet come to terms with every child's knowledge of his mother's feelings and of this aspect of his relationship with her.

Many mothers are keenly aware of the painful job of being there to be left at the time of their young child's entry into nursery school. In working with mothers at the Hanna Perkins School as well as in other preschool settings, we hear of their pangs of loneliness, the hurt of not being needed, their helpless inactivity when they sit for hours and days in the lobby or waiting room while the child grows accustomed to the new school and learns to enjoy himself there. We know that the child's mastery of this developmental step can occur only when the mother can allow herself to miss her child, to feel not needed, and to remain lovingly available for the moments when he chooses to return to her. He may need her help with his own conflicted feelings and worries about his new venture, or he may need her assurance that she can tolerate his absence and can even share his enjoyment of new relationships and independent activities (R. A. Furman, 1966; R. A. Furman and Katan, 1969; E. Furman, 1969b, 1978b). Later, many mothers feel the same hurt and welling up of tears when they stand at the door watching their kindergarteners march off to school with nary a backward glance. For years mothers make sure they are there at lunchtime and when the children get home after school. And still later, they stay up at night until their teenagers come home or while they entertain their friends in the home. Always available so as not to be needed, always there to be left, always bearing the pain and anger at being inevitably rejected, and, at times, feeling the joy at the children's growing independence and love of life turn bittersweet. It even continues after the children have moved out to work or study away from home, when every effort is made to keep ready a sleeping space, a special meal, and a warm welcome, and it sometimes shows in tears at a child's wedding.

When children are not made to feel guilty about all their growing up, they allow themselves to perceive and sympathize with mother's task.[1] They thank her at times and increasingly show their concern for her. They bring a little gift, they come home on time, they take mother's commitments into account when they make their own plans, they help around the house, they prepare a treat, they "mother" mother. Sometimes they also teach mother a few things by offering their own astute insight. One 9-year-old was getting ready for her first week away from home at a school camp. As she and her mother talked about writing letters and missing one another, the girl said, "Yes, I will miss you and you will miss me. But you will miss me more than I do because for me it's the beginning of life and for you it's the middle." She sensed well that a mother's tears are not only for the child but for herself, for the

---

[1] Winnicott (1957a, 1963a) also discussed the importance of the development of concern for and appreciation of the mother. He focused on the intrapsychic aspects of this process within the child, the beginnings of drive fusion vis-à-vis the love object, and internalization of aggression within the primitive mental structure.

passing of her own life and the passing on of it to her children—little step by little step, until they are the new generation of grown-ups.

As professionals we know only too well how matters look for child and parent when a mother cannot bear to be there to be left. She may have to drop off her child on the first day of nursery school or send him by bus. She may take on a new job before the child starts kindergarten, and she will then not be at home for lunch with him, or he will have to wait at a neighbor's after school. Or she may suddenly have to take a trip out of town. The child, in response, may disappoint and anger her by playing at the friend's house without letting mother know, by not getting home on time for dinner, and, later, by indulging in minor delinquencies on his way home from school. He may, alternately or at the same time, remain inappropriately dependent and demanding, careless of his clothes and possessions, unwilling to complete his homework unless closely watched, forgetful about assigned chores, and unwilling to keep to reasonable mealtimes and sleeping hours. In these ways the child shows that, through identification or by turning passive into active, he now decathects himself and his possessions as earlier he felt abandoned. At the same time, his immature and irresponsible behavior unconsciously serves to punish the mother for her past "neglect" and to force her into continued care. As these children get to be adolescents, there are apt to be battles royal over staying out too late at night, not letting the parents know of their whereabouts, never being at home when relatives visit or when they are otherwise needed, or taking the family car and making sure that mother is marooned. Yet even these adolescent forays of "I am never there when you want me" are not signs of true independence and object removal. They may go hand in hand with irresponsibility in learning at school, inability to stick with a job, dropping out of college, and generally demonstrating that they are not ready to take charge of their lives and feel badly in need of parental care.

At the other extreme, we recognize the mother who shows her difficulty in being left by clinging to her children when they enter nursery school or by making it, in one way or another, impossible for the children to enjoy their new ventures.

Regardless of whether mother's hurt manifests itself in tears and reproachful loneliness, or in angry or anxious control, the child is made to experience his age-appropriate independence as hurtful and bears the resulting resentment or guilt or both.

No true concern for the mother or appreciation of her can grow from such interactions, nor true joy in growing up. Acquiescence in mother's demands may show in the child's guilt-stricken refusal to take new steps, to like the teacher, to enjoy a meal away from home, to want to learn new activities, or to enjoy life on his own or with others. In this way he reassures mother of always being needed, yet punishes her ultimately by thwarting her potential pleasure in seeing him develop normally. He may combine spiteful spurts in independence with clinging in other areas or with always having to give up the very activity he so thirsted for. "Why don't you play on the jungle gym anymore?" "It's boring." "The teacher does not let us do the fun things." "There are too many children taking turns." Later on in latency there is lack of self-motivated learning and reluctance to engage in, or persist with, extracurricular activities. Periods of adolescent rebellion tend to be abortive and are counteracted by an inability to grow away.

I am not suggesting that these difficulties are solely due to a mother's inability to be there to be left. Nor are these the only difficulties that do result from it. Moreover, there are so many individual ways in which a mother experiences her being left and lets her child know, and again as many ways in which the child responds to her, that my examples merely illustrate some solutions to a complex ongoing process.

Actually, the preceding discussion only serves to remind us of the importance of the mother's job of being there to be left and that we appreciate that this job involves the mother's acceptance of the child's phase-appropriate rejection as well as her acquiescence in the role of assisting him in ultimately supplanting her as an adult. We recognize this parental task most readily when the children are adolescents, nearing adulthood, but we also perceive it at earlier points; for example, at entry into nursery school and public school. We know implicitly that the child's ability to grow up effectively, yet with appropriate concern for the parents and appreciation of them, depends to a considerable extent on the parents', and especially the mother's, ability to be there to be left. Insofar as she succeeds, she not only supports maturation and mastery in the child but helps these steps to become neutral ego achievements in the context of a relationship of adequately fused love and aggression. When she fails in this task, when growing up stands for instinctual pleasure and goes with aggressive annihilation, the child either has to protect the parent and cannot allow himself to grow up or he has to grow up in an angry and hurtful way. This jeopardizes his relationships with his parents, his own ability to parent, and his capacity to function as a feeling person with concern for others.

Obviously, entry into nursery school is not the first time that a mother experiences feeling not needed. During the toddler years the child daily impresses his mother with his belligerent independence. He wants to dress himself, he wants to run his bathwater, he wants to eliminate in his own time and place, he wants to walk away, he wants grandma for better treats or love. Mahler and her colleagues (1963, 1972; Mahler, Pine, and Begman, 1975) have described many aspects of this interaction. Another aspect, during this same phase, was discussed by Winnicott (1958), namely, the origins of the ability to be alone which lie in the experience of being alone in the presence of someone and are closely related to the mother being there to be left.

I should like to turn to an even earlier period of the mother's job of being there to be left, namely, weaning. Many authors have discussed this important developmental step. Many have spoken of the trauma of weaning for the child. Kleinian writers have specifically addressed themselves to the depressive position that accompanies or follows weaning (Klein, 1934, 1940, 1957). Winnicott (1954, 1957a, 1963a) prefers to think of it as the beginnings of concern, when the infant appreciates his separateness from the mother, struggles with his primitive aggression to her, and begins to fuse and internalize it to some extent to preserve mother as an object.

My experience suggests that the stress, even potential trauma, of weaning applies primarily to the mother's rather than the baby's feelings about it. It is often the first time when a mother is called upon to be there to be left. Since she is then still so utterly close with her baby and senses his primitive urges with a resonance of her own, she is especially likely to experience his turning away from her and reaching out for more advanced and independent satisfactions as a narcissistically hurtful rejection, abandonment, or attack. When she responds to it as such, the baby, in turn, is thrown into conflict, or confusion, or discomfort. We are then apt to view the infant's behavior as a reaction to the loss of his earlier state and satisfactions rather than as a response to his mother's upset at his leaving of her. In my observations of mothers and babies, I have always noted that the baby initiates the weaning and actively rejects the breast. This usually takes place when the baby's development is more advanced in the area of self and object differentiation and investment (see also Spock, 1963). When the mother heeds her child's signals and allows herself to be there to be left, the baby soon relishes his new achievement and invites mother to share in and admire his fun. When she is too hurt by his rejection, he misses out on this basic opportunity to learn that his growing up is safe for both of them, that it does not hurt or antagonize mother, does not render her unavailable, and does not jeopardize their relationship, although it may change its nature.

CASE EXAMPLES

Case 1

Lisa's mother, Mrs. L, had anticipated her first child with pleasure. She very much wanted to mother her baby well, in part because she had high standards for herself and in part because she had learned about the importance of the early mother–child relationship. She was therefore especially alert to the first signs of difficulty and distressed by them. Lisa was then about 7 months old, well developed, alert, and playful, but "fussy" in the evenings. Mrs. L had consulted her pediatrician and he had assured her that Lisa's trouble was a passing, not uncommon, phase and that she had nothing to worry about. Since she continued to worry, however, she came to me for help.

Whereas earlier, Lisa had gone to sleep peacefully and slept through the night, during the last few weeks she had cried. She did not cry desperately or to the point of being overwhelmed but long and plaintively enough so that Mrs. L felt she really needed to go in to Lisa and pick her up for a while. At first one picking-up helped, but then Lisa needed two or more. Sometimes she even woke up during the night. Mother and father were annoyed as well as upset by the nightly disturbance of their time and rest together. They talked things over and decided that Mr. L would go in to Lisa because Mrs. L had become so worried that she lay awake for hours and was perhaps too distressed to comfort the baby. They tried it one evening and it seemed to work, but the next night was even worse. And when they tried to let Lisa "cry it out," she did cry herself to sleep but soon woke again and sounded more unhappy. "I just know I am doing something wrong. I should not get so bothered, but I can't help it. And I can't help Lisa," said Mrs. L. Later she added, "Perhaps I send her a double message," but she could not explain this further because she was only repeating what her husband had told her.

We soon learned that Lisa's night difficulty coincided with her beginning to dawdle at the breast and turn away during feeds. One time she playfully bit her mother, who involuntarily yelped. Lisa was also teething a bit and spent much time and energy chewing on biscuits and hard objects. She had been so interested in the parents' eating and drinking that they had offered her liquids from the cup and bits of their food to hold and eat. The mother had thus readily recognized Lisa's wish to leave the breast for newer and better things and had helped her appropriately. She made new foods and new ways of eating available to Lisa. She allowed Lisa to reduce breast-feeding at her own pace—sometimes feeds were skipped and sometimes they were very short depending on Lisa's interest or disinterest. The mother felt that weaning was going well, and she spoke with pride of Lisa's new accomplishments, but she had not connected it with the onset of the sleep difficulty. She surprised herself when she made the link and then suddenly realized how much she missed the nursing. "It's like she doesn't need me anymore. It's the end of our closest time." Now she also knew what "double message" she was conveying. "If you don't need me at feeding time, you need me at night. I want you to grow up, but I can't bear being left." She now described in detail and with newly available feeling how anxiously she waited for Lisa's night calls and how, after holding her, she put her down with the thought, "This won't last for long. She'll want me again"; and yet how angry it made her that the child never left *her* alone so she could enjoy herself as an adult.

As soon as the mother gained this insight into her loneliness, resentment, mixed-up roles with, and expectations of, her baby, she was able to help Lisa at night. Her tenseness left her. She was calm and loving with Lisa through the evening routine and she told her, "It's okay to go to sleep. It's okay to be a big girl. Mommy loves you and we'll be glad to see each other in the morning." Lisa "drank in" all that was said and done and slept well. Mrs. L knew Lisa would. It was the end of Lisa's sleep disturbance.

Other babies' signals for wanting to wean are similar or different. It seems to me that mothers always react to them, though they may not consciously observe and understand them. I am not suggesting that a mother should not react at all—for example, that she should impassively allow the baby to hurt her by biting her breast. Indeed, the mother's appropriately attuned and attenuated reaction constitutes a vital link in the mother–child interaction, contributes to its healthy unfolding, and stimulates the child's progressive developmental responses. The crucial factors are how the mother experiences the child's growing up, how her personality deals with that experience, and how she conveys it to the infant within a normal range of variations or in pathological forms. Although Lisa's sleep trouble was not uncommon, there are many other ways in which babies respond to their mothers' upset and hurt.

The mothers I have worked with or been able to observe were mostly breast-feeding, except for one mother who felt just as strongly about her baby's refusal of the bottle. In a similar vein, some mothers are hurt by the child's thumbsucking or by his looking at the father during nursing, or by being sleepy, but these and other forms of the child's turning away are usually less upsetting than the child's wish to wean. Some mothers, however, already experience the baby's birth as an aggressive abandonment, an attitude which interferes with their initial adequate investment of the child. It is possible that, to some extent and under certain circumstances, this prototypical experience affects maternal responses to their children's later steps toward independence.

Some mothers initiate weaning in order to avoid having to be there to be left. Their active leaving of the children and introduction of the cup may be in tune with the children's readiness and may even come about in response to preconsciously perceived signs of the infants' wish to grow away, but the fact that the mothers feel they need to leave the children makes a special impact on their interaction. Their chances for coming to terms with the process of the children's growing up are diminished.

But surely there are babies who cling to nursing and do not want to be weaned! I suspect that, with some of these babies, their signals go unheeded and they give up, or give in, in time. With others, nursing may assume a different meaning and come to serve different purposes. Jenny is a case in point.

Case 2

Mrs. J came for help when Jenny was about 4½ years old. Her severe separation problem had completely foiled attendance at a nursery school and after one and a half years of trying, everyone had run out of ways to help Jenny take the step. A period of observation and exploratory work at the Hanna Perkins School revealed that this highly intelligent and potentially competent little girl suffered from an obsessional neurosis rather than from a mother who could not articulate appropriate expectations. In order to avoid the inner turmoil of indecision, which overcame Jenny with each independent function or activity, she used her mother to direct, initiate, and even function for her. For example, Jenny stood silent and motionless at the door of the schoolroom because she could not decide where to sit or what to do, but when her mother was at her side making suggestions, talking for her, and getting an activity or game started, Jenny could follow mother's lead. When that activity was over, Mrs. J coaxed Jenny into the next one. The mother fulfilled her role consistently and patiently. She knew Jenny had severe, temperlike anxiety attacks and felt she could not expose her child to such overwhelming distress.

For the purposes of the present discussion I shall select only one item from Jenny's earliest history. Her first year was uneventful except that she had been an avid nursling and she weaned herself only at the age of 2 years. Mrs. J had not tried to wean Jenny earlier because she had waited for the child's signals. She had not been surprised at Jenny's late weaning because she knew that Jenny had never wanted to "let go" of mother. The mother had deduced this from the fact that Jenny had not wanted to be held by others she knew, and because, at the age of about 6 months or so, Jenny had reacted with much protest and stress to mother's attempt to exchange baby-sitting services with a friend. The friend's baby did not mind being in Jenny's home for a few hours, but Jenny was so upset at the friend's home that Mrs. J quickly discontinued the arrangement. Later in our work, however, Mrs. J recalled with great guilt that, during that same period and for some months following it, she had taken on part-time work at home which made her unavailable to Jenny. "I don't know why, but I just felt I had to do something all on my own. Sometimes I heard her cry but I just couldn't let go of my work." The mother only interrupted her work for the nursing periods. Nursing became Jenny's way of keeping mother's love on mother's terms. Mrs. J's great guilt over her withdrawal suggested that she unconsciously rejected and left Jenny before Jenny could reject and leave her. Perhaps the mother's need to leave her baby was even prompted by Jenny's signals. This joint early experience did not produce Jenny's obsessional neurosis, but it possibly furnished a matrix for the later link between the temptations of growing independence and unresolved ambivalence in the mother–child relationship.

CONCLUDING REMARKS

I have shown that the principle of "mothers have to be there to be left" is well known to us in relation to some developmental steps and I chose the child's entry into nursery and elementary school to illustrate its more and less successful ways of operating. I briefly referred to some of its manifestations in the preceding toddler phase and subsequent latency and adolescence. I focused in greater detail on weaning, which, I believe, is the first significant developmental step when the mother is called upon to respond to her infant's maturational need to turn away from her by being there to be left. My findings suggest that, normally, the impetus for weaning comes from the baby, that the mother's conscious or preconscious perception of his signals upsets her, and that the infant's reaction to weaning (or unwillingness to wean) often represents primarily a response to the way in which the mother conveys to him her way of dealing with her feelings.

In other words, I suggest reversing a commonly held notion of weaning. Usually it is thought that the mother weans the baby and in doing so deprives the infant of an accustomed instinctual satisfaction and pleasurable closeness to her, to which he reacts with more or less intense feelings of loss, anger, and sadness. I put forward the idea that the baby "weans" the mother; that is, the infant lets the mother know that he prefers new instinctual satisfactions and more separateness. The mother reacts to this with more or less intense feelings of loss. In some ways *she* feels deprived of an accustomed instinctual satisfaction and pleasurable closeness. She views the child's step as a hurtful rejection, as an aggressive abandonment, as a threat of not being needed and being subject to replacement, and she imparts these feelings in some measure to the child, either directly or in defensive form. The baby responds to her mood and behavior, and this affects both his relationship with the mother and his attitude to the new developmental venture.

In discussing this prototypical mother–child interaction during a maturational step, I have picked out some general implications of the mother's job of being there to be left. (1) The child's spontaneous growing up, with each little or big step, implies his wish for new and better pleasures with more independence, and this inevitably includes a measure of rejection of the mother who supplied and participated in the early satisfactions. It also implies, more indirectly and at a less conscious level, the ultimate replacement of the mother as a sexually active, childbearing, and child-raising adult. (2) The mother senses all this in her child and experiences, over and over again, the hurt and inherent aggression of his maturation as well as the satisfaction in his progressive achievements. (3) She can allow herself to be there to be left, when she can tolerate the pleasure and the resentment and pain of her position, when her ambivalence in relation to her child is sufficiently fused, and when, at least in part, she can view his development as neutralized growth rather than as an instinctual battle. (4) When she fails to master these aspects in herself, she is bound to convey her inner turmoil to her child in one or another way and stimulates the child's response, which, again, may take many different forms. The ensuing mother–child interaction interferes with the development of their relationship and the healthy maturation of the child. (5) Under favorable circumstances, the mother's ability to be there to be left fosters the child's mastery of developmental steps and paves the way for neutralized progressive achievement of skills, activities, and even of functions. In the area of relationships it furnishes a model for the fusion of drives and the development of mature concern for others as well as appreciation of the maternal task.

This is not an exhaustive list of the many ways in which the mother's job of being there to be left affects the child's growth or the mother's own personality. In the same way, the specific developmental turning points I mentioned are merely examples of the many big and small developmental steps. They may encompass an entire phase, such as a child's toilet mastery (in contrast to toilet training, which implies the mother's control and activity),[2] or they may focus on a minor commonplace venture, for example, the child's simple announcement, "I told the neighbor I'd rake their leaves for them for money. Okay, Mom?"

I hope that this introduction to the theme of "mother has to be there to be left" will encourage others to think further, to note its many ramifications and applications, and to help deepen our understanding.

---

[2] I owe this thought and verbal differentiation to my husband, Dr. R. A. Furman, to whom I am also grateful for discussing this whole subject on numerous occasions and for encouraging me to put my ideas in writing.

5

Self-Care and the Mother–Child Relationship

When the Hanna Perkins Toddler Group began in 1984, my colleagues and I had already done much thinking about parenting and accumulated a lot of experience in working with families. We were well versed with the manifestations of parenthood as a developmental phase with its characteristic and changing investment of the child (chapter 2); we had come to understand the unique anguish parents and children experience when they are lost to one another through death (chapters 3, 10; E. Furman, 1974), and even how hard it is for them to negotiate the inevitable developmental losses engendered by the child's growing up and away (chapter 4). Inner interferences in parental investment had also been encountered and explored. In "Intermittent Decathexis" (R. A. Furman and E. Furman, 1984) we described a parent becoming temporarily unaware of her child's behavior or verbalizations, of his need for care and protection, even of his whereabouts, as though he suddenly did not exist, while the parent, at these times, is usually preoccupied with meeting his or her own need—all caused by a particular lability in the parental investment of the child. But when we added the Toddler Project, an intensive long-term research study, to our Toddler Group work, we had no specific expectation of studying parental investment. Indeed, we did not know what we would learn, and it was only when we integrated and reflected on our data that we realized how significantly the mother's investment affects the child's development.

The evidence amply confirmed and deepened our previous finding as to the important role of bodily self-care in the personality development of the toddler (E. Furman, 1987). At the same time, however, we were surprised by evidence of a reciprocal development in the mother, a change in her investment of her child which was crucially linked to her child's success in achieving autonomy as an individual. Actually, we found that rapid and extensive changes in her investment need to take place to facilitate his growth; that it is not any one specific milestone that has to be negotiated, but that the entire toddler phase is a period of drastic ongoing shift in the nature of the maternal investment, a shift from narcissistic toward object cathexis. Since it is a back-and-forth development, often changing from hour to hour, it also demands enormous flexibility of investment, a process which taxes a mother's capacity for change and resilience to its utmost. Our experience and research data of work with parents and children of all ages suggest that no other phase demands as much change in investment as the toddler phase. And, although this mutual mother–child process concerns all aspects of the child's growing personality, it is especially focused on his body and its care.

Many later difficulties result from not accomplishing this adjustment when the child was a toddler, and therefore understanding better the phase-appropriate changes in the mother–child investments also sheds light on the nature of the pathological solutions.

Owning One's Body and Taking Care of It

The child's mastery of bodily self-care is the vehicle by which ownership of his body is transferred from mother to him through identification with her. It is the fulcrum of change in the mother–child relationship, from a mutually more narcissistic to a mutually more object-oriented investment. It forms the basis for the child's growing concept of his body-ego, which integrates his developing functions and invests them as his own. As a first major secondary narcissistic investment, mastery also becomes a source of self-regard and self-esteem,

Self-Care and the Mother–Child Relationship

builds important tolerance for frustration and pleasure, and confidence in achievement through effort, all of which underlie the later ability to learn and work. The very process of mastery serves to further integration. It characterizes the youngster who is "with it," who is "all there," neither whiny, clingy, and diffident, nor oppositional for opposition's sake. Mastery of self-care, more than any other single development, makes the toddler feel he is a person, a somebody. Yet in the course of daily living, the path toward this achievement is long and arduous and fraught with obstacles within mother and child as well as in the interaction between them.

The child's wish for "me do" and the zest he brings to putting it into practice is one of the hallmarks of being a toddler. "Me do" encompasses all areas of activity, be it turning on faucets, hammering, cooking, everything he sees his loved ones do, but for the most part the young toddler is content to imitate or to pretend. Not so when it concerns his own body, for in this area he wants to do for real, becomes very determined, and interferes with mother's ministrations if he does not get his own way.

> Cindy, 20 months old, sits next to her Mom at the table, enjoying her snack with all of us. She is still quite messy. Juice and cracker crumbs dribble down her chin. Mom reaches over and wipes the mess off Cindy's face. Cindy screams irritably. A few minutes later Mom repeats her wiping and Cindy repeats her screaming. Whereas some mothers would soon understand and find a way to work it out, Cindy's Mom either continues her wiping or, embarrassed by her daughter's screams, lets the mess dribble till the end of snack when the wiping is more of a job and Cindy screams longer and louder and has to be held by Mom lest she escape. After some days of this interaction, I, the teacher, suggest: "Maybe Cindy wants to be asked about wiping her face and then Cindy could tell Mom if she is ready for it." Mother looks surprised, then smiles, looking at Cindy's beaming yes-nodding face. Soon we hear: "Cindy, are you ready to have me wipe your face? It'll feel better when it's clean." Cindy agrees, holds out her face for wiping, and then surprises mother again with a gracious "Thank you." Both are pleased. All goes well when mother repeats her request, but of course she forgets occasionally and now Cindy responds with pulling

away and yelling "No." Mother apologizes and promises to try harder. Cindy accepts her apology with dignity. After some days of this new, mutually respectful regime, Cindy fights for her next step in becoming Mommy to herself: she wants to do the wiping. Mother again has a hard time giving up, but this time I only need to say, "I think Cindy wants something more" and mother figures out that Cindy wants to do the wiping. She offers this to Cindy who agrees to the following compromise: Cindy will wipe herself and Mom will help her by guiding her hand with the bigger cleanup at the end of snack. Everyone is happy, and Cindy basks in her Mom's and the teacher's admiration for her new accomplishment.

Who owns the child's body, who gauges its needs, and who meets them are, for the toddler, the most crucial area of differentiating himself, of investing himself, and achieving bodily and mental self-esteem. He usually accomplishes this by internalizing mother's care of him and, step by step, learning to mother himself. He gauges his hunger and feeds himself, learns to know his sensations for eliminating and mastering toileting, dresses himself and cares for his clothes, learns to keep himself safe and avoid common dangers, is able to fall asleep on his own when tired. Although in Cindy's case, as in most others, the toddler's wish to take over his own care is manifestly signaled by impatience with or anger at mother's activity, by frustration at having to wait for her, or annoyance at the way she does it, the more important motivation for "me do" is the child's underlying admiration and love of what she can do and resulting wish to become like her. In the context of a good-enough relationship, this admiring wish for identification also helps the child to prefer doing to being done for, to persevere with trying in spite of his frequent frustrating failures, and to tame his anger at mother, which inevitably accompanies the long process toward mastery. Usually, the more positive the relationship and the more consistent and enjoyable the mother's care has been, the sooner and more insistently does the child want to identify with her and do for himself.

For the mother this area is also the most crucial, and usually the most difficult, as she now has to make some of her narcissistic cathexis of the child's body and bodily care available to him for his use and transform her relationship into a comparatively increased object investment. Cindy, like most healthy toddlers, leads the way and alerts Mom that the next step is due. Mother is not as ready as Cindy but, with just a little additional help, begins to catch up. She shows that it goes against the grain by forgetting to ask Cindy's permission, and by needing a little help again with the next step, but she also shows her success in her efforts by apologizing for slipping up and by finding pleasure in Cindy's achievement, and sharing Cindy's enjoyment of it.

THE SHARED STEPS IN ACHIEVING BODILY MASTERY

Sometimes the steps in the toddler doing for himself are miniscule, sometimes huge. They do, however, group themselves into four successive stages on the way toward full mastery, or internalization, and each stage requires its own characteristic interaction with mother: (1) There is the "doing for" stage, with mother doing the caring for the child who essentially enjoys being done for. Already during babyhood this is never a pure stage; even then most mothers respect and accommodate to some aspects of the child's active participation. (2) Next comes the "doing with" stage, where mother and child, in varying proportion, share in the tasks; for example, proceeding from the child holding up his arms to assist with getting off his shirt to the child perhaps putting on his own jacket with mother pulling out the collar and starting the zipper. (3) Then comes the "standing by to admire" stage, where the child is doing some aspect of self-care without any assistance—maybe using spoon and fork for eating, or protecting himself by carefully staying out of the way of a moving swing. Mother is very much needed still to stand by, fully invested, to appreciate her child's efforts and achievement, and to support and share his pride in it. (4) The final stage is "doing for oneself," where the child has internalized both the mothering of himself and the satisfaction it brings to such an extent that mother's bodily presence and emotional investment are no longer necessary. Whatever the achievement is, that aspect of his body, its needs, and care are now owned by the child and provide him with a sense of well-being and self-esteem, his secondary narcissistic investment.

Just as the first "doing for" stage already involves some "doing with" and long precedes toddlerhood in the bodily area, so the third stage of "standing by to admire," and especially the fourth one of really "doing for oneself" extend well beyond toddlerhood. But the important basics are best accomplished during this phase to enable the child to cope with the developmental tasks of the subsequent preschool phase. This phase includes the integration of concerns about sexual differences and the child's place vis-à-vis the parents' husband—wife relationship, and the ability to adjust in a nursery school where he has to relate with a teacher who is not a mere mother substitute, and where his investment in activities and play presupposes a considerable degree of independent mastery of bodily needs.

The child's success in getting to own his body and meet its needs depends throughout on his mother's ability to stay "in tune." Most mothers miss the toddler's first signals of readiness for "me do" and need his persistent help, usually in the form of protest and uncooperativeness, to help them along in their task of shifting investments. Most mothers find it especially puzzling and even exasperating at times to follow the zigzag line of the child's progress—protesting often, welcoming mother's taking over at other times, or even refusing to do for himself on some days the very self-care he had previously so proudly achieved. The best first signs of a mother's appropriately balanced investment and potential flexibility are the child's signals, and especially his persistence in signaling. It means he senses and trusts that she can respond to him, and she usually does. Even when, as with Cindy's mother, she seemed to need additional help from someone who could feel with both of them, the fact that mother can readily use this help and that the child has not given up signaling suggest that mother is fairly ready to do her part. We find that many mothers are able to use additional help to effect the necessary change, even when their interaction with the child has been at a standstill for some time.

When 22 month-old Jane's mother first arrived she asked where the changing table was. I explained that we did not have one, that we had learned that most toddlers like so much to stand on their own feet and take an active part in everything, and that therefore mothers work it out with their youngsters in this way in the adjacent private bathroom. Mother shook her head in disbelief and with some irritation but, when the time came, she and Jane did work it out. Jane emerged from the bathroom beaming, mother somewhat harassed. After a while we heard they had discontinued the being "done for" stage at home too, with Jane eager to dump and flush the diaper contents, pulling her own pants off and back on, even talking about using the toilet. Mother then added reflectively, "Getting her changed used to be such a struggle. I thought her standing up would be even worse, but it's really much easier now. I guess she was ready."

Such capacity for mother and toddler to get back in tune testifies not only to the health of their relationship but to the fact that help is most readily integrated when mother and child are still in the process of tackling this developmental task. But progressive steps are not always so easily taken. Sometimes a mother does recognize the child's wish for "me do," but begrudges it, and can't allow herself to enjoy it.

John's mother dressed her nearly 2-year-old in her lap, with him struggling and kicking and her alternating desperate pleas of, "But you need to help me" with strangleholds as she pulled on his snowpants or jacket. Finally she would stand him up and say angrily, "Well, you can just do it yourself. I am through!" John would then, with equal anger, push and pull at his garments, give up in frustration, and have a temper tantrum, or run around teasingly, or helplessly surrender to mother's renewed dressing efforts. When he did manage to get on his jacket, he looked more defiant and sheepish than proud.

Jeremy, just under 2, simply let himself be dressed, cuddling into his Mom. He had either never shown initiative or had long ceased to do so. Although a smart and capable boy, Jeremy sensed correctly that, with him as with his older siblings, mother especially enjoyed their bodily care and was very reluctant to surrender it. At the same time, mother's rather frequent absences and unavailability already posed a threat (he got very upset and angry at good-bye times) and perhaps made him reluctant, as it were, to leave her. Adapting to mother's need, he appeared to have surrendered his potential independence for the sake of keeping her infantile love—but at a cost. He would cast sidelong glances at his happy, accomplished peers and then look down as if shamed, and he often refused to attempt new activities, insisting on mother's help, never trusting himself to master anything. By pointing this out to them, mother and child could be helped to recognize Jeremy's wish to do for himself and to do well, and then they took the first steps in working on Jeremy's dressing together and building his self-esteem with each proud achievement.

The "doing with" stage, once embarked upon, is often a satisfying period for mother and child, but can also reach a plateau or turn into an increasingly unhelpful interaction. With toileting, for example, it often shows in mother continuing to wipe her child's behind ("He can't get it really clean"). The child then not only never fully takes charge of his body but also continues to experience a passive stimulation. Although this kind of getting stuck may be caused by many factors in mother and child, a significant one is the reluctance to face the next step. "Standing by to admire" is perhaps the hardest step of all for the mother, the time when she feels not needed, the time when she truly has to surrender her direct involvement with the child's body without withdrawing from him. It is the very time when the child needs her most to love him in a new way. Without it, his achievement has no value and cannot be internalized in a lastingly adaptive, satisfying way. Some mothers actually walk away to busy themselves with something else (most often with their own body—doing their nails, combing their hair, going to the bathroom). Some stand by, but their mind is not with the child. Some say, "I am so proud of you," as though the child's achievement were still theirs, instead of: "You really are doing a good job, how proud you can feel with yourself." Some show their persisting narcissistic investment in action.

Ellen's mother always had to improve her daughter's achievement, in fact making it her own. She did this not only with

Ellen's body, such as adjusting her clothes and adding decorative items, but also with Ellen's activities, such as adding items to her picture to make it look better or fitting in some of the pieces in Ellen's puzzle. Mother's pride in the final result was matched by Ellen's dissatisfaction and often led to her actually destroying the product because it had become mother's, Ellen's own part seeming inadequate.

Even skilled achievements are joyless and unstable when they lack mother's loving investment.

Jennifer's mother very much wanted to do the right thing and decided to set the pace by expecting her 2-year-old to dress herself. Jennifer had the necessary skills at her disposal, but neither she nor mother truly enjoyed either the process or the achievement. Soon Jennifer made a teasing, frustrating struggle out of it, dawdling or running around, or acting helpless until considerations of time often forced mother either to sit it out with constant firm exhortations or to end up dressing Jennifer. The little girl felt she was losing rather than gaining something by dressing herself. Mother's expectation reflected her narcissistic investment and was not accompanied by a change to object love. I commented to mother and child, "It looks a bit like Jennifer has to make such a big fuss to have Mommy close. Perhaps she feels that if you dress yourself you miss out on a loving time with Mommy." Jennifer understood at once. Mother needed time to work this out for herself in her weekly meetings with their therapist, but, to start with, even some extra hugs with dressing helped.

Regardless of whether a child actually knows how to care for his body, unless his admiring loving of mother's care motivated him to learn her skills, and unless they are internalized with mother's appropriate investment, they will not reach the last phase of "doing for oneself" in a reliable manner. Instead, they tend to remain subject to regression and/or do not add to the child's good feeling about himself. Lack of self-worth in bodily mastery tends to carry over to unstable mental self-esteem and remains, as our follow-up profiles indicate, a sign of this toddler development having gone awry. We have seen this occur not only in instances where the child learns to care for himself out of defiance of or compliance with mother. It is strikingly evident in cases where the child has learned aspects of self-care, such as dressing, from temporary caretakers (as in day care), or from siblings or peers, or even from the father. We have seen it also in instances where the child's self-care resulted from missing mother or her care and was accomplished during periods of mother's unavailability. When the child bypasses the step of, "I want to mother myself as mother does," and when the transfer of mother's love to loving investment of self-care does not accompany his accomplishment, it does not contribute to his self-esteem or loving self-regard. It may also adversely affect the mother's feelings for her child and pose an obstacle to her appropriate investment in him, even if, at one level, she is glad not to be needed. With some mother–child relationships, such leaving out or diminished use of the mother in acquiring self-care, appears to result from actual deficits in maternal investment and/or excessive unavailability. The child's accomplishment then suggests a defensive identification as opposed to the developmental ego identification, and therefore fails to serve as a helpful secondary narcissistic investment. This did not apply to the mothers of our toddlers. With them, our observations suggest that a mother's relative failure in effecting the necessary shifts in investment were often related to ambivalence. This was either part of an unconscious negative narcissistic cathexis of her child (e.g., her own lack of self-esteem as a mother extended to the child) or part of a considerable admixture of aggression in her object investment of her child. The former is, for example, evident in the vignette of Ellen whose mother always needed to improve her child's accomplishment and, in doing so, conveyed that anything Ellen did would not be good enough. The latter difficulty often shows in a mother's denial of her child's signals ("Oh, I don't think he's ready for that yet"), but she may then become very angry at her child when they finally work on mastery and the child does not perform well. In such instances, as in the case of Mary below, the mother's continued narcissistic cathexis protects her child.

> Mary's mother diapered her in a prone position until she was 2 years old, claiming that Mary was not ready to use the potty. Mother realized that she especially liked the infantile bodily

relationship with her children and Mary wisely adapted to this and submitted without complaint. But when, in part as a result of other progressive steps during Toddler Group, Mary finally asserted herself and mother embarked with her on the "doing with" stage, all loving patience left her in spite of her good intentions. She repeatedly burst out with harsh anger at Mary's incidents of wetting or soiling, much to her own chagrin. This difficulty with anger was a part of all mother's relationships, but had not manifested itself with Mary as long as mother owned Mary's body.

"I DID NOT EXPECT IT OF HIM"

A mother's attitude or verbalization of "I did not expect it of him" often encapsulates the essence of her narcissistic investment. It implies that the child's growth proceeds via mother's rather than the child's readiness, and often applies not only to matters of bodily ownership and care but extends to many other areas of his personality. On the one hand it reflects her sense of total responsibility, which is so crucial to her continuous care of him, and which, when something is wrong with her child, not only makes her feel guilty but fuels her efforts to put it right again. It is the very feeling we count on, for example, to help a mother initiate and support her child's treatment for bodily or emotional illness. On the other hand, however, and with her toddler especially, this attitude typically leads a mother to assume that she, and only she, is the cause of whatever the child feels and does, disregarding feelings and conflicts that stem from within the child or from experiences which were relatively unrelated to the mother.

> Tim, close to 2, did not know how to peddle a tricycle or climb up our small slide. Large motor skills were not his forte, but the striking thing was that he refused to practice, although he watched his peers with longing, some better than he at it, some not. His Mom told us she felt this was all due to the fact that her earlier illness had prevented her from doing these activities with him enough and she resolved to make up for it. She and Tim had many good outdoor activity times near their home

where Tim worked on these skills quite happily, and he also did so in our playground when he was out there first or last. But the moment the other toddlers were around doing the same activities, Tim gave up and refused to use the equipment. Mom practiced even more with him, and each time reported how good Tim was getting with his tricycle. She could not understand, sometimes puzzling, sometimes rationalizing, why he refused at certain times. It was quite evident to us that Tim felt inferior in the face of competition and our other observations as well as reports from home indicated that Tim's feeling derived from him comparing himself with his older brothers and father. It took much tactful work to help Mom appreciate that she could not help Tim by merely investing his motor control more lovingly but needed to assist him in facing and coping with his helpless envy of the bigger males in the family.

Holly, 26 months old, had waited with her mother in the toddler room before the start of class and had, with mother's permission, played with puzzles from the teachers' drawers. When we arrived and brought out these puzzles, Holly became furious at me, yelled at and attacked me, while at the same time backing away as though I would go after her. I told her it looked like she expected me to be very angry at her, which I was not, but perhaps she felt bad about something. The story of her use of the puzzles was then blurted out and Holly indeed was very guilty. We agreed that she need not feel so bad because the puzzles were not damaged, but that she would feel better if next time she would wait to ask teacher's okay before helping herself. Then we would plan ahead just what she could play with. Mother noticed how guilty Holly felt but was flabberghasted, "How could she feel guilty when I did not tell her it was bad?" In this as in other instances, mother had altogether disregarded her little girl's own feelings and conflicts, and hence been unable to empathize and help her.

Some mothers disregard not only feelings and conflicts but their child's ego functions. They may talk about him in his presence and claim he did not hear or know what they were saying because "I did not tell him," as though his perceptions and knowledge functioned only with what she selected for him. Or they may talk for him and answer questions directed to him as though his speech was really theirs, or urge him to tell the teachers specific events of their choosing about home experiences. They are then quite nonplussed and embarrassed when the child refuses to comply or, worse, tells what was meaningful to him. Thus Peter told us that at the zoo Dad told him to pee on a bush and Bart failed to repeat mother's nice account of going to a children's theater and blurted out instead that he tweeked a woman's nose because she came too close and touched his face. Less humorously, mothers frequently feel that they need to order and control a child's every move, be it in play, activities, or self-care, never crediting the child with remembering, knowing, having ideas of his own, or really wanting to do things well. And if he does make a mistake, they take it as proof of his inability to master for himself instead of sympathizing with the child's feeling of failure and assuring him that he can put it right and will soon learn to do it well.

Of course, the mothers who disclaim their responsibility and quickly put the blame for the child's difficulty on others are not feeling less but more guilty, hence the need for the defense.

> Alan's mother blamed his hitting on his older brother's mistreatment of him, but this only thinly and temporarily veiled her guilt about her own loss of temper and for not protecting Alan from the brother. Actually Alan's physical aggression also stemmed from other sources beyond mother's control but she could not consider these for some time.

In describing the effects of mothers' narcissistic investment I do not wish, like the mothers themselves, to disregard the child's contribution to their interactions. Toddlers' individual personalities, conflicts, and experiences may delay or interfere with phase-appropriate development in such a way that they do not signal their readiness for progressive steps or misuse their mothers' willingness to own them for defensive purposes.

> Bess, a 2-year-old with a very well-structured personality, had herself a rough day in Toddler Group. She was irritable and unable to settle down to activities. At the end of it she shouted

at mother: "I am very angry at you, you are a bad Mommy," which mother accepted, attributing it to that morning's argument between them. When I suggested that I did not know about Mommy being so bad, but perhaps Bess was pretty angry at Bess for having had a hard day, Bess suddenly looked guilty and seriously agreed, much to mother's surprise. Bess often used this defense to ward off inner conflict and found a willing partner in mother.

Sally, already past 2 years old, still wanted mother to diaper her. Sometimes she even wanted her diapers changed when they were dry, which mother attributed to Sally not being ready to use the toilet and not knowing when diapers were really wet. But Sally, it turned out, wanted mother, over and over again, to put on her, Sally's, bottom something else that was an appendage, hence the insistent demand for a ministration that never turned out satisfactory for long. She wanted mother to make her into a boy, but her demand for ever new diapers not only warded off this wish and expectation from mother but it also already served to defend against her feelings of inferiority and guilt, feeling that she might have spoiled her genitals.

A toddler's lack of zest of self-care and demands for or acquiescence in being done for quite often obscures low self-esteem and harsh early guilt, and finds secondary or defensive gratification in mother's infantile investment of him. Yet in each of these cases, the child's feelings of inferiority and his or her turning anger mentally against the self also grew out of mother not having responded to the child's readiness. She had not helped the child gain self-esteem through loving internalization of her investment, and had failed to channel aggression into purposeful activity in the process. Without this early self-esteem and well-directed energy, children easily feel incapable of coping with phallic concerns, instinctually as well as in the area of competent neutral achievement. They then readily fall back on mother doing for them as a solution to their difficulties.

Perhaps the most unhelpful way in which a parent's narcissistic investment may manifest itself is the use, or rather misuse, of the child for the parent's instinctual gratification.

Self-Care and the Mother–Child Relationship

We illustrated this, at the start of this chapter, when we mentioned parents fondling their child for their pleasure but without regard for his tolerance for stimuli. Tickling, bouncing him up and down, kissing him sensuously, or exposing him to parental nudity, toileting, or sexual activity are other forms, especially when the parents either fail to notice or actually prohibit or punish the child's response, or deny there even is a response. Alternatively, a mother may not limit her toddler's inappropriate sexual behavior, such as intruding on other's bathrooming, exposing their genitals to others, or masturbating in front of them during, say, storytime in a group. She seems unaware, at these times, not only of the reaction of other children, but of the fact that her own child has feelings and ends up either overstimulated or conflicted or both. Likewise, with aggression, mothers may fail to limit their child's aggression or be unaware of the child's feelings about mother's aggression. Although fathers are sometimes the main initiators in these interactions, the mother's compliance and failure to feel with and protect her child, points to her share in it.

The various manifestations of a mother's no longer phase-appropriate narcissistic investment in her toddler are of course widely encountered in her relationship with her much older or even adult children, as are the devastating effects on the child's personality. At later stages such interactions are usually related to many pathological factors in the parent's personality and overdetermined by many pathological factors in the child's personality. They tend to be rigidly fixed and difficult to change. During the toddler phase, by contrast, a mother's relative shifts in cathexis are a part of a phase-appropriate developmental task in her mothering and hence generally still quite flexible. Even when there have been delays or when the child's conflicts have complicated matters, limited assistance from the therapist and/or teacher is mostly well utilized. As long as the helper is able to feel with and respect mother and child and, instead of getting between them or posing as the better mother, assists them to reestablish communication, mother and child tend to appreciate the intervention—perhaps because getting in tune gives so much satisfaction to both. We find that a mother who gets in tune in this phase is likely to remain in tune in subsequent phases. Even a very partial success, however, is well worth achieving. So is a mother's ability to acknowledge her difficulty to her child, apologize for it, and encourage him to alert her when it recurs (as was the case with Cindy's mother who kept wiping her little girl's face). Even when a mother cannot consistently alter her behavior, attributing the blame to herself frees the child from undue guilt over his wish for independence, and enables him to feel good about his efforts.

Ultimately, being loved only as a part of a parent means not being loved, being unacceptable as oneself. The lasting personality adaptations to such a state vary enormously and may encompass the most severe pathologies, but basically they are a means of coping with a lack of positive investment in one's real self.

6

Early Aspects of Mothering: What Makes It So Hard to Be There to Be Left

Several of the preceding chapters, especially "Mothers Have to Be There to Be Left" (chapter 4) and "Self-Care and the Mother–Child relationship" (chapter 5), have described the mother's part in facilitating her young child's development as an ongoing process of her learning to love him in a new way, that is, as a person in his own right. The double investment of the child, as a part of herself and as a loved person, is, of course, the hallmark of parenting, but so is the necessary flexibility which allows for continuing shifts in the balance between narcissistic and object investment—caring about him as a part of herself and as a separate loved one.

But why are these shifts in investment so stressful for the mother? Why is she not merely reluctant to effect them but calls up so many defenses to protect herself from knowing and dealing with them? What is the nature of her affective experience and underlying anxiety?

CLINICAL MANIFESTATIONS

A mother drives her daughter to the airport, bidding her good-bye after a brief, mutually enjoyed holiday from college. Returning from the flight gate to the parking lot, she is well aware of her heavy-hearted sadness at the separation, which will now again be bridged by weekly letters and phone calls. In her mind, she begins to write the next letter. She also thinks about the laundry and cleaning up, the bittersweet aftermath of each visit that awaits her at home. Then a panic seizes her as she reaches into her purse: she has lost her keys! She rummages around in the purse and in her pockets. She begins to retrace her steps lest they fell out. Were the keys left in the car? Did someone steal the car? The panic becomes unbearable. She feels she cannot think straight, cannot remember when she last held the keys, cannot plan what to do next—all so unlike her usual competent self. Suddenly she holds the keys in her hand. They had been in the purse, in their usual place, all along. The panic leaves. She feels like herself again, shaken but relieved.

A mother's oldest son starts to attend kindergarten. Despite being pregnant and having a younger child to care for, she decides to help him with his new experience by driving him to and from school herself. The big busy parking lot, the playground full of youngsters chasing and milling around, feel strange and overwhelming. She parks and waits with him until his teacher rounds up her class and, after a last mutual wave, leads them off. Within a few days he knows the routine, recognizes some of the children, spots his teacher, and happily runs to take his place in line. The mother is aware of her pride in her son's coping, of her relief that he is "making it," of a tinge of loneliness in herself as she walks to the car. She reaches for her keys but cannot find them. A panic grips her. She realizes her purse was left unzipped and, sure the keys had dropped out, she begins to search the playground. No luck. She doesn't know what to do. Finally, she decides to phone her husband from the principal's office, increasingly distraught at the thought of not reaching him. She reaches into her purse to get out a hankie and pulls out the keys. They had been there, in the right place, all along.

A mother readies her 4-year-old, her 15-month-old, and herself for the daily morning drive to the older boy's nursery school. They are in good time and good spirits, but she cannot find her keys. The little daughter likes to hold the keys. Mother is convinced she let Annie play with them and the child dropped them somewhere, as has happened a few times lately. She finds herself becoming furious at Annie for losing the keys and at herself for letting the child have an item so vital to her functioning throughout the day. Mother, son, and even Annie search the house, every crevice is checked, all the garbage is sifted. No trace of the keys. The mother borrows grandmother's car. After later returning the car and walking home, mother realizes she lost her purse. Now her earlier fury turns into panic. She feels she is falling apart, going crazy, can't think. Something is wrong with her. Grandmother catches up with her and hands her the purse which had been left in the car. The mother has no idea how she managed to leave the purse and her panic gets worse. Suddenly, she looks up and sees her keys on the kitchen hook where they always hang and where they were all along, only partly obscured by a board hanging next to them. Annie had not held the keys that day but she had sinned in another way which mother realizes later on reflection. Just the previous day the mother had happily and proudly related to the grandmother what a "with it" little toddler Annie was becoming, how much interest she showed in the world around her, and how eagerly she now approached and engaged with other familiar adults.

Keys are not the only item to get lost and found in these situations. Glasses, purses, jewellery, driver's licence, airline tickets, almost any personal essential item will do, as long as it is urgently needed to carry on daily functioning. Less common, but not infrequent, is the idea that a commitment, such as an appointment, has been forgotten. Characteristic in all these instances is the fact that the content of the anxiety is objectively unwarranted (the keys are where they should be, the appointment was not missed), and that the degree of distraught panic does not fit the situation in these usually very competent persons; that is, the presumed loss of, say, keys under other circumstances causes annoyance, frustration, followed by thought-through goal-directed measures. Some mothers experience the vague panic without a specific content, and some feel it in a bodily way, such as being ill in some fatal way. Anna Freud (1967) similarly related losing things and being lost to the mother's narcissistic investment of her child. She also reminded us that Freud (1916–1917) had referred to the link between the narcissistic investment of children and possessions when he stated, "The preserving of *things* may be subject to the same influences as that of children" (p. 77). However, both authors were discussing real, as opposed to presumed, loss, and they did not mention undue panic or bodily sensations.

Annie's mother's insight was unusual. As a rule, a mother has no awareness of the connection between her anxiety state and the loss of a part of herself due to the child's developmentally increased, and independent personality functioning. The anxiety is separate from and unmitigated by her pleasure in her child's growth as well as by her ability to recognize and feel sad that his new achievement implies a loss of earlier closeness in their relationship. However, she responds at once, and with great relief, when she is told that her anxiety feels as if her sense of being a whole person is threatened, as if something that holds her together has disappeared, and that this something is the part of herself that is vested in her child but is now taken away, or taken over, by him. It has become a part of him and ceased to be hers. Sometimes she then knows at once what the child's developmental step was. Sometimes she finds it, or can be helped to find it, quite shortly.

One mother, with whom I had worked on her young child's difficulties, asked to see me many years later when one of her other children prepared to leave home to go to college. She felt terribly anxious, "undone," worried that something was "wrong" with her. She was vaguely aware that it had something to do with her daughter and needed little help beyond the contained setting of our long-standing relationship to figure out the connection with the impending narcissistic loss. Relieved by her new awareness and by the reassuring knowledge that she was coping with a typical maternal experience, she smiled and, touching her abdomen, asked, "And when will the hole go away?" 'Never," I replied, "but it will become more manageable." I told her the truth as I have come to understand and feel it through years of working with mothers. I also thought, but did not share, that this mother's ability to encompass and symbolize her previously formless severe anxiety as a hole in her body represented a partial, but very helpful ego mastery. Similarly, the lost-but-not-lost keys are important ego means of binding and mitigating the primitive overwhelming fear of disintegration. The mothers who can feel and tolerate the unspeakable anxiety and can bring to bear some ego means to contain it, such as in the form of a pseudolost item, usually function consistently well in their maternal capacity. That, no doubt, is also the reason why they profit so readily from offered understanding of their predicament.

There is also a developmental factor, in that the anxiety is generally less pronounced and more easily tolerated when it is prompted by the loss of self-investment with an older child, for example, in adolescence. With less of a threat and more ego means available, there is space and time to integrate insight and understanding. The younger the child, the more intense is the threat, and the more quickly are defensive measures instituted.

However, even with older children, the mother's relief and ability to reintegrate her self result not merely from the intellectual and verbal conceptualization of the deeply unfathomable. The knowledge is most, and most immediately, helpful when it is conveyed within a contained relationship, symbolically in the context of being held, and held together, by an empathic mother. When the mother's own mother is in tune and available, the mother turns to her and she meets the need intuitively, without words. This is one of a grandmother's major roles and, at the same time, meets her own need. Often, a supportive husband can provide containment, and this is a major maternal role he fulfill's as the child's father, just as he was needed to be the container and protector of the mother–baby couple when the child was first born (R. A. Furman, 1986; E. Furman, 1987). Sometimes a friend may be available. Sometimes it is the therapist, especially when the focus of the therapeutic work is the child and the mother–child relationship, as is the case in treatment via the parent (R. A. Furman and A. Katan, 1969; E. Furman, 1992a).

THE MOTHER'S CHARACTERISTIC
DEFENSES AGAINST LOSS

It is the anxiety generated by the partial developmental losses of the youngest children that prompts the mother's defensive measures most quickly and causes interferences in the child's mastery as well as in the mother–child relationship. It is therefore with these age groups that therapeutic intervention is so useful, preferably combined with a containing setting, such as the Hanna Perkins Therapeutic School (R. A. Furman and A. Katan, 1969; E. Furman, 1992a). The mother of the young child tends not to experience conscious anxiety. Instead, she turns the tables by leaving her child first, bodily or mentally, and unconsciously puts him in the situation of experiencing the overwhelming anxiety. She may decide to go to work, or become preoccupied, or take a trip, or go out one night, leaving the child to waken to an unfamiliar sitter. Intermittent decathexis of the child tends to increase (R. A. Furman and E. Furman, 1984).

There are many other defensive measures, such as misinterpreting or denying the child's readiness for steps in self-care or for exercising his newly developing functions. I have previously described numerous clinical manifestations of this syndrome (E. Furman, Chapter 4, 1984, 1992a). With many mothers, their timing and use of day care is significantly determined by the impelling need to ward off the anxiety of losing a part of the self to the growing child. Many "ordinary devoted mothers" (Winnicott, 1949), however, while unaware of their anxiety and of their ways of warding it off, become concerned about the resulting developmental interferences in their young child—sleep disturbances, delays or complications of toilet mastery, eating difficulties and excessive reliance on pacifiers or bottles, problems in speech development, separation troubles, tantrums. The list is endless and so varied that each presenting manifestation needs to be individually explored and understood. Insofar as it relates to the mother's difficulty with adapting her investment of the child to his changing needs, she has to gain some understanding of the child's response to, and interaction with, her defenses, and she needs to tolerate some of her underlying anxiety in order to marshal adaptive coping mechanisms. Many mothers can be helped relatively readily in this way during the child's later infancy and toddlerhood, the period when the mother–child relationship undergoes the most frequent and drastic changes in the area of shifting from a mutually largely narcissistic investment to one in which object love assumes a much bigger part. Despite the hardship, or perhaps because of it, mothers deeply appreciate the therapist's understanding of their distress and help with mastery. Mother and child share the benefits of their increasingly phase-appropriate relationship.

MOTHERS WITH SPECIAL NARCISSISTIC VULNERABILITY

There are, however, also some mothers whose maternal functioning is more seriously affected by the threat of narcissistic loss and whose defensive measures are rigidly adhered to. They cannot invest their children as separate loved persons. They cannot utilize developmental help, despite their professed wish, and, even in their own intensive analyses, achieve only very limited improvements, and do so very slowly. With their young children they can sometimes make promising changes but these are soon undone again when the least bit of loss threatens.

A most distressing aspect of their difficulty is that the impact of the threat of narcissistic loss generates in them extreme aggression toward the child. A certain amount of anger, conscious or unconscious, directed at the child, self, or a displaced target, usually accompanies the mother's anxiety. In the example above, Annie's mother's anger at herself and her daughter about the lost keys is quite typical; but Annie's mother did not act on her anger nor did she fear that it would get out of control and harm her child. Most often the mother's anger at the child shows in not recognizing his wish and attempts to care for himself, and in blaming him for what she perceives as his contrariness. But the most vulnerable mothers tend to respond by disinvesting their child, actually walking out on him or handing him over to another's care in order to keep in check their aggressive impulses experienced at that moment.

Some mothers manage to protect the child from their own harm, but expose him to the aggression of others (siblings, peers, doctors, sitters) or to unsafety in the environment (traffic, open windows, electric appliances). Some, instead or in addition, actually attack the child, sometimes in the crudest ways, such as biting, hair pulling, sticking his face in water, and sometimes in the more rationalized manner of hitting and other punishments. These mothers usually feel very guilty about their abusive breakthroughs and are often unaware that their disinvestments and abandonments represent attempts at protecting the child from their abuse. They are not abusive with others, except, in extreme cases, with those who care for, teach, or treat their child, and who thereby threaten to disengage him from the mother's narcissistic orbit. Some of these mothers want help to the point of tenaciously clinging to the therapist, almost the more so the less able they are to effect inner changes. Struggling valiantly to contain her aggression, one such mother described her state as "My whole body is aggression." Regardless of its overt manifestations, the children sense from earliest on the nature of their mothers' aggression, and they adapt their personality growth accordingly, with inevitable unfortunate consequences (E. Furman, 1992a).

METAPSYCHOLOGICAL CONSIDERATIONS

By this time, some readers will be fully in tune with what I have described, some will be hesitant but eager to follow my thinking further, and some will be put off and critical. I assume these responses from my experience in discussing the topic with professionals and parents, and I shall later offer some reasons for them. First, however, I want to share some of my thinking which has helped me understand the clinical phenomena, at least to an extent.

Working with children who have lost a parent through death and with parents who have lost a child through death, we have learned that the narcissistic and object libidinal elements in the parent–child relationship affect the mourning process in different ways (E. Furman, 1974). The narcissistic aspects were, of course, most dominant with parentally bereaved infants and toddlers, and with parents whose infant or toddler died. In these situations the impact of the loss and the means of coping with it differed markedly from the usual bereavement task (chapter 3).

The obvious similarities between the mothers' responses to the death of their baby and to the partial developmental loss of the child, are all the more striking (chapter 4). There is the common feature: the nature of the anxiety, namely fear of disintegration, and its cause, the actual or threatened loss of the part of the mother's self which is invested in her child.

THE MOTHER'S PRIMITIVE EGO STATE

The sense of fear of disintegration, the difficulty in conceptualizing and integrating it ("I don't know what's happening to me"), the bodily sensations or symbolic body parts so often associated with it, all indicate that the threat to the narcissistic investment of the child constitutes a threat to the integrity of the basic body-ego. It harks back to a period when its investment and boundaries were still very labile, when the object was primarily a part of the narcissistic milieu (Hoffer, 1952), and object cathexes proper were only just beginning. The fact that the mother invests her child as a part of her own body, in the form of a bodily narcissistic cathexis, was described previously (E. Furman, 1969a, Chapter 3, Chapter 4, 1984, 1987, 1992a, 1992b), but I had not appreciated the early developmental state of the ego which effects this investment or the related consequences, three of which will be discussed.

The first is that it helps us to understand the primitive aggression which accompanies the mother's intense fear and sense of disintegration. Parts of the aggression can be viewed as reactive to the anxiety, may actually substitute for the anxiety, or represent an attempt to encompass it and direct it outwards, along with the child who caused it. But that does not explain the raw unmitigated nature of the aggression which often contrasts so markedly with the mother's usual anger and her way of dealing with it. If, however, we take into account the immature state of the body-ego which is threatened, we have to take into account too the fragility of its libidinal investment and the as yet minimal capacity for drive fusion and integration (E. Furman, 1985). Not only can such a primitive ego not judge the difference between a small and big loss, but even minor losses of this early libidinal investment cannot be compensated, cause a sudden drastic imbalance of the drives and result in defusion with discharge of raw aggression. Since a mother usually extends the most positive aspects of her self-love to her child ("As long as he is wonderful, it doesn't matter what's imperfect about myself"), the least loss of it represents indeed a considerable libidinal depletion, followed by barely controllable, even uncontrollable, aggressive impulses.

A second consequence is that it throws light on the different experience when the mental, rather than bodily, self-investment in the child is threatened. These losses usually concern the older child's and adolescent's newly independent mental functioning, activities, and relationships. They cause a narcissistic injury or diminishment and are felt as a mental hurt, with lowered self-esteem. There is no primitive overwhelming anxiety, no bodily symptoms. There is often anger at the child, but it tends not to surface so suddenly, harshly, and seemingly unreasonably; the parental ego is more in charge. The difference between a threat to the bodily as opposed to the mental narcissistic investment is blurred in the mother, but it stands out clearly when we compare the mother's with the father's responses. The self-investment in the child characterizes both parents' entry into the developmental phase of parenthood and is essential to their parenting (E. Furman, 1969a). The father's narcissistic cathexis is, however, mental, whereas the mother's is mental and bodily. Even fathers who are consistent and fully invested primary caretakers do not experience the primitive fear of disintegration or the related bodily sensations when their baby weans himself or takes over bodily self-care. Sometimes they feel some nostalgia, sometimes they become controlling, but for the most part they welcome the child's early, growing autonomy. The youngsters sense this difference. For example, the process of learning to dress himself, as well as the way this skill becomes integrated in and serves the toddler's personality, differ when the father, rather than mother, is the facilitator (E. Furman, 1992a). Many fathers feel they can relate better with an older child, and many shy away from early bodily care of him. Although fathers often kindly support mothers, they have no empathic understanding of the distress she experiences with the young child's growth.

By contrast, fathers and mothers share their strong reactions to their adolescent's emancipation, but even then many mothers complain "But it's so different for him. He misses him/her in such a different way." They are then relieved to learn how and why it is different, and this in turn helps parents to reconcile and overcome the sense of being at odds and estranged as a couple. Otherwise there is a tendency at these times to turn the tables, to leave each other, or to undercut the child. This was brought out by the provost of a prominent university. His address at a national pediatric meeting consisted of exhorting the pediatricians to exercise their influence with parents so they would neither have a divorce nor sell their home; both events were cited as the major causes of first-year college students' failure and drop out.

The third consequence of the mother's primitive ego state, evoked by the narcissistic loss of her child, is the relative difficulty mothers manifest in using their object investment of the child to compensate for the loss. It is never an easy immediate transition, even for mothers who maintain an age-appropriate balance between self and object investment and whose object relationship with the child is not burdened by undue conflict. It is much harder, even impossible, for mothers who have a predominantly narcissistic investment, especially one with many negative aspects, and for mothers who unconsciously dread the marked ambivalence which would invade their relationship with the child as a separate person (E. Furman, 1992a). This difficulty makes sense when we realize that the evoked ego state is one in which object representations and investments are tenuous and not yet fully gratifying, feelings are not yet available in ego filtered form, the drives are largely unfused and discharged bodily, and there is minimal integrative capacity. Such a primitive ego can respond only with fear of disintegration. It does not have the means to cope with the inner disequilibrium and to reach out for alternate compensations. Instead, it is the later, more mature, parts of the mother's personality which shoulder the task of recognizing, containing, integrating the breach, and of offering their resources—much as an empathic mother would help her baby when she finds him in this kind of distress. Thus, the more mature ego parts "mother" her own distressed, vulnerable ego part as effectively, or ineffectively, as her own mother did in earliest childhood.

When a mother's earliest body–ego distress could not be sufficiently assuaged, or her later personality did not reach sufficient maturity, she cannot "mother" herself well enough, cannot utilize later means of coping, and remains subject to ever-threatening, barely mitigatable fears and states of ego disintegration. Perhaps the reason for all mothers' deep appreciation of an understanding, containing person relates to the genetic need to be mothered through these vulnerable periods with their child. It may also account for the most vulnerable mothers' clinging to a therapist. Even though they cannot use the therapeutic work to develop adequate means of self-integration, they try to use the therapist as a containing mother who provides stability and safety from outside, and in this way protects the positive progressive aspects of the mother–child relationship.

The mental narcissistic investment of the child is accomplished by a developmentally somewhat more advanced ego, not as primitive as the earlier bodily investment, not as mature as the later object investment. Thus the loss of the mental narcissistic investment does not focus on the basic bodily integrity, has more capacity to compensate by reinvesting in the self, but cannot yet readily find compensation by reinvesting in the object.

In my focus on the early economic and structural aspects, I do not wish to eliminate the later dynamic ones, the intrapsychic conflicts which contribute so prominently to difficulties in the mother–child relationship. I only wish to stress that these conflicts, important and complex as they are, derive from later developmental phases within the parents. The phenomena I have described stem from a much earlier preconflictual and largely prestructural personality core, devoid of phallic–genital or even anal–sadistic drive components. It is of course likely, and experience indicates, that mothers who are very vulnerable to narcissistic loss at these earliest levels, tend also to suffer from later conflictual interferences in their relationship with their children. For example, the mother who appropriates her son as her penis is likely to have superimposed this phallic–sexual component on an earlier presexual and preconceptual body-ego unit with him. Individuals, no doubt, vary in the extent to which the early vulnerability affects the later personality development, or in the extent to which interferences in later development caused inadequacies in coping with the recrudescence of earlier ego states. Probably both factors contribute to individual functioning.

DEVELOPMENTAL AND ADAPTIVE ASPECTS

This brings us to the last part of the metapsychological considerations, namely the developmental and adaptive aspects, although these too have already been mentioned, since all aspects are of necessity intertwined. The adaptive nature of the parents' narcissistic investment of their child is self-evident. It enables them to empathize with, care for, and protect the child in a continuous way as a most valuable part of themselves, and to meet his needs ahead of their own, often at the cost of their own gratifications. In order to make such an investment, the personality has to have access to a part which still maintains very flexible boundaries with minimal differentiation between self and object.

We do, of course, make many narcissistic investments—in possessions, work, hobbies, causes, not to mention the narcissistic aspects of all our relationships—but we rarely care for and about them in quite the way we do with our children (E. Furman, 1974). Moreover, most of our narcissistic investments are mental. Yet it makes sense that the mother's narcissistic investment has to include bodily aspects and utilize a phase of unstable body-ego because, during pregnancy and, to a lesser extent, nursing and bodily child care, she has to be able to rely on sufficiently flexible ego boundaries to include the child within her bodily self. A man's body is never faced with such a task. Years ago a colleague told me jokingly, "Now I know what it's like to be pregnant and give birth: I lost 25 pounds in two weeks!" He, unlike most men, could allow himself to try and feel the characteristic maternal changeability of the body-ego. The comparison between a mother's and father's narcissistic investment of the child (and response to the loss of it) links with observations of very young boys' and girls' behavior, suggesting some basic differences in the development of their body-ego and distribution of cathexes.

Toward the end of their first year and well into the second, youngsters begin to like to carry something. Boys tend to choose an attaché case or toolbox like Dad's; girls prefer a bag or basket with handles, similar to Mom's handbag. Both like to fill their containers with momentarily precious possessions. Parents vary in their appreciative participation and in offering suitable items, but essentially the impetus and pleasure are the child's own. Boys and girls also invest and carry around soft toys, different from and in addition to the transitional object. Boys tend to trail their teddy along, Christopher Robin fashion; girls usually hold it hugged tightly in their arms. As time goes on, the boys no longer carry their case or box, and their interest shifts to real and toy machines, what they do and how they work; playing with cars, trucks, and trains becomes an invested activity. Elsewhere (E. Furman, 1992a) I described Chris in whom this development paralleled increasing ownership of his body and its care, culminating in asking his parents to draw a chalk outline of his body on the ground (as he had seen other children do), to which he added the outline of his penis in the correct spot. His bodily self-image now had firmly contained boundaries. The girl toddler, by contrast, continues and increases her doll-in-the-container and take-care-of-doll play. At 16 months, Janie often suddenly thought of her doll and rushed back to where the doll lay to hug her or, on the walk, she had to be assured that the doll was safe at home and they would reunite.

Obviously children vary and there is overlap between the boys' and girls' early interests. Kestenberg (1956a, 1968) clearly and helpfully related these behaviors to the investment of the inner genitals. T.-B. and V. Hägglund (Hägglund and Pika, 1980; Hägglund, 1981) elucidated the role of the mother's womb in male and female development. I would like to stress another aspect, namely, the growing differences in the distribution of boys' and girls' narcissistic investments, as well as the fact that the boy closes and firms up his body-ego boundaries, whereas the girl takes pleasure in keeping hers flexible (e.g., including the doll), although its absence upsets her. These early male–female differences predate phallic–genital sexual interests and are unrelated to the children's knowledge or ignorance of sexual differences, but they are closely linked to later attitudes to bodily integrity and to mothers and mothering. Winnicott (1964) thought along similar lines when he described man as being all unto himself, isolated from others, and woman as always being also someone else, with mother, grandmother, and little girl interchangeable within her.

The woman's changeable and so very vulnerable body-ego certainly poses a threat to the boy and man who once were similarly vulnerable. The greater the threat of reexperiencing early states of bodily disintegration, the more he needs to defend his bodily integrity, to the point of avoiding feeling contact with women as mothers and with their mothering experiences. A thoughtful and insightful father who willingly devoted himself to the full-time care of his little children after his wife's sudden death found that he needed to withdraw, in part, to do other things, and employ a housekeeper. He was unhappy about it but said, "The mothering is a threat to me—not to my masculinity, but to the very integrity of my person." But many women too feel threatened by mothering for this reason. They may opt not to have children; they may opt for work or hand over the child's care to distance themselves; they may envy men and try to emulate them to protect their fragile boundaries.

In a very small way, perhaps, this has some bearing on the reader's relative willingness to endure and feel with the contents of this chapter. I sympathize. I too found it hard to immerse myself in these early experiences and to give conceptual form to the formless, however imperfect the result.

7
Helen, Andy, and Their Mothers

INTRODUCTION

There are aspects of being a mother and of having a mother that we usually are not aware of (chapters 2–6). By that I do not mean that these aspects are very rare and special, or that we have defensively prevented our conscious encounter with them, but rather that, at least for the most part, they had never been consciously invested. They originate in and belong to such early primitive parts of our personality that they predate symbolic representation in words or images and predate the capacity to think about them in secondary process form. It has not been easy for me to feel my way into that level of experience and to try to make sense of it. Using inevitably imperfect words, it is harder yet to convey my findings to another person. Sometimes it helps us to get in touch with the feel of it when we observe mothers' interactions with their somewhat older children. Helen and Andy, described below, attended kindergarten.

HELEN AND HER MOTHER

Helen's mother had, all along, found it extremely hard to let her much loved little girl proceed with self-care. Although she consciously encouraged steps toward independence, she often unconsciously delayed them, left before being left by way of turning passive into active, and became quite irritable. Helen took great care not to ask for too much. Working in treatment via the parent during Helen's attendance at our Hanna Perkins School from early on, the mother had become aware of her mixed feelings about Helen's steps toward independence. She took many opportunities to reassure Helen that she still loved her and was very happy with her growing up skills, even though a part of her missed "doing for" Helen. Hair care (shampooing, brushing, combing, barettes) remained mother's domain for years without Helen protesting at all. When Helen finally worked at putting in her own barettes, she did a good job but could not be proud of her achievement or show it to her teacher. Within a few weeks, mother fell ill. She was not incapacitated but uncomfortable. Helen at once discontinued her hair care, insisting that mother do it for her. As mother and Helen came to discuss this, Helen told her she had thought that doing her own hair had made mother ill.

Just how vulnerable a mother feels, how much flexibility she can allow, and how readily she can recoup, will all depend in large measure on the way she formed her own body-ego out of her own early mother–child matrix, as well as on the help she gets from an empathically containing husband, friend, her own mother, or therapist.

ANDY AND HIS MOTHER

During one of my weekly conferences with the teachers in our Hanna Perkins Therapeutic Kindergarten, I learn that 5½ year-old Andy, my little patient, has begun to lose his daily assignment sheet and demands that his teacher find it. Reminded that this is his responsibility and he needs to look for it, Andy remains in the middle of the classroom, glances around perfunctorily, and demands more insistently, "I don't see it. *You* have to find it." Andy does not relent. Ultimately, the assignment sheet turns up, usually found by another child. Andy is more annoyed than grateful. One senses that he still blames the teacher for not having performed, as he views it, her assigned part. Is Andy lazy? Yes. Is he a bit bossy? Yes. Does he let us know that he has trouble with his conscience, that it is a harsh taskmaster when it comes to judging how a boy should take care of his equipment, and that he therefore projects the blame and externalizes the responsibility to his teacher? Yes, that too is true. But there is also a deeper, underlying truth, namely Andy's longstanding difficulty in firmly delineating his personality boundaries from those of his mother. On the one hand, this makes him very vulnerable to intrusions and loss of an integrated sense of self, but, on the other hand, it allows him to blur the boundaries for defensive purposes.

When Andy's mother is told of the trouble with his assignment sheet, she at first thinks that such situations don't arise at home. On second thought, though, she realizes that they happen quite often these days with various items of his equipment, from backpack to tennis racquet, but she had not paid much attention to it. In other words, she had readily functioned for him as though he were an infant or toddler. In that phase he would have still been a part of her, she would have still been in the business of keeping his body and soul together, and he would have still taken it for granted that she would function for him in this undifferentiated way.

Are we dealing with a major pathology? Not necessarily. The teachers and I laughed heartily when we reminded ourselves that not only Andy but also our children and even husbands tend to turn to us with an expecting "Where is such-and-such?" that we then describe just where the item is stored (it may even be in one of their dresser drawers) and, after they have gone off to look for it without ever finding it, they return with a more demanding "It isn't there," implying that it is our job to find it. And most of the time we just go and get it. As with Andy, we simply consider it mother's job. When some important belongings, parts of oneself, are missing, they must be with mother and she has to hand them over. As mothers, we accept the situation and act accordingly.

When I speak of Andy's equipment and of husbands' belongings, I am not implying that these are necessarily phallic symbols. I am referring to parts of the body-ego at a developmental time when the older infant and toddler are in the process of extricating them from the matrix, shared with mother, when they make these parts their own, and fit them together into a whole. These body-ego parts, as with the early hand, mouth, and ego integration described by Hoffer (1949), encompass external and internal perceptions related to bodily needs and need-fulfillment. Owning one's hands, digestive sensations, tummies, and behinds serves to integrate the body-ego around meeting the needs of hunger and elimination. This often precedes the steps of integrating one's sexual parts and gender identity. And therefore daughters, like husbands and sons, look to mother to furnish their parts—at least until they get to function as mothers themselves. Investing our body-ego, sensing it as the permanent core of a "me," and enclosing it in its own space is a long and difficult process at best.

As already mentioned, Andy, our kindergartner, and his mother had found it very hard to achieve separate enough body-egos and, mentally, were still very essential to one another's narcissistic equilibrium. The period of losing his assignment sheet coincided with Andy preparing for first grade in a new school and losing his relied upon teacher. It also coincided with moving into latency and needing to give up his under-5 relationship with his mother who could not really tolerate being there to be left (chapter 4). At the time of this new step in becoming a separate person, Andy dealt with the stress, in part, by relating with his teacher as though she were his mother and he were much younger, having regressed from a more mature teacher–pupil relationship.

Although we had learned early on that Andy's mother's difficulty in keeping boundaries was quite marked, it was not an unusual pathology as such, representing merely an intensification of what all mothers experience insofar as their personalities function as mothers.

Andy's mother struggled with her trouble during the years of her little boy's growth. In her own analysis and in treatment via the parent on behalf of her son she had worked hard on gaining insight into her behavior and feelings, but, as is the difficulty with very early personality elements, she could not master her responses, could not anticipate and control them. She could often recognize and correct them after they had occurred. And so it happened this time too.

At the time of the loss of Andy's assignment sheet in kindergarten, she had not noticed that she had increasingly functioned for him at home, such as by assuming responsibility for finding his mislaid belongings. In this way she prolonged and tightened her owning of him. At the same time, however, she had already responded to her upcoming developmental loss of him by leaving him first. When his school difficulty came up for understanding in treatment via the parent, the mother suddenly realized that about two weeks earlier, just about the time when he began to lose his assignment sheets, she had precipitously enrolled in a special body-building course which caused her to be away from home every week night during Andy's bedtime, a time of bodily need-fulfillment which had always been an important link between them. Mother had arranged for a familiar sitter, but she had not appreciated that her sudden need to invest her own body so intensively was related to the threat his anticipated independence posed to the integrity of her body-ego, nor did she realize that, instead of supporting his development, she was sending the opposite message of, "You can only have me when you are a part of me." Andy received the message. Losing his things and insisting that mother/teacher function for him served also to assure himself of not losing mother/teacher by being too independent and self-reliant.

8
Early Steps in the Development of Gender

INTRODUCTION

The development of a boy's or girl's gender concept is usually linked with two sources: (1) their experience of phallic and genital sexual impulses in their own bodies, self-engendered or stimulated by sensory contact with others; and (2) their internalization of the parents' image of them as male or female, conveyed verbally and nonverbally through many parent–child interactions. In this chapter I want to focus on some underpinnings and beginnings of gender development which do not include phallic–genital impulses, or only in a marginal way. Some of these early steps predate gender development as such but, nevertheless, affect it in important ways.

THE DEVELOPMENT OF THE EARLY BODY-EGO

It is impossible to think about the ways and sequences in which boys and girls establish their body-ego and delineate its boundaries without keeping in mind that this entire process is a bodily matrix originating within the narcissistic milieu of the mother–child unit. Mother's and child's body-ego are in flux for a long time, with separateness as well as engulfing and being engulfed bringing deep satisfactions at some times, threats of annihilation at other times.

The 6-month-old who begins to hold and munch on his biscuits and, with mother's blessing, progresses quickly to independent self-feeding shows that he has formed a core of his own body-ego with hand–mouth integration. Yet, at 10 months he may still feed or pretend feed mother and teddy and self at the same time in a manner that indicates that boundaries between them are blurred. At a year or even later, he may, at a moment of distress, reach into mother's shirt as if her breasts were still his. And when he gets to be nearly 20 years old and gets sick at college, he is likely to call home first and only then contact the infirmary—still drawing on the old bodily link.

Important though the first year is, the bulk of body-ego integration and delineation takes place during the toddler period, with mother–child interactions focused on mastery of toileting and the related anal-sadistic and urethral impulses.

Some mothers "toilet train" their toddlers without surrendering to them a single aspect of the whole process, even owning the child's bowel movements and urine. At the other end of the curve, some mothers assist their child in truly gaining mastery by helping him own every aspect, from recognizing and gauging the internal signal sensations of his urge through to wiping himself, flushing, getting dressed and, of course, acquiring his own reaction formation and pride in achievement (R. A. Furman, 1984b). Most mothers, like their toddlers, combine the two approaches, going back and forth; for example, when he wiggles and withholds, she may, at times, patiently help him recognize and meet his needs, reminding him perhaps also how good he feels when he can stay clean, and, at other times, she may anxiously pressure him and, in the end, either drag him to the toilet or dash to the bathroom herself as if his urge were still hers (E. Furman, 1992a, 1993a).

Data gained from observation and treatment indicate that handing over the wiping is one of the hardest parts for mothers. Yet, for the child the use of his or her own hand is crucial to the integration of their body-ego. The hands have this role in the first year with hand–mouth and ego integration (Hoffer, 1949), will have it again in the next phase of integrating the genitals, and they are just as helpful for the young toddler. Wiping with his or her own hands helps integrate them to their invisible behind. Holding his penis to urinate, wiping herself after urinating, helps them to integrate these organs in their urinary and excretory function, invested with anal-sadistic and urinary impulses, and serving the need of elimination. This step in body-ego integration and boundary delineation forms a very important underpinning for the upcoming integration of some of the same bodily parts in their role as sexual organs with primarily phallic–genital impulses.

SOME FACTORS FACILITATING EARLY BODY-EGO DEVELOPMENT AND GENDER CONCEPT

Just how well integrated this underpinning is and how helpful it will be to the next phase of gender development depends on a number of factors. I shall highlight three: (1) The first is the extent to which the mother has been able to transfer her bodily ownership and care of her child's excretory functions to him, and to effect this transfer in such a way that he can feel safe and good in owning them while trusting her ongoing emotional availability. In analytic terms this means that the mother has given the related parts of her body-ego to her child and transformed her narcissistic investment of them into object investment of her child as a separate loved one. (2) The second factor concerns the father's role in helping mother and child with their difficult task. A father can ease and contain the mother in her vulnerable period of transition with its unarticulated fears of bodily disintegration, and he can help her feel whole in their relationship. When he, whose boundaries are so different, can appreciate her mothering with its necessarily flexible and partly open body-ego, he helps not only her but also his child. He conveys something like this: "My own boundaries are so safe that I can love your mother's difference without feeling threatened by it." He further helps his child's still vulnerable boundaries by offering a relationship which resists mutual engulfing: However much the child or the father might wish to become a body-ego unit, it cannot happen. This is one of the many reasons boy and girl toddlers need and seek out their fathers. This crucially important role of the father with mother and toddler is not sexual and their threesome is not of an oedipal nature, but it paves the way for respectful mutual consideration in a triadic setting. (3) The third factor is protection from excess stimulation. The young toddler's vulnerable boundaries are matched by his having as yet few self-protective means for dealing with stimuli. Toddlers are hyper-alert to all perceptions, often cannot yet make good sense of them or screen them out, just as we are alert to and bothered by every little noise in a new house. In contrast to the later sexual curiosity, this hyperalertness is not impulse driven and subsides when the child gets to feel safer in his own house, his body-ego, and understands better what could or could not impinge on it. But in the meantime he is easily subject to overstimulation. It can result from uncontrollable impulses or unmet needs within and from without through painful or exciting experiences which exceed the child's coping mechanisms.

The nature of the overstimulation as well as its effect on the individual toddler varies considerably. As Weil (1989a,b) documented, at one extreme are incidents of sexual or aggressive abuse and major medical–surgical interventions, all of which tend to be totally overwhelming and a severe interference with personality growth. At the other extreme are common practices whose unhelpful effect is widely disregarded or misunderstood. For example, physical punishment interferes with the toddler's loving investment of his early body-ego, not only because it inflicts pain, but because the parent who hurts or lets others hurt the child conveys his or her lack of protective love for the child's body, an attitude the child is likely to make his own.

Premature and excessive stimulation of phallic–sexual excitement often constitutes a similar interference with loving self-investment of the body-ego. For example, toileting is sometimes taught by having the child watch the parents' excretory activities or being exposed to their bodies during bathing or dressing. My colleagues' and my data from work at the

Hanna Perkins Center show that in each such instance the perception of the manifest differences, in size and kind, of others' bodies and of their different ways of eliminating constitutes a greater or lesser narcissistic injury. It may threaten the toddler's phase-appropriate attempt to own and invest his excretory organs and functions in a loving way. Just as we are often especially upset about the least spot on a new dress or scratch on a new car, so the toddler is upset to find that his newly owned body and its functions appear flawed or endangered when he is faced with comparisons. Moreover, in his global way of thinking and feeling, one thing wrong means everything wrong. It is not just a part of him that is not perfect, all of him feels inferior. Once he has coped with the developmental task and established pleasurable confidence in ownership and mastery of his excretory functions, seeing others look and do differently is much less disturbing and much easier to understand and integrate (E. Furman, 1992a, 1993a).

The child's concerns are often accompanied by marked, even uncontrollable phallic–sadistic excitement. This is heightened when the caring adults are unaware of the child's feelings, or even when they prohibit or punish his behavioral responses, or when they are themselves excited and/or engage the child in excited interactions, such as excessive fondling or roughhousing. We traced these causative factors in our work with many toddlers and their parents when we explored the manifest difficulties with toilet mastery, the youngsters' stated feelings of inadequacy or wish to be someone else and, especially, their avoidance of neutral activities, dissatisfaction with what they could do and constant worry about comparing poorly with others (E. Furman, 1992a, 1993a). Sadly, their excitement and its gratifications did not provide the modulated pleasure, so essential for effecting a loving bodily and mental genital self-investment.[1]

---

[1]These findings contrast with those of Galenson and Roiphe (1971, 1974, 1980). The reasons for this difference are discussed by R. A. Furman (1984) and in E. Furman (1992a, 1993b).

EARLY STEPS IN GENDER IDENTITY AND THE INTEGRATION OF THE GENITAL ORGANS

The preceding discussion of facilitating and impeding factors in early body-ego formation has focused primarily on areas where the parents, especially the mother, played a crucial role and where, therefore, we have much opportunity to do prophylactic work in assisting parents to help their youngsters negotiate these complex developmental tasks. I shall now focus on developmental aspects which concern the early developmental steps in gender identity per se and in the integration of the boy's and girl's very different body-ego, the former circumscribed with stable boundaries, the latter relatively open with flexible boundaries. It is an aspect of development which proceeds relatively autonomously, compared to those previously described, but it too, of course, benefits from the parents' appreciative tolerance.

Katan's (1960) observation of a 13-month-old boy pretend feeding his penis illustrates an early step toward forming a male body-ego at a time when mother, self and penis begin to be separately conceived within the narcissistic milieu of the mother–child matrix. I have described elsewhere how, in this early phase, children invest external items, such as toys, which they carry around—a step quite different and succeeding the adoption of a transitional object (E. Furman, 1992a, 1993b; chapters 6 and 14). Soon the boys tend to drag these things along Christopher Robin fashion, whereas the girls hold them tightly in their arms. Next, boys start to put things into their pockets and to build enclosed spaces, such as railroad tracks and corrals for toy animals. Chris's development illustrates many of these early steps.

According to his mother, Chris had clearly been a boy in his own and others' views as early as 10 months old. Other than from general appearance and manner of movement, she judged this by his closeness to his Dad and delight in having things like Dad; for example, carrying around a briefcase, filling it with papers, and often taking them out to scribble on them, and then putting them back and closing up the briefcase, all in obvious imitation of his father. Later, as a young toddler, Chris delighted in cooking and cleaning with his Mom and he cared for his teddy and other stuffed animals in a maternal way, all just like Mom. But he very much missed his father when the latter was at work and nothing thrilled him more than to be with Dad doing "Daddy things" on weekends. He initiated efforts at self-care early, and when he began to work on toilet mastery he became pleasurably fascinated with faucets and spent much time pouring water into and out of containers during his bath and at the sink. Watering cans and anything that had spouts were the favorites. At the same time, machinery of every kind, but especially large machines worked by men, became a special interest. He soon differentiated the garbage trucks, power shovels, backhoes, cement trucks, tractors, and was especially happy when he was allowed to sit for a while in the driver's seat of one of these parked vehicles. He achieved toilet mastery at 23 months. By this time he could independently direct his urine stream, had asked about his testicles and scrotum, and integrated the whole organ into his body-image.

Shortly after, and having observed the neighborhood children draw their body outlines in chalk on the pavement, he asked for help in similarly drawing the outlines of his mother, father, and himself. They did. Chris then took the chalk and drew on his outline a longish loop between the thighs and, when asked about this, said it was his penis. He was concerned when he learned that the rain would wash away all the drawings, but readily accepted the assurance that this would affect only the drawing and that his body would remain safe. Chris had never seen his parents or anyone else in the nude. He was not concerned about the details or rain resistance of his parents' body outlines (E. Furman, 1992a, pp. 166–167).

Girls, by contrast, become increasingly interested in containers. They adopt purses, boxes or bags to keep precious things and often fill them with a little figure. Their soft toys and dolls assume the role of babies in their play. Lilly's development was characteristic in these respects.

We came to know Lilly when she and her mother joined our Toddler Group during the latter part of Lilly's second year. She was still preoccupied with toileting, just far enough along to like herself better clean. Sometimes she was angrily insistent on doing everything herself and at other times she was just as angrily insistent on mother doing everything for her. She had a favorite Raggedy Ann doll who was often left waiting in their car. Increasingly, we heard Lilly talk about this doll: Was it all right? Will it sit in her lap on the way home? Was it wearing a coat? Mother reported how Lilly would rush to the car after Toddler Group to hug her doll and say how much she had missed her.

About this time, too, mother shared her puzzlement about Lilly's new preoccupation. Lilly had found and appropriated a round box and several small rectangular ones and she spent much time quietly playing with them in her room. She put things into them, covered and opened them, arranged them. The round box was evidently a favorite, with a little doll or toy animal in it. At first mother had been suspicious of Lilly's sudden preference for alone time in her room, especially as not so long ago Lilly would sometimes hide out there when she had soiled herself. But mother had checked on Lilly several times and found her clean, calm, and focused. Asked about her play, she was not defensive, saying she just liked to play with her special things, but she was not eager for mother's company, nor did she accept mother's suggestion of showing her box to us in Toddler Group. No, it was for home; Lilly did not want to move it. When I asked mother, "Did it seem like Lilly was looking within, putting herself together?" mother looked like a light had gone on. "Oh, I see. Of course," and she smiled at her little girl.

As with Chris and Lilly, these steps allow us to follow the toddlers' efforts at delineating their body-ego—the boys in a physically enclosed space, the girls encompassing the externally invested doll-baby along with its container, the internal space. T.-B. Hägglund, V. Hägglund, and P. Ikonen (1978), V. Hägglund (1981), Kestenberg (1956a, 1956b, 1968), and Torsti (1993) are among the authors who have addressed some aspects of these developmental steps.

Strikingly, throughout the toddler months, girls and boys continue at the same time to delight in wheeling their soft toys around in strollers or buggies, reminding us just how fluid their boundaries still are, how tenuous their gender identity and their separateness from mother. Whereas adult observers, including fathers, tend to find the manifestations of such unstable boundaries somewhat disconcerting, mothers are quite comfortable with them, accept them readily and join in games related to them.

During a discussion of this developmental phase, a colleague, Dr. Silver (personal communication, 1994), related the following anecdote: On a neighborhood stroll with his wife, they met a mother wheeling a baby buggy and her 2-year-old son with his toy stroller. Looking at the carefully bedded and blanketed interior of the child's stroller, they asked him what was in it. He lifted the blanket lovingly, revealing his toy gun. We do not know the intricacies of this young man's ideas about mothers, babies, boys and penises, but it is easy to appreciate how vulnerable his body-ego still is, poised at a point where he is a babybuggy-wheeler like his mother, with his penis gun still more like an external baby than a solidly attached part of himself.

Susan, 26 months old, often entertains two dolls and a teddy at her pretend dinner parties. Mother is always asked to join. Susan never varies her role of cook and server of food and beverages, but the role of taking care of the babies varies greatly and changes so rapidly that Susan herself confuses a plan she has just made. One moment mother is told to hold and feed the "babies," the next moment they *are* mother's babies but Susan gives them their bottles. One doll may then remain mother's, another one becomes Susan's, and then Susan forgets which is to belong to whom, or she may ignore the babies altogether and just serve mother, now treating her as the little girl. Susan does not seem conflicted nor is she distressed. She plays, in Winnicott's sense, with the mother-baby-child boundaries and, at least at these times, derives comfort, even pleasure, from not delineating herself.

When boys and girls have a chance to come into their own more fully and can feel safe, these early phases will serve them adaptively and creatively in their adult roles as partners and parents as well as in their work and hobbies. When too much of their development remains arrested at the early unstable levels, their pleasure in being a part of the mother–child matrix and of its narcissistic omnipotence is overtaken by its entailed threat—the fear of being engulfed and annihilated whenever internal and external circumstances endanger the vulnerable integrity of the body-ego. Such concerns burden all subsequent maturational phases, distort the phallic-oedipal conflicts and identifications, and contribute to many unhappy and maladaptive later solutions. Among these are women who cannot invest and mother their children and men who continue to invest guns outside their bodies and can never feel safe from "big Mama's" encompassing reach.

With later difficulties often so hard to treat, the toddler period offers a most valuable opportunity to those of us who can feel with mother and child at that time in their relationship and who enjoy helping them get in tune so that they can lay solid, safe foundations for future personality development in general and gender identity in particular. It is our experience at the Hanna Perkins Center that mothers who are helped to get in tune with their toddlers remain in tune through subsequent phases, conserving the early gains and finding satisfaction in parenting—goals much harder to achieve when help is given during later phases (E. Furman, 1992a, 1993a).

9
Mothers, Toddlers, and Care

Throughout the ages, the twosome of the early mother–child relationship has been subjected to interruptions, not least due to the mother's need or wish to engage in work or other pursuits which necessitate her absence. Substitute mothering in the form of day care, home care, or care by members of the family, by nannies or nursemaids has always been practiced (de Mause, 1974). No doubt there have also always been mothers who were concerned about the adequacy of their substitutes and the effects of separation on their children, and who have struggled to mitigate the perceived difficulties. The difference today lies in our efforts to understand via studies the many contributing factors and to assess their relative importance and impact on the child, the mother, and their relationship.

The goal of this chapter is to explore the stresses and hazards that substitute mothering may pose to a toddler's personality development and the primary mother–child bond. We shall consider what happens when substitute mothering overtaxes the mother's and child's tolerance for the stress and interferes with growth, and, last, how we can adapt substitute mothering to lessen the inherent stresses and perhaps avoid ill effects.

WHAT IS A TODDLER?

A toddler toddles. He is mobile; he is on the go. He can choose to stay with us, to leave us, to come back. This characterizes the state of the toddler's development as a person. Unlike the younger baby who cannot, of his own accord, physically leave the mothering person, and who also mentally can hardly exist as a person without her, the toddler has begun to view self and mother as separate people.

The behavioral hallmarks of the toddler's beginning development of the self are his wish and ability to take over some of his care, to meet some of his own needs. The baby begins to become a toddler when he can feed himself, with fingers, cup, and spoon; when he can, to an extent, comfort himself and make himself feel good, by using a part of his own body, such as thumb-sucking, and by using a "transitional object" (Winnicott, 1953), a blankie or soft toy that he has made his very own, because it links him to mother and bridges the gap between them. He is becoming a toddler when he can recognize and dislike pain and discomfort, can protest, can make his feelings known to his mothering person, and seek and accept comfort from her, saying, though not in all these words, "I am hurting, I don't like it, I want you to know, and I trust you to make it better." The toddler not only wants to do for himself what he already can do (pushes away mother's arm when she tries to feed him, or refuses to open his mouth for her spoon-feeding, screams and struggles at being picked up when he can walk, and later yells, "Don't carry me"). He also wants to do for himself a host of things that he cannot yet do so well or that mother does not trust him to do well—be it getting the cookie box off the shelf, turning on the water faucets, crossing the street. The unrelenting zest for "me do, me by myself" provides enormous pleasure, especially when it leads to mastery, and also brings anger and frustration when it is interfered with.

At the same time mother has begun to matter as a person. The older baby recognizes her as different from everyone else and thinks about and mainly looks for her when need arises. When he gets closer to being a toddler, mother's part in meeting his needs is so special that he often foregoes need fulfillment when she cannot minister to him, even when others do it in much the same way—does not want to eat, go to sleep, be cleaned up, or "kissed better" when she does not do it with him. This means the infant has reached that crucial developmental point when the relationship with the person has begun to be more important than the way his needs are met. Now, mother's companionship, their social interactions and feelings for each other are the thing. Everything mother does with her toddler means a lot, and he observes everything she does without him and wants to do it with her and like her—cooking, cleaning, talking on the telephone. He even stops doing some things or does them her way for the sake of keeping her love and for the pleasure of becoming like her. At the same time, her presence and her good feeling for him are necessary to sustain his zest for independence, his wish to do for himself, and even his wish to get away and to turn to others for additional fun, to Dad and siblings and other family members. When she is not there, the harbor is gone and venturing out feels less safe and less fun. Without her, the toddler's activity becomes less purposeful and his achievements may crumble.

Not surprisingly, toddlers often want to leave mother or send her away, but do not want her to leave them. Yet, for stretches of time and under favorable circumstances, toddlers can keep mother in mind during her absence and can keep their feelings for her and with her. This enables them to relate to a mother substitute and to maintain their own personality achievements during limited periods of separation.

It takes a lot of healthy mental and physical endowment on the child's part, and a lot of good mothering on the mother's part, for a baby to grow into a toddler. We usually see significant indications of this developmental achievement by the first half of the second year.

THE MAIN DEVELOPMENTAL TASKS OF THE TODDLER PHASE

We often say of a thriving child, "He's all put together." In the case of a toddler, this describes very aptly that he is succeeding in the business of putting his self together, body and soul. This implies not only that he develops the many new functions, activities, and skills we shall enumerate, but that he comes to know them and to enjoy them, that he values them and makes them his very own, fits them together, and uses them for purposeful functioning, for coping with himself and his world, and for interacting with others. It is not enough when a toddler knows how to walk and to manipulate things with his hands. He has to enjoy his motor control, has to make it a precious part of his "me," and has to want to use it for himself, be it to run to mother or push her away, to retrieve his teddy, to put on his shoes, to make his way in the world. It is only when a toddler can invest and use all these parts of himself that they can afford him satisfaction, and it is only when he can integrate them into a coherent idea of self, of "me," that they can contribute to his self-esteem. To be "put together" means not only that one thinks of oneself and functions as a whole person, but also that one likes oneself. A toddler who develops a sense of self and of self-esteem is a person who is "with it," a person who has zest and initiative, a will to master, and has fun as well as pride in doing so. We can tell him from a compliant automaton who does what he is made to do, from the chronically contrary ill-humored child who only wants to do the opposite, and from the incompetent, bewildered child who responds to most situations by feeling overwhelmed and helplessly falls apart.

Among the many new personality parts the toddler has to develop and encompass are the use of large and small muscles for effective motor control, the use of language for thinking and purposeful communication, a grasp of the outer outline of his body, of where it begins and ends, including the parts he cannot see, such as his behind (when toddlers first learn to wipe themselves they usually aim for the general area, but later, when their behind has really become part of their body concept, they manage to touch the exact place). And because he likes his body, he learns to avoid common dangers and shows or tells his caretakers about specific discomforts, a scratch or bruise or sore ear, and solicits their help. He even extends his sense of ownership to his clothes and possessions, recognizes, treasures, and looks out for them. He also gets to know what goes on inside his body, differentiates his needs and knows what to do about them, to eat when hungry, to sleep when tired, to control elimination. A wish for and mastery of self-care become manifest in proficient self-feeding, in considerable accomplishments in self-dressing and washing, in falling asleep on his own, and in independent toileting (chapter 5). He makes most important strides in the area of feelings which are no longer simply pleasurable or unpleasurable sensations, but become more subtly varied and modulated, and which are no longer only discharged bodily, but experienced mentally and increasingly recognized, tolerated, even named and shared in words—happy, mad, lonely, excited, sad, envious, bad, good. Along with these steps we see new interests in play, such as blocks and tricycles, rhymes and songs, which serve to practice skills, and dress-up and role play, which serve to differentiate himself from others, to interact with them, and to "put himself in their shoes," to try out how it feels to be like them.

This brings us to another aspect of the toddler's personality development, namely, the new and different way he relates to his mother and the tasks he has to accomplish in the context of this relationship. The toddler's lack of consideration for others is well known, as he grabs things from other youngsters and even steps on them to reach something or to go somewhere. Equally well known is his unattenuated, intense mixture of love and aggression for those closest to him, especially his mother. Both feelings manifest themselves together in his aggressive hugs and in the twinkle in his eye when he teases and torments her; each is expressed alternately when he lovingly cuddles her one moment and attacks and rages at her the next, or when he angrily sends her away and wants to exchange her for a better mommy, perhaps over just a minor frustration. These characteristics do not change of themselves. The hallmark of the toddler's achievement is to tame and tone down his raw aggression and to overcome his self-centeredness for the sake of mutual love. He learns to maintain his loving feelings and loyalty in spite of disappointments, to transform his rage into anger, and to express it without harming his loved one. In doing so the toddler brings about a real change in the nature of his impulses, in his ability to tolerate frustrations, and in self-control. At the same time, this makes his relationships more stable and consistent, makes him more considerate, and paves the way for new and more mature relationships with peers and adults. Most important, it enables him to take into himself admired aspects of the parent's personality and thereby to enrich his own. A toddler who has taken this step masters his toileting because he wants to be clean the way his mother is and is pleased with himself when he is like her. Having made cleanliness into his own valued thing, he will extend it to his possessions, his room, his schoolwork, his job, and take pride in it. A toddler who has not taken this step may become toilet trained, but his achievement will not add to his self-esteem, is apt to be unreliable and easily subject to regression under stress. He is not likely to extend cleanliness to other areas and will consider cleaning up as a nasty chore at best. Cleanliness will not be truly his own. This ability to take in attitudes and ideals through a relationship, and to make them a permanent part of one's own self, is crucial for later learning, for character development, and effective conscience formation. Without it, all such gains tend to be unstable; what is there one day may be lost the next, or enables him to function in one setting but not in another.

WHAT DOES THE TODDLER'S PERSONALITY DEVELOPMENT DEPEND ON?

Obviously, the toddler's personality development depends on many factors, such as good health, an adequate bodily and intellectual endowment, reasonable stability in his physical environment, space and safety to be active in it, and a large measure of good luck. Above all, however, his development depends on a continuous enough and good enough relationship with the mothering person who has helped him to become a toddler in the first place. This relationship is the crucial facilitating factor. It does not mean that the mother needs to be perfect or that she should actually be with her toddler every minute. It means that she thinks of herself as his mother always and feels responsible for his well-being at all times, even when she is not with him. It means that she has invested herself in him as a part of herself and as her loved person.

This special, ongoing inner bond with her toddler usually enables her to gauge whether and when he is ready to be without her, with whom and for how long, how he feels and copes when he is away from her, how to reunite with him, and how to bridge the gap of separation by sharing their mutual feelings and individual experiences, what they did and what all happened. If, during a separation, the child cannot keep his inner tie with the mother, he cannot continue to make developmental gains and may lose what he had already acquired.

If the mother cannot maintain her inner tie with her toddler, she may lose her capacity to progress in her maternal development, may get stuck at relating to him at the current level, and fail to appreciate his changing needs. For example, we often see that a mother who is with her toddler only at night continues to care for him as if he were an infant. She may even regress in her mothering ability and lose touch with her child, and in extreme cases, may cease to function as a mother with him. Even their physical reunion may not serve him or her to reestablish the vital link. For example, one day at her day-care center a child suddenly bit Mary's arm. She made no response. Even when her careworker, who happened to see the incident, rushed over to comfort her, Mary remained completely impassive. At pickup time, when the careworker told Mary's parent, showed her the toothmarks, and apologized, Mary remained expressionless, while the parent remarked, "Well, she used to bite so I guess it serves her right." The parent had lost her feelings for and with the child, just as Mary had lost her own.

Mothering is not a given. The ability to enter the developmental phase of parenthood (E. Furman, 1969a) and to progress adequately as a parent, depends in no small measure on the ongoing mutual interactions with the growing child. The child's response to the mother and their physical togetherness are almost as important to the mother's development as it is to the child's. Klaus and Kennell's (1976) work has highlighted the value of postnatal contact with the baby for the mother's "bonding." But this holds true not only for the first few days. All mothers need to be with their infants and care for them actively to get their mothering under way and to achieve that special stable investment in the child which enables them to help their child grow and to grow with him, and to maintain their mothering ability during separations. Mothers vary in how much togetherness, caring, and interaction they require to facilitate their maternal development; they vary in how long it takes them and in the extent to which separations from the child endanger it. For most mothers, however, the child's toddler phase is still a vulnerable period during which insufficient opportunity for ongoing active mothering may interfere in the nature and consistency of their ability to parent effectively and cause lasting damage to its further development. In terms of assuring harmonious growth, we tend to be more aware of the child's need of his mother than of the almost equally important mother's need of her child. I am not implying that being with the child is the only factor in maternal development or that other factors cannot seriously impede it, but I wish to stress that it is a crucial, often neglected factor, and one we need to keep in mind, especially in considering the role and effects of substitute mothering for young children.

I also wish to stress that the concept of a mother's stable investment in her child, the hallmark of mothering, has nothing to do with the currently fashionable term *quality care vs. quantity care*. Being "all there" for the child at certain times, at times especially set aside for that purpose, is a most desirable attitude in those who maintain additional relationships with a young child, such as fathers, grandmothers, baby-sitters, or at a later time, teachers. They fulfill their function by being fully invested in their role with the child at specified times, but can essentially go about their own business at other times. Not so with mothering. Its quality depends on the uninterrupted mental investment which is always there and enables the mothering person to feel with her child regardless of whether she is with him or away from him. It enables her to wake up and attend to him, though not necessarily cheerfully, at night when he is sick, to drop everything in the kitchen and charge after him into the living room, though not necessarily with a smile, because she sensed an ominous silence which told her he was in trouble, or to feel a twinge of regret and pain when she watches him march off happily on a drugstore expedition with Dad while she stays behind to go about her business on her own.

WHAT AFFECTS THE MOTHER'S AND TODDLER'S ABILITY TO MAINTAIN THEIR RELATIONSHIP DURING SEPARATIONS?

Experiences in working with mothers and caretakers of infants and toddlers suggest that the following factors contribute significantly. The list is not exhaustive and does not explore their interaction, nor does it attempt to describe the additional effects of events and circumstances in the past and present lives of the mother–child couple, such as illnesses, family constellations, socioeconomic conditions, births and deaths of other family members, or even the relative emotional health of mother, child, and their relationship. I shall focus specifically on those factors that are directly connected with the mother's, toddler's, and caregiver's handling of temporary separations.

First, there is the time factor: How often do the separations occur, how long do they last, and do they include periods of bodily need fulfillment? Mothers and toddlers generally best tolerate separations of a couple of hours in the morning or afternoon, during periods when the toddler is awake and active and does not need to be fed, bathed, dressed, go to sleep, or wake up. In other words, when his body is under least stress and his mind functions optimally.

Then there is the place factor: Does the toddler remain in his home during the separation or does he stay elsewhere? If he stays elsewhere, does the place resemble his home, is it a totally different kind of setting, is he fully familiar with it? Especially, has the mother been with her toddler in this other place long enough and in such a way that she has experienced everything and everyone there with him, so that he can rely on her full knowledge of him in it and so that she has a complete mental picture of all that happens there with him? Similarly, is he familiar with where she is and what she does there (has he visited her place of work, for example) so that he can picture her in her surroundings? Obviously, it is easier for a child to maintain his concept of self and of mother when he remains in his home, and progressively harder the less homelike the setting is and the less familiar he is with it. Similarly, the more intimately mother and child are acquainted with one another's whereabouts and activities, the easier it is for them to maintain the mutual link and to bridge the gap of separation after reunion.

The factor of shared preparation for the separation and follow-up after it, is important too in that it helps both partners to master the separation. Sudden and unexpected leavings of each other, without a transition period of leave taking, and uncertain times of reunion, are quite stressful. Many of us know how poorly children react to the mother's "disappearance" and how badly they tolerate her absence when it has no predictable end. We can similarly remind ourselves of how distressed, frantic, and furious a mother is when she has unexpectedly lost sight of her child, when he perhaps "disappeared" behind the counter in the department store or when father or an older sibling takes him along on an errand without letting her know.

This brings us to the factor of who is with the child during the separation. Is it someone mother and toddler both know well, someone with whom they have both shared togetherness, someone who has learned how they are with each other, and who therefore carries the trust of their togetherness and becomes a constant reminder of it? And does this person actually receive the toddler from the mother and hand him back to her? This, of course, makes it easiest for mother and child and obtains most often when the child is cared for by a member of the family or by someone in a similarly close relationship with both. Maintaining mental contact with each other becomes much more difficult, even impossible, when the caretaker is relatively or totally unknown to mother or child, when the mother does not personally participate in the transfer of the child to and from the caretaker, or when the child goes from one caretaker to another or even a third one during the separation period. For example, toddlers are often brought to a center by a relative, handed over to an early-duty caretaker, then go on to someone else to join their group, are switched to a next person during nap to allow for the regular caretaker's "break," and, on a late day, are transferred to another special group or are picked up by another family member with whom they stay until mother gets home.

Equally important is the factor, does mother stay in charge? Do mother and child take it for granted that the temporary substitute cares for him at her direction, that she knows about and has sanctioned everything the substitute does with him and the way she does it? Is she called upon to decide what and how things are to be done if there is something unusual ("Would you like Jimmy to wear his snowsuit today?" "Do you want him to go outside yet after his recent cold?"). Does the caretaker report to her what the child did or said and what happened while she was away, and does the mother inform the caretaker of particular events or circumstances that occurred, how they may have affected the child, and how the caretaker could help him with them, be it a family upheaval, or his tummy ache the previous night, or a car accident witnessed on the way? When mother remains responsibly in charge, when the caretaker works at her behest and under her direction, the mother–child tie is much safer for both partners than when she hands over her child, in mind as well as in body, and lets others do for him as they see fit and does not even get to know just how they go about his care. Unlike the older schoolchild, the toddler can only share with mother those parts of his life that she already knows. This is not only important in the case of employed sitters or caretakers, nor does it concern only "bad" things that the substitute may do to him or with him. It applies just as much to family members and to things they do which the child may like very much but which go against mother's wishes or are not cleared with her; for example, staying up late, eating certain foods, playing games, or watching TV programs that are usually off limits, to mention but a few of the more harmless indulgences. If the mother has not okayed these things, happy ones and unhappy ones, they inevitably burden and threaten the mother–child relationship and affect the role it has to play.

This brings us to the last, but by no means least, factor, the attitude of the caretaker. Does he or she do mother's jobs without taking her place? And does he or she build and use the relationship with the child in such a way as to help mother and child maintain their vital link? This is the hardest part of being a good substitute—to be at one's best by accepting oneself as second best. Early on in my professional training,

Anna Freud told us that a good child psychoanalyst keeps in mind, feels with, and deals with, three facets: the child, the mother, and the mother–child relationship. This applies even more to being a good mother substitute, especially with a young child. The caretaker's helpful attitude shows itself in so many ways: She understands and supports the child's thinking and feeling for the mother during the latter's absence, and reminds him of her when he seems to have to shut her out from his mind or seems in danger of forgetting about her. She accepts the child's complaints when she does not come up to par in her handling, does not do as well as mother does; and when she does things that seem to him more fun than what mother does, she reminds him that Mom wanted him to have that fun while she was gone and that they will tell her about it so that she can share in it. When the child welcomes mother on her return, the good sitter accepts being dismissed, and when he teases mother on her return, keeps her waiting and wants to do one more thing with the sitter, she tells mother and child that he probably missed Mom a lot and wants to give her a taste of how hard it is to wait for someone we love, that that matters really more than the extra game with the sitter, and that, anyway, it is really time to be with Mom now. It is a difficult task to be a good sitter, especially when the mother is very far from perfect and when the child is very loving with us. It is hard then to remember that his ability to be so nice with us stems from his relationship with his very imperfect mother. Without that he could not relate to a substitute at all.

A substitute cannot help mother and child to maintain their relationship when she does not have a relationship with each of them herself and is not in feeling touch with them, when she does not know the mother or does not consider her maternal needs, or when she cannot adequately relate with the child, perhaps because she has too many children to look after or because she is only geared to meeting his bodily needs. A substitute also cannot fulfill her true task when she views herself as the mother, be it in the sense of being the child's second mother or even of being his primary mother. This happens in day care when it considers itself the "home away from home," or sometimes assumes that it is actually the child's primary home because he spends so much of his day there. It happens even more frequently when the mother substitute is a family member or resident caretaker in the home, a father or grandmother who regularly shares in the toddler's care, or a nanny or housekeeper. Caretakers who take over as mothers usually invest themselves very intensely in the child and feel very close and loving toward him, but they leave out the mother and the child's relationship with her, or compete with her for the child. They handle the child in their own way, may even feel they do a better job of it. They do not keep the mother in close touch with what they do and with what the child experiences while he is with them, do not readily follow her directions and wishes, and do not support the child's thinking and feeling for his mother during her absence, but often welcome his apparent lack of response to being away from mother. And when the child states a preference for being with them, they see it as a good sign of his fondness for them rather than as a danger signal of the child's difficulty with loyalty, difficulty in dealing with his anger at mother, and difficulty in maintaining his vital relationship with her. Double mothering is very different from substitute mothering, and poses its own special threats to the primary mother–child relationship.

WHAT HAPPENS WHEN SEPARATIONS BETWEEN MOTHER AND TODDLER OVERTAX THEIR TOLERANCE AND ADVERSELY AFFECT THEIR RELATIONSHIP?

In the normal course of development toddlers seek out familiar people, enjoy new and special activities with them, and form meaningful relationships with them which are maintained in addition to, not instead of, the primary relationship with the mothering person. Prompted by their as yet unresolved mixed feelings about their mother, toddlers often also seek out or wish for others to be new and better mommies—the proverbial better cookies at the Joneses. Sensible mothers and "others" do not allow this actually to happen because they realize that, far from helping the child, it would interfere in his task of coming to terms with his dissatisfactions with his own mother and with the reality of his situation. In the normal course of development, however, there also inevitably arise circumstances in which the mother has to arrange for substitute care during limited periods, at least for such occasions as her own doctor's appointments, an older child's school conference, or a special shopping trip. If these separations are helpfully managed, they are good learning experiences, times when mother and child can test and practice their means of coping. Masterable stresses may serve to build mental "muscles." By contrast, extended, repeated separations of mother and toddler tend to become unmasterable stresses for one or both partners and endanger the mother–toddler relationship and the personality growth that depends on it, especially if they involve double mothering, multiple mothering, or unhelpful substitute mothering.

These kinds of interferences are not new or newly prevalent. They are not limited to this country or to specific socioeconomic groups. The very affluent in all countries always employed caretakers for their children and still do so; the very poor have always left them with family members or neighbors out of necessity, while mothers helped with farming, or later, with industrialization, flocked into factories. Wars and the ravages of epidemics and of economic hardship have always disrupted family lives and mother–child relationships (Thomas, 1977; Tate and Ammerman, 1979). A historic exhibit in one of South Carolina's plantations shows pictures of the slaves' day nurseries, a big room supervised by a black daycare worker with many little mats on the floor, each occupied by an infant. This is how the slaves' children spent their days while their mothers were at work, some of whom were no doubt providing double mothering for "the master's" children. All slave cultures were run on similar lines through the ages. And the extended families in many culture patterns fall far short of the imagined ideal we tend to attribute to them. Not only do they involve double and multiple mothering, but youngsters are often dropped off at a moment's notice with relatives or friends whom the child does not know, just as in this country children are sometimes sent to grandparents far away who are close with the mother but near strangers to the child. Indeed, early extended separations and substitute care are not new or limited. What is new is our efforts to understand their effects.

To my knowledge the first scientific inquiry originated with Anna Freud and her coworkers. In Vienna, during the years of extreme depression which followed the First World War, she ran a day-care center for toddlers from deprived families. It was called the Edith Jackson Creche, named after the generous American colleague who financed it. The toddlers' day there started with a bath in the early morning. Later, during World War II, Anna Freud and Dorothy Burlingham ran the Hampstead nurseries in London. They cared for infants, toddlers, and preschoolers who were separated from their families, to protect their lives during the blitz bombardments and to enable their mothers to participate in the work of the war effort. Again American generosity helped out and the now famous descriptions of Anna Freud's and Burlingham's (1943, 1944) findings originated for the most part with the monthly reports to the funders, among them this country's Foster Parents Association. Shortly after the war, it was again Anna Freud who was sought out to consult with Israeli mental health professionals and educators. They had noted some of the distressing effects on many children raised in kibbutzim in which extended substitute parenting was the rule.

Since the seventies there has been a profusion of research and findings, especially on the effects of day care on young children. Some of these have lacked adequate data, some have focused their field of inquiry too narrowly or over too short a period. Few have recognized the enormous inherent difficulty in comparing the highly individual experiences of youngsters and their parents in settings which also vary greatly, not only one from the other, but even from day to day when, for example, a trusted caregiver suddenly leaves and thereby changes the crucial personal milieu of a center. I would still list some of the earlier publications among the most thorough. They include the study of English day care by Bain and Barnett (1980) and in the United States the related publications by White (1978) and Provence, Naylor, and Patterson (1977). Among the developmental interferences stressed in these studies are delays and deficits in language development, both during the toddler phase and during the later school years, especially difficulties in using speech for comprehension and communication. Also noted, at the time and in later schooling, are increased aggressive manifestations and difficulty in impulse control. Those who have mainly studied schoolchildren, in follow-up, find a prominent tendency to learning problems, characterized by academic performance below intellectual potential; lack of motivation; difficulties in concentration, in ability to invest and enjoy interests and activities, and in integrating and using what has been learned. Bain and Barnett also point to "damage or severe interferences in personality development."

My experiences with the care of infants and toddlers have taken several forms. They began in the 1940s, when I cared for youngsters in residential settings, and have become an ongoing focus of interest for me since the 1960s. My most detailed data have been gained from the psychoanalytic treatment of five school-aged children who had experienced substitute care or double mothering in their earliest years. With each seen in individual sessions five times weekly for about four years, their symptoms and personality functioning could be unraveled and traced to their origins. Their early care experiences proved to be important causative factors in their pathology (E. Furman, 1967). Several preschoolers with emotional difficulties were the source of detailed data. They had experienced similar early care experiences and attended the Hanna Perkins Therapeutic Nursery School. Observations at the school and weekly sessions of treatment via the parent for two to three years enabled us again to relate some of the children's troubles to the effects of earlier care. My colleagues at Hanna Perkins and at our Center's child analytic clinic also worked with such cases. In 1984, when I became the director of our own then newly established Toddler–Mother Group, the ongoing study of toddlers, their mothers, and their relationships, including the effects of interferences, became my main area of research (E. Furman, 1992a, 1993a). Through our regular scientific meetings, I had a chance to compare data and to extend and confirm findings. At the same time, my regular consulting work with day-care centers afforded an opportunity to learn how toddlers, mothers, and careworkers respond to these experiences at the time when they are actually taking place, and to apply the understanding gained through therapy in the form of preventive educational measures. This work began with my participation in the Home Start Project, a family day-care program under the auspices of the then Cleveland Day Nursery Association. In more recent years, our Center responded to community need by offering an ongoing yearly course, "Toddlers in Day Care," which I have taught and learned from. In this course directors and careworkers from about ten day-care centers for toddlers and infants meet with me every other week to discuss the children's development, educational practices, contacts with parents, individual youngsters' difficulties, and ways of helping them.

What, then, has it been possible to learn? First of all, it is noteworthy that the observations of toddlers' and mothers' responses to various forms of care confirm the retrospective knowledge gained from the therapeutic work with older children. The personality difficulties that are seen to underlie the older children's problems can be observed as they take shape during toddlerhood, and they manifestly interfere with the toddler's mastery of his developmental tasks even before they contribute to his trouble with later ones. For example, the toddler's difficulty in developing his valued independent self-concept may show in not wanting to take over care of his body, while the older child's similar difficulty interferes with his self-motivation in learning, prevents him from making his learning his own thing, and from investing his interests and activities.

Although even during the toddler's process of development a variety of factors interact to produce an interference, it is often possible to pinpoint the effect of substitute care when we can alter it to mitigate the stress and observe the child's responses to such a change. For example, we have noted repeatedly, that toddlers who neither recognized nor cared about their own and others' property in a day-care setting, began to treasure their own and respect others' belongings, including the Center's toys and equipment, after they were encouraged to keep one of their mothers' belongings (a scarf, a glove, a coat) which they could carry with them or deposit wherever and whenever they wished to, without anyone interfering. This measure was one of several designed to help the child maintain his inner tie with his mother and his self. Such instances helped substantiate the link between the effects of care on toddlers and on later development. Treatment of some of the older children with trouble in caring for and respecting property revealed a connection with early care experiences, but it was by then harder to isolate this factor from other contributing factors.

In contrast to other studies, which tend to single out several specific areas of difficulty in connection with early care, our findings suggest that any or all areas of personality development may be affected, but especially all those we have listed as the developmental tasks of the toddler phase and which, as such, form the basis for later growth. This, we must remind ourselves, includes not only many aspects of the development of self and self-esteem, but particularly the ability to form and maintain stable caring relationships.

Obviously, not all children suffer or suffer equally. No two individual experiences or personalities are alike, but a sufficient number of them manifest problems or interferences in development to indicate that there is a risk for all.

CAN WE ADAPT "CARE" FOR TODDLERS TO AVOID ILL EFFECTS?

The insights gained from therapy and years of work with gifted and dedicated caregivers in our course are consistent with national professional standards for toddler care. They have enabled us to develop many approaches and measures that have lessened the stress sufficiently for some toddlers to overcome difficulties and have perhaps helped others to avoid potential troubles. We have not been able to follow the children long enough or closely enough to know whether all ill effects were avoided. We do know that it is difficult to bring about the many necessary changes in attitudes and procedures. It makes many demands on the mothers and caregivers, but it also brings them many pleasures and satisfactions and a greater sense of shared effort.

The onus falls on the caregiver. If she is a person who truly enjoys toddlers and feels in tune with them, which, by the way, is very different from being good at relating with preschoolers, she can probably also learn to feel with and understand all the things we have just discussed. She will know when a toddler really is a toddler and can relate to a substitute, what his developmental tasks are, what the mother–toddler relationship is about and the role it plays, how separation may affect this relationship, and the many factors that help to bridge the gap during absences. Above all she will appreciate that she is a substitute, that her role with the mother is to help her realize her importance, that her role with the child is to help him maintain his relationship with his mother and to do so in a setting that meets his developmental needs. Given that, she will find the many practical ways that serve to put this attitude into practice. I shall mention a few such practical measures, but want to stress that they work only when they are used within an overall helpful context, not when they are isolated gimmicks.

An initial interview with the mother when she first visits the care center while it is in session, without her child, serves as an opportunity to listen to her, to get an idea of her expectations, and of her understanding of what substitute care will mean to her and her child, and to ascertain whether he has mastered the pretoddler developmental steps. This helps to gauge how best to introduce her to the realities—that her relationship with her child is and needs to remain the most important part of his life, that their separation will inevitably put a stress on this, that the caregiver's main task will be to help her child to keep his mom in his mind and in his heart. She, the mother, will also need to participate, to help him with his feelings, and to cope with his responses which may show in unwelcome ways, like contrariness or sleep troubles or regression in toileting, and that, to start with, she will need to free up time to help him with the new experience. This will take at least one or two weeks, during which she will be attending with her toddler, starting with an hour or so and gradually extending it to the full period. This will give her a chance to know fully all that happens while he is there, and especially, to get to know his caregiver so that all three of them can begin to relate and trust one another. One skilled director reports that mothers' initial reactions range from "Oh God!" to "No problem" or even "I like that." It is never easy to work out the necessary schedule. Many a letter is sent to mothers' employers to enlist their cooperation, sometimes by telling them that a mother's comfort in settling in her child helps her ease of mind at work and ultimately makes her a better employee. Most mothers do manage to participate fully and effectively, enjoy being truly welcomed and involved, and after the separation is effected, use many ways of keeping in touch—joining the child for lunch, phoning at certain times, picking him up early whenever possible, accepting and sharing feelings. Many mothers also find ways of shortening the separation period in order, for example, to assure that the child's stay will not exceed his caretaker's work hours and he will not need to be cared for by an additional substitute.

The caregiver uses the introductory period to understand the mother–child relationship, their ways of being and doing things together, and to learn their language (all caregivers are multilingual because, in addition to special family words for special things, each toddler speaks his own language in words and behavior which usually only his mother really understands).

As mother begins to leave, the caregiver's main job starts, picking up, supporting, and verbalizing the child's feelings about mother's absence and return. It is very difficult for toddlers to sustain feelings without their mothers, not only feelings about her, though this is the first step. When they are helped to recognize and tolerate their angry, sad, lonely feelings about mother, it helps them to keep the tie with her and to build a relationship with the substitute, and this in turn helps them to tolerate and share feelings about other things, be it a current pain or an event at home. Without help with feelings the toddler survives, but does not function as a person. For some time, children may only be able to feel when mother arrives; for example, one caregiver noticed that a rather new little boy kept touching his ear. Although his face was bland, she surmised he might be in pain. She told him so, telephoned his mother, and he silently accepted her comforting lap. As soon as his mother walked in he ran to her, clung to her, and burst into tears. It turned out he had a painful ear infection. This boy could recognize and feel discomfort and seek help, but not yet with a substitute. When mother and caregiver tell one another of the child's experiences with them, each can help the child maintain his appropriate feelings and make them a part of his continuous self. Mother helps similarly by talking about the caregiver at home and supporting his feelings about missing her, especially during holiday breaks or when the worker is ill. Remembrance tokens, such as little toys, from the center to home are a useful concrete link.

A steady rhythm of daily and weekly activities helps youngsters to gauge when to expect mother's return as well as the leaving of the center for the weekend. It develops their sense of time and helps them master the changes; for example, "Now it's lunch, then it's rest, then it's music, then Mommy comes," or "Today is washday, then is take-home-your-bags day, then is weekend-stay-at-home day." Transitions from and to mother are the hardest times for everyone. They are the times when loyalty conflicts and stored up feelings on the child's part surface, and when tensions between mother and caregiver about their respective roles with the child become most touchy. Good caregivers look out for these times and help and support the mother when she is "on the spot." When little Janie had a spell of really giving her mother the business at pickup time, the caregiver did not take over and do it "better," did not pretend to ignore it, did not even just stand by and watch. She caught the runaway Janie at the door and handed her over, then called mother up in the evening and said, "I am sorry that Janie still shows in this way how much she missed you. She really makes it very awkward for you. How would you best like me to help at these times? Let's think it through together and work out a plan."

When mothers feel in charge and respected, they also respect the caretaker, watch and learn from her ways of handling children, ask for advice, want to share concerns, and talk them over. These are not opportunities for posing as the "expert," but for listening, for sharing what "other mothers sometimes do" or what "we have found helpful at the center," or, if necessary, for paving the way toward suggesting professional assistance, preferably with someone directly or indirectly connected with the center.

But what about the care setting, its equipment and opportunities for intellectual stimulation? One then-new member of our course who was planning to open a new day-care facility, asked for suggestions for toys and apparatus. The experienced caregivers were unanimous. "Ask your mother and aunts and neighbors for all their spare kitchen and household utensils, their pots and pans and plastic containers, their old spools and jar tops. That's what you will really need." They were basically right. Create as homelike an atmosphere as possible and help the toddler explore and understand his world which is the home. His best "field trips" are the kitchen, the laundry, the broom closet; let him do things there, if at all possible. Toys and materials are best introduced singly and slowly, in keeping with individual children's readiness and the caregiver's ability to play and do with them. It is through the shared pleasure of the loved ones that skills and activities gain lasting investment. This brings us to the most important aspect of the "curriculum": have as few children as possible to one adult. After all, a mothering person has her hands full with one toddler, just because he needs all of her.

We can tell that a youngster is mastering the stress of substitute care when he pursues his developmental tasks with zest and self-motivation and enjoys his achievements with his loved ones, with the mother and with the mother substitute.

WHAT ABOUT MOTHERS WHO HAVE GREAT DIFFICULTY IN MOTHERING, DIFFICULTY IN FEELING WITH THEIR CHILDREN, DIFFICULTY IN HELPING THEM WITH DEVELOPMENTAL STEPS?

Obviously we cannot change people nor can we serve everyone. We can only do our best to help those who want to work with us. "Our best" in such cases, however, is not to focus on the child and give up on the mother or to discount her importance for the child. The more tenuous and burdened the mother–child relationship is, the more important it is for the substitute to help the toddler maintain it and to underline its positives. A mother who has even just managed to help her child live to be a toddler, must have devoted a considerable amount of effort and care to the task, prepared many meals, changed many diapers, got up many nights. In some such cases the most helpful approach is to admit mother and child to the center, support her care for him there, and let her help with and join in the activities. A number of mothers could in this way be helped to feel worthwhile and invest their children more lovingly.

10

On Trauma: When Is the Death of a Parent Traumatic?

As my contribution to a Panel on "Trauma Revisited" (1984), I was asked to discuss the potentially traumatic effects of parental bereavement in childhood. This assignment gave me the opportunity to trace again, for myself, the history of the term *trauma* as an analytic concept, to review the material gained from the treatments of traumatized children, both my own cases and those of my Cleveland colleagues, and to formulate some thoughts as well as questions about the topic. Although I shall limit the case examples and most of the discussion to children who had lost a parent through death, my thinking is also based on data derived from the analytic study of other traumatic experiences, such as sexual and aggressive abuse, life-threatening accidents, illness, injury, and medical–surgical procedures.

WHAT IS A TRAUMA?

In analytic papers the term *trauma* is frequently used in the sense of connoting a severe stress, and a child's parental bereavement is commonly referred to as a traumatic experience. I do not wish to minimize the crucial importance for a child of his loss of a parent through death or to underestimate the potentially devastating effects this may have on his personality. I do feel it is necessary, however, to differentiate instances where a parent's death is traumatic from those where it is stressful, because the impact on the psychic system and the means the personality employs in dealing with the tragedy differ, and this in turn affects therapeutic handling as well as preventive measures. This differentiation is in keeping with A. Freud's (1964) view. She urged us to use the term *trauma* according to its original analytic definition, "to rescue it from the widening and overuse which . . . lead inevitably to a blurring of meaning and . . . abandonment and loss of valuable concepts," and she suggested that we exclude "notions of the accumulative, the strain, the retrospective, the screen trauma . . . [because they make it difficult] to differentiate between adverse, pathogenic influences in general and trauma in particular" (p. 222).

According to Freud (1920) and A. Freud (1964), the essence of trauma is an influx of stimuli from within or without which wholly or partly breaks through the ego's protective shield and floods the system with excitation. Such an occurrence may be caused by the sheer quantity or nature of the stimuli, or by the relative lack of preparedness of the system through prior hypercathexis, or by the system's inadequacy in coping with stimuli, due to immaturity, anomaly, pathology, or individual variations in the level of tolerance for excitation. In the youngest children, the traumatic break through the stimulus barrier may be related to insufficient availability of the protective containing function of the "holding" environment, a point repeatedly stressed by Winnicott (1960a, 1960b, 1962, 1963a, 1963b, 1963c) or, as A. Freud puts it, a failure in the mothering person's function as her infant's auxiliary ego. Thus, a trauma may be caused by factors in the id, ego, and external world, and these factors are usually closely related and mutually dependent, so it is difficult, if not impossible, for the outsider to determine what the cause or causes may have been unless they become revealed in the course of an analysis. We need therefore to heed A. Freud's reminder to herself, "I shall remember not to confuse my own with the victim's appraisal of the happening" (p. 239). This applies to parental bereavement as the potential cause of trauma. We can never say before treatment that the death of the parent as such was traumatic. The later case vignettes will illustrate that, in each instance, different combinations of internal and external factors proved to have been traumatogenic—the circumstances of the death, the incapacitation of the ego through bodily injury at the time of loss, the antecedent experiences, existing ego mechanisms and instinctual impulses, the role of the environment, developmental factors, and many more.

Irrespective of the varied individual causes of trauma, however, its immediate effect on the organism is always the same. The ego and pleasure principle are put out of action when the psychic system is either altogether overwhelmed by the excess of excitation or cannot prevent the pouring in of stimuli through a limited breach in its protective shield. In the case of total flooding, all ego functions are suspended, the entire defense organization which served as the protective shield becomes inoperative, and the mental apparatus is reduced to what A. Freud (p. 238) calls "physical responses via the vegetative nervous system taking the place of psychic reactions," or what Yorke, Kennedy, and Wiseberg (1980) term *vegetative excitement,* which may behaviorally resemble a temper tantrum. In the case of a breach in the protective shield, the reparation process, according to Freud (1920), begins at once by a massive anticathexis which drains off all the available energy and extensively reduces or paralyzes the remaining functions. This manifests itself in states of shock (Freud), in states of paralysis of action or numbness of feeling (A. Freud), in battle exhaustion (Yorke et al., 1980), in some types of apathy (Greenson, 1949; E. Furman, 1974), and in some forms of depersonalization.

These traumatic or immediately posttraumatic states may last for minutes, hours, days, months, or years. They may recur, even recur repeatedly under certain conditions, a point I shall return to. When we can actually observe these states in patients, they can serve as one indication that the patient experienced a trauma. However, since these states sometimes last only for brief periods, and since both the patient and others may not notice them or may misinterpret them, such observations are often omitted from the personal history and from reports on current behavior. Moreover, even professionals find it hard to differentiate posttraumatic states from other disturbances, especially in prelatency children. I know of two cases misdiagnosed as "minimal brain damage and retardation" and several others termed *psychotic* (E. Furman, 1956).

THE PROCESS OF RECOVERY

After the catastrophic event, the psychic apparatus is faced with the problem of binding, or mastering, the noxious excess of stimuli and of restoring all areas of ego functioning and their phase-appropriate maturational progression.

According to Freud (1920), the gradual process of binding takes the form of repetition compulsion until all stimuli have been mastered and brought under the domain of the pleasure or reality principle. Among manifestations of this process Freud includes certain forms of children's demands for repetition and passive-into-active play, repetitive dreams, fate neuroses, and analytic transference phenomena. Yorke et al. (1980) further include children's pavor nocturnus and stage IV nightmares, and their accompanying motoric discharges.

A. Freud (1964) points out that we should differentiate between two types of repetition. One is a pre-ego process, the repetition compulsion; the other is an ego mechanism "repeating an experience with variations suitable for its assimilation, such as turning a passive experience into an active one" (p. 237) or employing defenses such as denial. Such a transition from pre-ego mechanisms to ego mechanisms indicates a progression in the recuperative process.

Another measure of the nature and rate of recovery mentioned by A. Freud is the reemergence of ego functions—either residual or reinvested—and how fast or slowly they reach their pretraumatic level and pick up their phase-appropriate maturational momentum.

The nature and role of anxiety are other important elements in our understanding of trauma and of posttraumatic developments. Freud relates the failure of signal anxiety, and aspect of the system's preparedness, to the occurrence of trauma and views the need to repeat as an endeavor "to master the stimulus retrospectively, by developing the anxiety whose omission was the cause of the traumatic neurosis" (p. 32). Yorke and Wiseberg (1976) and Yorke et al. (1980) trace the developmental line of anxiety from vegetative excitation which is bodily, to terror/panic which is primitive mental, to signal anxiety. Winnicott emphasizes two further stages in the development of anxiety which follow the purely vegetative excitement and precede the essentially mental terror/panic. Both of these anxiety states combine mental and bodily responses. The first (Winnicott, 1960a, 1963c), the developmentally earlier one, happens when the traumatic impingement awakens the ego's awareness to experience an interruption of its "going-on-being" (1963c, p. 256). The second, later one is characterized by annihilation anxiety or "unthinkable anxiety." Its contents are "(1) Going to pieces. (2) Falling for ever. (3) Having no relationship to the body. (4) Having no orientation" (1962, p. 58). I am uncertain as to the developmental point in earliest infancy when vegetative excitement begins to be accompanied by the mental experience of an interruption in "going-on-being." Clinical experiences with babies suggest that the second stage, annihilation anxiety combined with bodily responses, is present in the latter half of the first year.

Some of my analytic patients have clearly described the overwhelming fears Winnicott lists during their recurrent states of traumatic overwhelming. These take the form of awake episodes of terror and frantic motor discharge, sometimes accompanied by bodily distress or nausea, abdominal discomfort, and an urgency to urinate or defecate, and sometimes ending in total bodily collapse in a fetal position with paralysis of all functions. In the most severely affected patients any excess of stimuli, such as a minor change in their environment, can trigger such a recurrence of the traumatic state. They are sensitized to trauma in general. Their reparative measures include withdrawal, avoidance of all stimulation, and insistence on sameness; preoccupation with things as opposed to people (the latter being less predictable and controllable); a frantic separation anxiety, using the mother as a protective auxiliary ego. At a later point, denial and passive-into-active may be used, for example, in the form of actively bringing on the traumatic state to avoid being surprised by it and to "traumatize" the helpless onlookers. It also is a sign of the healing process when these patients' traumatic states begin to occur in response to specific stimuli or situations, which in some ways remind them of the original trauma, and it is further progress when the recurrences take place primarily or exclusively in the analysis and are linked to the transference. Some patients are at the stage of situation-specific traumatic recurrence when they start treatment, and it is not always clear whether they ever were generally sensitized to trauma or perhaps experienced only a brief period of that stage during the immediately posttraumatic time. The next milestone in the recuperative process is reached when, in the course of the analysis, and sometimes prior to it, these states of situation-specific annihilation anxiety become linked with and supplanted by later developmental anxieties and by contents which apply directly to the original trauma.

These clinical experiences have led me to regard the presence of annihilation anxiety in its various forms as another manifest indication that a trauma did occur, and to view the defenses against annihilation anxiety, as well as its gradual change to other forms of anxiety, or even an admixture of other anxieties, as a measure of the ongoing reparative process.

Let me now turn to another aspect of trauma damage and the healing process which has seemed particularly important to me. In her study of adult analysands who were raped during childhood, A. Katan (1973) found that these patients were most severely affected in two areas, impairment of integration and drive defusion. These damages permeated their personality structures and functioning and could not be improved much through analytic treatment. My own work with children who could not feel good showed that these patients invariably also suffered from marked difficulties with drive fusion, integration, and ability to develop and maintain neutral interests and to be creative in whatever form. All these characteristics proved to be psychically related to one another, and one of the genetic causes was the experience of trauma. In 1985, I attempted to trace the mutual dependence of these characteristics, discussed the factors which facilitate and impede their development, and suggested some clinical approaches to the problems they pose for the afflicted patients and their analytic work. In the context of the present focus on trauma, one finding is especially pertinent: Drive fusion can take place only when there is a sufficient quantity of libido in relation to aggression and when the libido is sufficiently bound to be securely under the sway of the pleasure principle. Binding the libidinal energy, and indeed all stimuli, is in part if not wholly, accomplished through the function of integration. At the same time, integration depends on bound, as opposed to free-flowing, libido because it draws on this very source of energy to fuel its own functioning. Freud pointed out that the impact of trauma, the break through the ego's protective shield, and the flooding of the organism with excessive stimuli, put the ego and the pleasure principle out of action. This means that drive fusion can no longer be maintained and that the integrative function which helps to bind excitations is totally or largely incapacitated. The damaging effect of trauma on drive fusion and integration is therefore particularly severe. The clinical manifestations of defusion and impaired integration are especially prominent in the personality functioning of traumatized children. This is most marked in those who experienced trauma during their earliest years because in them drive fusion and integration were interfered with during the initial, most vulnerable phases of development. As a result, drive fusion and integration fail to mature normally and cannot appropriately contribute to the progression of other areas of personality growth.

Yet it is just in these two most damaged areas of drive fusion and integration that we also can most readily follow the reparative process. It takes the form of gradually integrating the traumatic noxious excess of stimuli by libidinizing them—bringing them under the domain of the pleasure principle—and, at the same time, accomplishing the first steps in drive fusion. This shows itself in increasing sexualization of the traumatic event, alteration in some of its features, and linking with other more adequately mastered life experiences. In this form, the trauma may be incorporated in anxiety dreams and nightmares with an element of wish fulfillment (succeeding the mere repetition compulsion of pavor nocturnus and stage IV nightmares with motor discharges). It often becomes the content of masturbation fantasies; it infiltrates behavior patterns and actively provokes interactions with others which partly serve instinctual gratification. It affects the formation of the superego and instinctualizes its interaction with the ego, and it may even libidinize the posttraumatic forms of anxiety. The primitive degree of fusion attained through this aspect of the reparative process is usually of a crudely sadomasochistic nature. This may be clinically distressing for the patient, his loved ones, and the analyst, and may indeed lead to secondary pathology, yet it represents definite strides in assimilating the trauma and in restoring maturational progression of drive fusion and integration.

TRAUMA IN PARENTALLY BEREAVED CHILDREN

Since the publication of *A Child's Parent Dies* (E. Furman, 1974), the original number of twenty-three parentally bereaved children treated by my Cleveland colleagues and myself has more than doubled. In assessing which of these patients were traumatized by their experience of the parent's death or by factors related to it, I have used the criteria listed above which indicate traumatic or posttraumatic responses. With some patients the data were gained during analyses that took place after the loss; with others, whose parent died during their treatment, the data include the actual time of bereavement. Many patients did not experience the death of the parent as a trauma, but a number did, and from amongst this latter group, I shall briefly describe four, to illustrate some of the earlier points and to raise further questions.

Miriam was the eagerly welcomed, healthy first child of a happy young couple. By 3½ weeks of age she thrived, seemed comfortable and well-contained, and had just begun to extend her sleeping periods at night. When Miriam was 4 weeks, her mother fell ill and died of a viral infection within twenty-four hours. The maternal grandmother immediately took over Miriam's full-time care and soon invested the infant as her own. I began to work with the grandmother a couple of months later. By that time Miriam was at peace and thriving again, but the grandmother described Miriam's immediate response to the upheaval. The baby screamed and fretted almost incessantly, refused food, suffered interference in all bodily functions, and could not be comforted. This state lasted for many days and only gradually diminished. One suspects she experienced a state of vegetative excitation or possibly an interruption in the "going-on-being," caused by the loss of what Winnicott calls the "holding environment," and what A. Freud terms the *auxiliary ego* provided by the mothering person. I worked with the grandmother for several years. She was unusually empathic with infants. This seemed to have mitigated even her own initial severe distress so that the child's traumatic response was all the more noteworthy. During her early years Miriam then weathered a number of stresses, and during her fourth year she experienced a near-total loss of her grandmother when the father's new wife insisted on taking her over and placed her in a day-care center. Miriam was deeply distressed but at no point showed a traumatic reaction. The development of drive fusion and ego functions was neither delayed nor impaired.

Danny (Fiedler, 1974), the third child in his family, was 11 months old when he and his father were hospitalized with a viral infection. The father died of it within forty-eight hours. The mother, distraught and preoccupied with her other more mildly ill children at home, could not visit Danny during his week-long hospital stay during which he underwent many medical procedures. When she came to take him home, he was pale, listless, and did not respond. He no longer walked or crawled, had lost his early speech and intense emotional interest in people and the world around him. He was limp and apathetic and only clung like a little baby. The family moved to a new home, and work with the mother began within a month. With the help of the mother's empathic efforts, Danny resumed crawling at 17 months, which soon turned into heedless hyperactivity and accident proneness, and he spoke a few words again by nearly 2 years. Testing showed him to be of at least normal intelligence, but his persistent lack of affect and response made him appear mentally retarded.

The therapist's ongoing weekly interviews with the mother continued when Danny entered the Hanna Perkins

School at nearly 3 years. His previously constant separation terror had subsided by this time but still reached panic proportions when he thought mother would leave him suddenly; for example, when he momentarily lost sight of her in a store, he screamed in terror to the point of turning blue and lost consciousness. His analysis, begun at age 4, showed that he remembered and missed his father, and that his death troubled him in many ways. The real trauma, however, was the temporary loss of the mother at 11 months and some of the medical procedures he endured during her absence at that time; for example, when he was to be photographed, the idea that someone would take his picture reminded him of his X-rays during the early hospitalization and resulted in a episode of terror for him. Although these recurrences of terror states surfaced in barely mitigated form for many years, they were in time supplanted by heightened developmental fears, especially castration anxiety and early superego anxiety. He also began to use passive-into-active repetitions, instinctualized some aspects of the trauma, and linked it with other experiences. This showed itself in his running away, refusal to care for himself, magical denial of masturbatory dangers, and insistence that his mother could cure everything because she was a nurse. Danny's difficulty with drive fusion contributed to particularly harsh, early superego forerunners.

Ruth was 3½ years old when her father was murdered. She learned of this from her mother's frantic, instinctualized account and behavior. The impact was intensified by the mother's chaotic response during the following year and her propensity to externalize her fears, anger, and excitement to everyone, including Ruth, overwhelming them with gruesome details and unrealistic speculations. After a lovingly invested infancy, the child had already suffered repeated, overwhelming trauma through sexual and aggressive abuse and, during the months preceding the father's death, she had helplessly witnessed the parents' violent arguments and fights. During the period immediately following the father's death, Ruth seemed to have suffered very frequent states of being totally overwhelmed, suggesting posttraumatic recurrences. These were sometimes ignored and sometimes punished as naughty temper tantrums. There also was evidence that, at least within the year, she overwhelmed others, turning passive into active. Her unfused aggression manifested itself in physical sadistic attacks, especially on younger children, and in self-hurting masturbatory activities.

Ruth's analysis began in her sixth year during her attendance at the Hanna Perkins School. Highly intelligent and verbal, she was plagued by symptoms in all areas of functioning, many fears, extreme ambivalence, and inability to tolerate any increase in stimuli, for example, a change in routine or someone talking to her unexpectedly. Although it was difficult to disentangle to what extent Ruth's earlier experiences affected her response to her father's death, and to what extent her integration of its trauma linked them together, some post-traumatic symptoms were understood to relate primarily to the murder: pavor nocturnus, a horror of everything related to violence and death, and recurring episodes of overwhelming fear of annihilation, accompanied by frantic motor discharges and bodily collapse into a fetal position, and by sensations of pain and an expectation of being killed. During the years of analytic work, her pavor nocturnus changed to repetitive nightmares and, later, specific phobic fears at bedtime. Her episodes of trauma recurrence became less frequent and more situation-specific and were mostly limited to transference reactions in the sessions. She also gradually achieved better control of the episodes, first by bringing on the overwhelming when she sensed it coming over her, then by experiencing it mentally without bodily sensations, and still later by being able to withdraw into a closet and calm down when it had barely started. By age 9, almost 6 years after the trauma and 3 years of analysis, Ruth showed evidence of signal anxiety. She could feel the threat of "it's coming" but could prevent feeling or manifesting terror. She coped at those times by asking to be left alone and playing quietly for a while. The contents of the trauma also became integrated in the form of passive-into-active provocations, sadomasochistic masturbation fantasies, and instinctualized aspects of superego, representing murderer and victim internally. Although drive fusion and synthesis were seriously impaired, Ruth could be helped to address and cope with all aspects of mourning the loss of her father through death. Its form, the murder, was the real trauma and has been much harder for her to master.

Jim (Schiff, 1974) was 7¼ years old when he experienced a car accident while driving with his mother, his twin, a younger brother, and another mother and her four children. The car hit a bridge abutment and both mothers, Jim's twin, and three of the other family's children were killed. Jim sustained serious head injuries and only recovered consciousness after several weeks. For three months he was cared for in a hospital room he shared with his brother who was casted for limb fractures. He learned of the deaths there but did not acknowledge them, although his later analysis revealed that he had clearly remembered the pretraumatic and traumatic events. Jim's initial confusion and hyperactivity were probably organic but persisted after neurological impairment was ruled out. In addition, while he had been pathologically aggressive, he became quite passive and defenseless in his interactions with others and suffered frequent spells of sitting motionless, staring and losing touch with the world so that he failed to respond to what was going on around him, even to his family's efforts "to get him out of it." These symptoms were unchanged when he started analysis at age 10, almost three years later, and could then be understood and resolved.

Jim had experienced overwhelming terror and subsequently heightened anxiety at all levels. Castration fear contributed to his passivity and hyperactivity. His episodes of apathetic withdrawal ultimately warded off overwhelming sadness. In part these manifestations were posttraumatic, related to the nature of the deaths and injuries, as well as to the loss of the mother and unavailability of emotional support and adequate care during the succeeding period. Jim's analysis revealed, however, that, at least by that time, his symptoms also had become linked with earlier separations during which Jim had been aggressively abused and neglected. These earlier experiences had heightened his developmental anxieties prior to the trauma and shaped his early defenses, serving especially to ward off extremely helpless feelings of unsafety, sadness, and longing.

DISCUSSION

These vignettes raise rather than answer many questions. The very selection of the cases and the sequence in which they were arranged imply that I wish to draw attention to the significance of developmental factors in our attempts to understand trauma. Following Freud and A. Freud in recognizing that the causes of trauma, at any age, depend on the unique individual confluence of internal and external circumstances, we may yet take it for granted that the immature ego is more vulnerable to traumatization. Whereas under good enough conditions the auxiliary ego of the mothering person compensates for the infant's and young child's ego weakness, his very reliance on maternal functioning also increases his vulnerability. He may be traumatized because the mother's auxiliary ego does not function effectively, or because it becomes totally unavailable, or even because the mother actually causes the overwhelming excess of stimulations instead of protecting her child from it. In assessing the developmental factor we therefore have to take into account the interaction of two variables, the developmental status of the child's personality and the nature and availability of the auxiliary ego of the mothering person.

Experience suggests that this two-pronged developmental factor affects not only the initial experience of trauma but the recuperative process. Young children sense this. Regardless of who or what inflicted the trauma, unless the mother is actually absent or emotionally altogether unavailable, they turn to her to avail themselves of her protective and healing ego functions. They cling to her and react to separation from her with renewed annihilation fear or panic. Analytic data show us, time and again, that the child's healing process is greatly facilitated when the mother is not only physically available but emotionally aware of the child's experience, active in assisting him with integration, and supportive of his efforts. Unfortunately, this applies in reverse as well. Although Miriam was almost too young to view her experience as equivalent to the trauma in a more differentiated personality, it seems likely that the immediate and consistent availability of her grandmother's auxiliary ego favorably affected her subsequent satisfactory progress. Danny's mother was truly helpful and devoted in her assistance to him, but she had been absent for a long time during the traumatic period and was a very different mother when she became available to him once again. Sad, drawn, and burdened by the many demands of her changed life situation, she presented quite a contrast to her earlier happy, smiling self, tackling life with zest and optimism. This had a profound effect on Danny, mitigated but not erased by the mother's, and later the analyst's, acknowledgment and discussion of it. Ruth's mother, though invested in her child, could not fulfill her role as auxiliary ego and was often driven to add new stresses and overstimulation. Even when she could feel with her little girl, she could not help Ruth to contain and integrate the experiences. In part this left Ruth to struggle on her own, in part it led her to identify with the mother's unhelpful ways of coping, for example, it intensified her use of sadomasochistic sexualization and her passive-into-active tendency to overwhelm others. Jim's mother was dead. Although the analyst, from the time of the trauma on, assisted the family in a consultative capacity, it took three years before they could provide a measure of physical and emotional parental care. This delayed the start of Jim's analysis and perhaps also contributed to the delay in his recuperative steps. He was still showing the same posttraumatic symptoms.

While wanting to underline how significant a role mothering plays, I am not suggesting that optimal availability of the mother's auxiliary ego cures the effects of trauma or that it is the only deciding factor. We know only too well that mothers cannot prevent all stresses in a child's life, and that recuperation from trauma can be impeded by unavoidable further debilitating experiences, and no doubt by factors within the child. However, as with bodily traumatic injury, the posttraumatic milieu and protective as well as facilitating nursing care contribute considerably to the recuperative process.

The younger the child, the more total the overwhelming, the less available the mother's auxiliary ego, and the more stressful the posttraumatic period, the slower are the steps in the reparative process. We note this in the general sensitivity to traumatization, the recurrent experiences of annihilation fear or terror/panic instead of progression toward signal anxiety, the damaging impact on all functions which are in the process of development, and especially on integration and drive fusion. The impairment in these latter two areas may cause uneven development, even when maturation again gets under way, may interfere with progressive personality growth, and may contribute to chaotic clinical pictures, such as pseudoretardation and atypical or psychotic disturbances (E. Furman, 1956).

The older traumatized child is more likely to be able to "wall off" the trauma in the form of pavor nocturnus, episodes of withdrawal, affect block, and related posttraumatic symptoms. To an extent this protects him from recurrences of traumatic anxiety and helps him to preserve a measure of adaptive functioning until his ego can begin to use defenses and libidinization to assimilate the traumatic event. But whether or how soon such reparative steps are taken again seems to depend in part on the posttraumatic support and experiences.

This division into earlier and later developmental phenomena is not clear-cut. There are overlaps and other significant factors, among them the child's internalization of the mother's ways of auxiliary ego functioning, as was evident in the case of Ruth, and as I discussed in greater detail in another context (E. Furman, 1985).

There are also developmental phenomena which are even harder to understand. Traumatized children, especially the younger ones, invariably reexperience the trauma in the transference, with the analyst as the agent who inflicted the trauma. In fact, this is how we usually learn about traumas in child analysis. When I asked several colleagues, among them A. Katan (1973), about their experiences in analyzing adults who had suffered a trauma in childhood, they told me that the patients hardly ever bring the trauma into the transference in this form and that their transference reflects only some aspects or features of it. Does this mean that the transference in childhood operates more strictly under the repetition compulsion? Does it mean that there are different developmental levels in the transference?

Of course, developmental factors do not account for all the many variations of posttraumatic manifestations or of the rate and nature of reparative steps. Nor do I think that the differences can be attributed simply to variations in individual endowment. It seems more likely that other specific factors play a part, either before the trauma or afterward. For example, recurrences of traumatic anxiety are, in some patients, not a sign of difficulty in recuperation but may at certain times point to progress. They sometimes signify that the psychic system has reached a point of transition from pre-ego to ego mechanisms and can begin to admit the anxiety to consciousness as a way of starting to deal with the hitherto unbound traumatic stimuli. Also, some manifestations associated with traumatic injury may stem from different sources. For example, severe damage to integration and drive fusion may be caused by factors other than trauma (E. Furman, 1985).

We also know very little about recovery. A. Freud suggested that complete recovery is impossible, that a vulnerability remains, perhaps unrealized until the individual encounters certain life situations. Miriam's good progress during her early years does not guarantee invulnerability. We would have to follow her analytically throughout her life to gain reliable data. Most cases, followed at least long term, show that the inner work on a trauma never ceases. Even when the patient achieves signal anxiety in relation to his or her traumatogenic events, the personality continues to expend a great deal of energy on using such signal anxiety to remain on the alert, to differentiate past from present, and to integrate the remnants of the original experience which surface at such times—a form of working through.

This brings us to the role of treatment. Since its historical beginnings, psychoanalysis has been helpful to patients who had suffered a trauma. The very process of tracing a person's earlier traumatic experience and making it available to his consciousness assists him with integrating it, as do many other aspects of the analytic work, not least the transference. However, there are limitations. An analysis can be helpful only within the givens of the patient's own rate and stage of recuperation. When a patient's ego is not ready to assimilate the traumatic event, or when the analysis forces his pace of integration too much, the treatment itself is experienced as a repetition of the traumatic intrusion. This may impede a

When Is the Death of a Parent Traumatic? 139

patient's ability to engage in the analytic work in the first place, or to persist with it when he feels threatened. It may also cause some patients to experience setbacks in the reparative process if they have not been able to protect themselves with sufficient defenses. The analyst's awareness of the patient's precarious integrative capacity and his empathic skill in working with the patient is therefore especially important in these cases, as is an understanding of the steps in the recuperative process and a recognition of the limits of analytic help at certain points.

With children the analyst has an added task, namely, to apprise the parents of the child's psychic state and to enlist and support their functioning as auxiliary egos in relation to the posttraumatic recuperative process—a role that exceeds their usual age-appropriate caring and educational function with the child. The younger the child, the more is it helpful, nay essential, that the parents understand and undertake this role. It is an ongoing round-the-clock job and provides the milieu for the child's effective use of the analysis. With the analyst's support, many parents can and do fulfill this need when they are helped to appreciate the reasons for it, just as parents often rally to nurse their child through a bad sickness in cooperation with a caring physician.

Obviously, we know far too little about trauma, but I find that parents, physicians, and professional caretakers know even less. They tend not to appreciate the difference between trauma and stress, between long-term, perhaps lifelong, damage and potentially masterable upset. For example, in my consultations with Child Life workers in pediatric hospitals I have frequently noted that staff and parents are tempted to regard suggestions about the need for a mother's availability or preparation for procedures as optional frills which, at best, reduce children's unhappiness and, at worst, interfere with "getting on with things." Since prevention is so much easier than cure, especially in regard to trauma, perhaps the child analyst should take part in clarifying these issues with parents and professionals, not only after the trauma when the child needs or is in treatment, but before. Not all but many traumas can be avoided.

11
Parenting the Hospitalized Child: Consulting with Child Life Workers

Since this chapter describes an aspect of my ongoing consulting work with Child Life workers, and since most readers would not know what Child Life workers are, much less why and how they consult with me, a few words of explanation precede the main text.

Child Life work is a fairly recent, very important profession.

> The professional task of Child Life workers or, as they often call themselves, Child Life specialists, is: First, to assist sick children and their families in coping with the emotional stresses of illnesses and hospitalization, and second (for the more ambitious), to help adapt the hospital milieu, its procedures, and treatments as much as possible to the emotional needs of the children and their families. Currently, Child Life workers are employed in many of the larger hospitals' pediatric departments around the country. In Cleveland, many now also work in the hospitals' pediatric out-patient clinics, emergency wards, and special units, such as the NICU (Neonatal Intensive Care Unit), PICU (Pediatric Intensive Care Unit), burn center, oncology center, radiology [E. Furman, 1996, p. 90].

Since 1976, it has been my privilege to learn from and with them through our ongoing fortnightly meetings within the framework of the "Hospitalized Child" course, one of the consultation courses under the auspices of the Hanna Perkins Center. Child Life workers from several hospitals in the Greater Cleveland area attend and set their own agenda for the many harrowing and heroic aspects of their stressful daily work with the child patients and their families.

> The topics addressed, even repeatedly addressed, encompass a vast array, from sick prematures and young children with urinary diseases, to all forms of cancer and its debilitating treatments, to deteriorating adolescents suffering from cystic fibrosis or sickle cell anemia. R. A. Furman (1988a) has written about the Child Life workers' important role with preparation. I have described their work with victims of sexual abuse (1993b, 1995), with dying children (1981a, 1992a), and with children who visit in hospitals (1981b). But these accounts barely begin to tell the story[E. Furman, 1996, p. 93].

> The biggest topic . . . is the Child Life workers' striving to understand and gain insight into the nature of their own work in order to increase their effectiveness, to further their professional growth, and to deepen the satisfaction they gain . . . . In this report, I shall take up an aspect of this last, big topic, namely, the Child Life workers' relationship and work with the hospitalized child's parents [E. Furman, 1996, p. 94].

LEARNING TO UNDERSTAND THE PARENTS' ROLE IN THE HOSPITAL

During the early years of our seminars, parents were not a prominent topic. We were preoccupied with the daunting task of how to prepare patients for, and assist them with, stressful and difficult procedures, which is often viewed as the Child Life workers' primary task. Also, despite the fact that the original severe limits on visiting hours had been replaced by allowing parents to remain with their child at all times, and a comfortable facility near the hospital had been provided for those who lived out of town, parents were more conspicuous by their absence than by their presence. The Child Life workers were very kind to them, sympathized with the strain and stress they suffered, helped to provide a lounge for them with coffee, TV, and magazines, but bemoaned the fact that so many parents visited little if at all.

In keeping with the general attitude, they also felt it was their role to "protect" the parents. After all, parents would not only lack the technical knowledge to explain upcoming procedures to their child; it would also be too painful for them, be it blood work, NG tubes, or amputations. In the same vein, when patients were scheduled for surgery, the parents were asked to bid their child good-bye at the elevator door, and it was the Child Life worker who accompanied the children on the long ride in the elevator and corridors to the induction room. After all, the parents would get too upset, would even upset the child, and could not enter the surgical division anyway. All on-the-floor procedures were performed in a treatment room, with the Child Life workers assisting the child, while the parent waited outside. After all, the treatments would not only be too upsetting to the parents but the child might blame them for what was done to him if they were with him. Likewise, parents had to be protected from too much exposure to the stress of the neonatal and pediatric intensive care units. And with special emergencies, like resuscitations, the parents were relegated to a distant lounge.

Like all the hospital staff, the Child Life workers were very busy and very active, yet always feeling that they were not active enough, were not doing enough for the patients, and even for the parents, and feeling very responsible and distressed when things did not quite work out for the best. In discussing this need to be active, they came to realize that it also served to ward off the painful helplessness in the face of terrible suffering and tragedy. They were soon able to extend their insight to appreciating that this passive helplessness must be even worse for the child patients. Perhaps even their well thought out preparations might not be helpfully integrated, partly because the Child Life worker could not know all the past experiences and current context of a child's personality, but even more so because it was just another thing that was done to him and for him. Counteracting the need to be active themselves, the Child Life workers began to focus on ways of helping the patient to be active, not just by letting him play with medical paraphernalia, which was standard fare, but by eliciting his ideas and feelings and by finding ways in which he could actively and helpfully participate in whatever he needed to undergo. It became their byword in the treatment room that the rougher things are and the more you feel you have to do something helpful, the more important it is first to find something helpful the patient himself can do. It always worked.

Our discussions around preparation brought out another issue, namely, that under-fives did not listen to preparation, or did not understand it, or did not believe it. One Child Life worker related the poignant situation of a 3-year-old who just turned away his face and hid in his mother's sweater as he practically crawled into her. Almost in exasperation, the Child Life worker then said, "I can see you don't want to hear me, I'll just tell it to your Mom." She repeated the preparation to the mother who then told most of it to her now intently listening son. The Child Life worker understood that, with a young child, only mother's words count. It became a rule to prepare the parents of young children and to assist them in broaching the subject to their child. If the parents could be helped, not only to understand but to accept what was going to happen, they could prepare their child well. For the few parents who could not quite bring themselves to talk with their child themselves, it was still essential for them to let him know that they knew about it, that it was really going to happen, and that they wanted him to listen to what Ms. or Mr. So-and-So would tell them.

Soon we came upon another situation: The patient was a prepubertal girl whose father was with her when the Child Life worker approached them and explained that she had come to prepare the girl for an upcoming procedure. The father got up and went into the hall to wait while the discussion with the girl took place. The Child Life worker brought this up for discussion that very day because she had felt badly for the father, although she had spoken to him in a friendly way on leaving. Should the father have been asked to stay? Should the girl have been given the choice of having him stay? The Child Life worker went back to them that afternoon and said how sorry she was to have acquiesced to the father's leaving, especially since she knew how much father and daughter meant to one another and had already gone through together. It turned out that the father knew the procedure well, had undergone it himself, and his daughter had known about it through him. He talked about it knowledgeably and with feeling, and was ready to sustain his child through it. Deeply touched, this sensitive Child Life worker shared what she had learned: By the mere way one walks in, one can deprive a parent of his parenting function, render him passive and helpless, deprive his child of his support, interfere in their relationship, and put in its place something that is much less helpful. The striking thing was how immediately the father had accepted his wordlessly assigned exclusion and would have never mentioned his experience, had the Child Life worker not apologized and, as it were, "reinstated" him as a valued parent. As all the Child Life workers began to involve the parents more as parents, we learned of many similar situations.

They now wondered whether "protecting" the parents did not imply depriving them of their parental role and making them feel helpless and useless. Instead of spending hours holding and rocking sick babies, they sought out their mothers and persuaded them to do just that because mothering was so important for each infant and constituted such a helpful part of his care, something mothers could provide best. Mothers were encouraged to assist their children in the treatment room and did so. Parents were permitted to accompany their children into the operating room and to hold them during induction. Parents were supported in caring for their dying children. They were given the option of remaining nearby or even looking in on resuscitations. They stayed with their youngsters in the intensive care units. And they were encouraged and helped to take care of their children's bodies and needs, even when this required some specialized handling.

These were momentous breakthroughs, thoughtfully supported by some physicians and nurses, vehemently resisted by others. Dr. Gauderer (Gauderer, Long, and Eastwood, 1989), who instituted outpatient surgery with parental presence at Rainbow Babies and Children's Hospital, received our first Annual School and Center Award (1991). Each change required much tactful handling, but each was also helped by the experience that parental participation worked. Patients and parents were happier and more cooperative, procedures went faster and more smoothly. News began to trickle in, in the form of occasional articles, that similar parent involvement was being tried in a few places (Hanson and Strawser, 1993) and that some parent groups were negotiating for more active participation (Harrison, 1993). Even for the Child Life workers, it was not always easy. One of them had worked particularly hard with several staff groups to permit parents to accompany their children through induction and was working just as hard with the parents who were assisting their children. He told us that, on one such occasion, he then found himself alone outside the operating room, feeling utterly useless and helpless, until he suddenly realized that he was needed as much as ever, albeit in a different way, namely, to support the parents. Their deep appreciation and the children's greatly decreased stress were ample reward.

The parents' concerns and complaints were also listened to in a new way and responded to respectfully. For example, they were encouraged to ask for a conference with their child's doctor if they had a worry, or they were supported to discuss perceived problems with appropriate staff members, or to bring difficulties to the attention of the administration. But they were equally encouraged to put in writing their frequently voiced satisfaction and gratitude. Positive or negative, their opinions counted because they were the parents—and customers.

Previously, parents had either stayed away or stayed in the background, not only because they felt helpless and useless, but also because they feared that any complaint, demand, or even question might turn them into a nuisance and backfire on their child's care. Indeed, it used not to take too much for a parent to get a "reputation" which certainly reverberated at least in the form of hostile tension and inevitably increased the stress of hospitalization for everyone.

More and more, the children, their parents, and their many special helpers worked actively together in their shared goal-directed task, each contributing in their own role. The divisions between those who are active and those who are passive, the doers and the done to, the good guys and the bad guys, the ones all-knowing and the ignorant, receded into the background.

WHO IS THE CHILD'S BEST PARENT?

The changes in procedures, however, did not always eradicate attitudes. Although parents were welcomed and respected to a greater extent, the Child Life workers noted that a comfortable armchair or rocker for holding and resting was rarely available, that parents were not assisted with sleeping facilities in their child's room, that the patients' bodily care was often only reluctantly surrendered to the parent, even when it did not require special handling, that parents' knowledgeable and potentially helpful observations about their child's status were sometimes treated as a nuisance (especially when they exceeded what the staff knew).

Such subtle signs of disregard could assume hostile proportions when the parents showed difficulties in the hospital setting, and also when they were known or presumed to have had difficulties in their home setting. Cases of sexual or aggressive abuse, shocking and upsetting to the staff, are particularly prone to focus hostile suspiciousness on the parents who tend to be barred from contact with their child. Regarding them as unfit, the staff wants to rescue the child by taking him away from them, keeping him in the hospital, and later transferring him to a foster home or institution.

> It was a major step in our work when one Child Life worker described her ultimately successful efforts in a hospital staff conference on behalf of an abused little girl of 3½ years. The child, genitally molested by her mother's ex-boyfriend, had already been on the ward for several months with foster placement at that time in the offing. The worker had previously sought out the mother and managed to arrange regular visits for her with her child, and had noted many positives in what was obviously a viable relationship between them. She had also arranged for a social worker to see the mother regularly, which the mother appreciated. Observing the little girl, however, she had pinpointed one reason why the child had become

everyone's darling and why everyone wanted to "rescue" her. The girl pranced through the halls in the most flirtatious manner, smiling at the doctors, getting them to pick her up, hug her, and bring her special treats. The worker addressed with the staff the child's symptomatic seductiveness, predicting that she would readily provoke any foster father and thus expose herself to more danger than if she could be allowed to maintain her relationship with her mother with the help of supervision and ongoing therapeutic help [E. Furman, 1993b, p. 1].

Sometimes, however, the staff's hostile reaction to a parent comes from less tangible motives: A 10-month-old was brought to the Emergency Clinic by his teenage mother because of high fever. He was admitted and the mother was sent home. I learned about him five days later from the very concerned Child Life workers. His fever and viral infection had subsided quickly but he was being kept on the ward because he was totally apathetic and withdrawn, refused food and people, and was getting worse. Tube feeding was to be instituted that day. The entire staff had decided that he was a failure-to-thrive baby due to the neglectful lack of care by his much too young and irresponsible mother who had been forbidden to visit. Nobody had met her. I pointed out that he suffered a typical anaclitic depression due to the separation from his mother, a reaction that could indeed prove very dangerous. The Child Life specialists alerted the staff in a special conference and, despite many misgivings on everyone's part, the mother was allowed to come. The infant immediately welcomed her comforting and feeding and, within twenty-four hours with mother, was discharged as a fully recovered happy child. A follow-up visit, a month later, showed that he had maintained his good bodily development and was functioning above his phase-appropriate level emotionally. Obviously, many factors contribute to produce such unfortunate situations. In our seminars we focused on the following prominent aspects.

All of us who, in whatever capacity, have elected to work with children share a smaller or larger element of motivation—to be the child's better parent, to do something for him or with him that his parent can't or won't do. On the one hand, this unconscious motivation helps us to invest the child and our work with him; on the other hand, it tempts us to take him over and to forget that the parent, good or bad, is both an essential part of the child's personality and his most important, most intensely invested relationship. In short, we are all potential mental kidnappers—sometimes more overtly, especially when we can righteously justify our attitudes and actions by underlining the individual parent's shortcomings.

This usually unacknowledged part of our motivation is, however, always keenly, albeit unconsciously, perceived and reacted to by the child and his parents. Prompted by their own concerns, they may respond with manifestly cooperative, even submissive, or uncooperative interaction, or with emotional withdrawal. For example, the parents may relinquish their parental role, accept us as their "superparent," and admonish the child to do our bidding as well; or they may protest, fight with us over unrelated issues, and denigrate us in the child's eyes; or they may hand the child over to us and become physically or emotionally unavailable to him. The child, for his part, may cope with his loyalty conflict by favoring us lovingly and looking down on his parents, or by refusing to have anything to do with us, lest he burn his bridges behind him. Parents and child may do all these and more things in sequence. Regardless, the parent–child relationship suffers and their chances of establishing an appropriate, mutually respectful, and cooperative goal-directed working relationship with us are interfered with.

This problem has been described and exemplified in regard to parent-substitutes in the home with caregivers of toddlers in day care (E. Furman, 1984, 1992a, 1993a), in regard to preschool and kindergarten teachers (E. Furman, 1977a,b; R. A. Furman, 1971; Hall, 1991), in regard to child analysts (E. Furman, 1992b), and also in regard to the parents vis-à-vis one another (R. A. Furman, 1983; Chapter 13; E. Furman, 1991, 1992c, 1993a).

Variations among individuals apart, the helper's wish to be the best and therefore most loved parent (especially the mother), is generally more pronounced the younger the child, the more his bodily care and need fulfillment are involved, and the more our services are essential to the child's well-being and healthy growth. It is easy to see where the hospitalized child fits in, the child who is always seriously and often fatally ill. Those who have made it their job to rescue and cure him take on a special responsibility that requires a special investment. Performing this special service and doing so, as it were, on their own home ground, the hospital, it is not surprising that their little "kidnapper" part leads them to forget that theirs is, after all, only a temporary service for which the parents employed them. It tempts them to feel that the child *is* theirs by virtue of their important role with him, a role the parents cannot fulfill.

Some basic facts are then readily disregarded: that the ill child—functionally always younger than his chronological age because he is ill—has a much greater need of his parents than the healthy child; that his incapacitated personality relies on their functioning for him; that, as his most intensely invested people, he uses them to replenish his diminished resources for pleasure in living which help him to cooperate with and benefit from the prescribed treatments (E. Furman, 1985); that, without their parental availability, the chances of treatability itself may be jeopardized. "Just as dehydration can dangerously upset the basic body chemistry, so the absent or inadequate maternal care can dangerously deplete [the child's] personality leading in many instances to depressive mood or apathy and, in extremes, culminating in mental and bodily death, as Spitz (1945, 1946) showed" (E. Furman, 1992a). Disregarded too may be the fact that parents, whose self-esteem is already shaken by their child's illness and further diminished by being rendered useless as they hand him over to the "superparent," lose their capacity as parents to sustain their child; this breach in their relationship with their child may not heal when they are finally asked to take him back home or when they are left to mourn him without the soothing memories of having parented him to the last.

The better we know about our "kidnapper" part, the better we can channel it toward investing—as Anna Freud (personal communication, 1950) put it—not only the child but the parents and the parent–child relationship.

PARENTS ARE NOT PERFECT

Parents, of course, are not perfect either. For the most part, they are no better or worse than we are. Sometimes they are much better, occasionally they are much worse. In our seminars we often have to remind ourselves that illness does not strike only the best families, the ones who can cope well with almost everything. In one respect, however, parents of ill children are different: They bear the special stress of having an ill child. Their intimate investment of their child as a loved person reacts to the child's illness with extreme distress and concern. Their parental investment of him as a part of themselves causes them to experience his illness as a deep narcissistic hurt and depletion. Both kinds of investment combine to produce guilt and a sense of responsibility. These intense responses can be so threatening that parents may not be able to tolerate them consciously and have to ward them off by unconscious defenses which may lead to maladaptive behavior. For mothers, there is the additional unique stress resulting from their bodily investment (i.e., their experience of the child's body as a part of their own body). His illness affects their own bodily well-being and integrity. They feel ill with him. Mothers sometimes voice this to the Child Life workers, either in terms of feeling generally ill or in terms of literally experiencing the exact pains their child suffers.

I have discussed the nature of parental investment and its far-reaching implications in many articles since 1969, and again as recently as 1994. Some implications are particularly pertinent to working with the parents of ill children: (1) The effects of the specific stress of having an ill child have to be taken into account in assessing a parent's basic capacity for parental functioning. This is difficult in a hospital where we can only observe the parents with their ill child and where their other or secondary stresses stand out more clearly, such as the need to care for siblings at home, financial worries, illness in the wider family, transportation problems regarding visiting, and not least, parental pathology unrelated to the child (divorce, delinquency, drug addiction, etc.). (2) The stress of having an ill child and its effect on parental feelings needs to be understood and empathized with in order to build a productive working relationship with the parents. (3) Their stress is considerably alleviated when the parents are given opportunities to be appropriately active in their parental role with their child. Helpless distress subsides with active caring; self-esteem is raised by doing positive things for and with the child; guilt is assuaged by participating helpfully in ameliorating his affliction.

Since only respected and self-respecting parents can take their rightful and necessary role with their ill child, we cannot dismiss them on the basis of their manifest difficulties but have to reach for and engage their potential strengths. This task is perhaps hardest with the ill neonates whose parents have not had a chance to establish themselves as good parents in their own minds and often experience serious interferences even in entering the developmental phase of parenthood (E. Furman, 1969a). I am continually amazed how often Child Life workers succeed in helping these parents to become parents, to value themselves as such, and to make a crucial difference to their babies' well-being.

Even parents of adolescents, however, with some years of good enough parental experience, can be thrown off course by their child's deteriorating condition and become quite unavailable until a Child Life worker helps them bridge the gap. I have described such cases earlier (1981a). Let me here quote a Child Life worker's own experience.

> A 21-year-old cystic fibrosis patient had, several years earlier, become estranged from his parents. An argument at the hospital abruptly ended when the patient told his parents to leave and never return. When I met this young man he was at the end stage of his disease. One particular [morning], as I quietly sat with him, he asked if I would help him with something. Would I call his parents, who lived in another state, and ask them to come? On entering the room, a staff person, who had known the patient for many years, overheard the request and later suggested not to call the parents because they wouldn't come. There were strong feelings against these parents by the majority of caregivers. After speaking with the attending physician, who shared his skepticism as well as blessing, and with shaking body and a mental prayer, the call was placed. After

determining it was the mom who answered, I proceeded to introduce myself and explained that although she didn't know me, I had come to know about her through her son's reminiscings. I knew she made delicious bread that tasted best right out of the oven. I came to hear about the family fishing trips that her son and his dad had taken and the tasty catches they would prepare. I told the mom their son had requested I call and ask them to come. The mom said, "I have been waiting for this call for two years. We will leave as soon as possible." At the parents' request, I met them as they entered the division and the recollection of that reunion will forever be etched in my memory. The patient was so weak he barely had the energy to raise his hand. Mom and dad entered the room and following a tearful embrace, dad proceeded very slowly to unwrap a foil package. To his son he presented a beautiful smoked salmon, then broke off a small piece and slowly raised his hand to his son's open mouth. I can still hear the son's response "um .. umm .. umm. . . ." The remaining months of the young man's life were filled with familiar pleasures. Mom stayed, borrowed a waffle maker, and the smells of the son's favorite childhood breakfast frequently came from his room. It's hard to know the various components that can keep a family separated during such difficult times, yet, during those last months, mother, father and son made their peace and there were good feelings among them (and all of us as well) [Niklas, 1993, pp. 2–3].

As occasionally happens, in one of our recent seminars the Child Life workers took stock, thinking through how they had grown and where they were going. This time, their self-assessment had been prompted by their experiences of presenting and discussing aspects of their work with Child Life workers and other hospital staff in several cities. One Child Life worker stated with astonished conviction, "We are different. We work differently with the children and with the staff. But, above all, we are different because we work with the parents." She described that when others hear of her work with parents, they invariably respond along the lines of "But we can't do that. Our parents are not like that. They won't come, or they are too overwhelmed, or they make a nuisance of themselves." And they are incredulous when she explains that such parents are everywhere and that is where the Child Life workers' task begins, by going out to them, understanding them, tapping their strengths, helping them with their ill child—an effort that benefits all parties.

We have come a long way, but there is always further to go.[1]

---

[1] I am most grateful to the Child Life workers whose contributions I have specifically quoted—M. Barkey, D. Bline, M. Bowers, S. Niklas, and B. Smith—as well as to the many others who have participated so productively in our course over the years and taught me so much.

12
Children of Divorce

REVIEW AND DISCUSSION OF DATA

Since the early 1970s, child analysts associated with the Cleveland Center for Research in Child Development and Hanna Perkins Therapeutic School have had the opportunity to study children's reactions to parental divorce as well as the subsequent effects on their growing up in families with only one of the original parents. Contacts with the other parent varied from regular to sporadic or were altogether discontinued. To date, we have worked with fifty-five children of divorce, including two raised out of wedlock. Initially, our interest in these children grew out of our research on parentally bereaved children. They also live with only one original parent but their family disruption was caused through death and contact with the deceased parent is impossible. When our findings of this latter study were reported (E. Furman, 1974), we had worked with twenty-three such cases but noted already then that children who suffered a bereavement and a divorce encountered very different psychological hurdles in coping with each of these stresses and in fact could sometimes be helped to master the parent's death better than the divorce (W. Goldman, 1974). Since that time we have treated thirty more cases of children who lost a parent through death, so that their current number is fifty-three. The ongoing opportunity to compare the data emerging from the treatments of these differently yet similarly afflicted youngsters has added to our understanding of the psychological tasks they face and the vicissitudes of their ways of coping with them (R. A. Furman, 1980, 1986; Chapter 13).

Our data derive from children of all ages seen in five times weekly analyses for three to five years and from children under 5, observed and treated via the parent for two to three years at the Hanna Perkins Therapeutic School (R. A. Furman and A. Katan, 1969). Of the fifty-five children of divorce (including the two raised out of wedlock), twenty-five were in analysis and thirty were treated via the parent. Of the fifty-three bereaved children, twenty were in analysis and thirty-three in treatment via the parent. Several of the analytic cases in both groups were treated via the parent in their earliest years, before they started their individual therapy. A few of the analyses were conducted by the author privately; the majority were seen by child analysts at the Child Analytic Clinic of the Cleveland Center for Research in Child Development. In this Clinic as well as at the Hanna Perkins School there is a sliding fee scale, some able to pay the full fee, others as little as a few cents. This has made it possible to extend our services to families of very different economic and social backgrounds and to include members of varied ethnic, racial, and religious groups. At intake, the youngest children at Hanna Perkins are under 2 years, participating with their mothers in our Toddler Group; the oldest children accepted at the Child Analytic Clinic are 14 years. Over the years, many families have maintained contact with their analysts or the school after the end of therapy and this has facilitated follow-up during the children's later development, in some cases into adulthood. There was also one formal follow-up study (R. A. Furman and A. Katan, 1969).

It should be stressed that none of these patients came to us because we sought them out or publicized our interest in the effects of divorce and bereavement. In some instances, the parental death or divorce occurred during the child's treatment but had not been anticipated at its start. In others, the disruption of the family had taken place but the effect of this on the child was not the main reason for referral. The parents wanted help for a wide variety of symptoms, usually manifestly unrelated to the special family constellation. Even when the parents recognized that the bereavement or divorce contributed a special stress, particularly when some of the child's difficulties flared up in current situations (such as around visits with the absent parent in the case of divorce), neither they nor we could truly understand the nature of the child's responses. In each instance only the slow and painstaking therapeutic work helped gradually to unravel the intricate fabric of underlying causes and their connection with the manifest pathology.

All participating child analysts repeatedly present their ongoing cases at the weekly Monday night and/or Friday afternoon child analytic meetings, both chaired by Dr. A. Katan. Year in, year out, these study groups have afforded us an opportunity to share our analytic material and experiences, to discuss our questions, and to learn with and from one another. I am most grateful to Dr. A. Katan and to my colleagues for the data and insights they have made available. I am particularly indebted to my husband, Dr. R. A. Furman, who has all along collaborated with me in studying children of divorce and in formulating our findings, including some of those presented here.

The wealth of accrued data highlights the complexity and diversity of the children's individual experiences and the multitude of factors affecting their ways of coping. Above all, it underlines clearly that parental divorce is a legal entity and does not represent specific events or changes in a child's life situation. Tolstoy was so right to begin *Anna Karenina*, the most famous work on divorce, with "Happy families are all alike; every unhappy family is unhappy in its own way" (Tolstoy, 1876). Not only does the actual divorce rarely coincide with the separation (some parents have left the home years earlier, even before the child was born, others return to live in the home even after the divorce), but the parents' relationships with one another and with the child vary enormously before and after the breakup of the family. For some parents, marital tension and unhappiness is alleviated by divorce and they are better able to communicate and support one another as parents afterwards; for others, a superficially calm and cooperative marriage comes to an almost sudden, calamitous end, followed by lasting hurt and bitterness which preclude any form of helpful interaction; in still others, particularly where there is a marked sadomasochistic relationship, the divorce hardly marks a change in the nature or intensity of the ongoing contacts. For the child, this implies not only very different, or perhaps no experiences with the parents as a couple, but also very different opportunities for relationships with each. Some youngsters have never known relationships with both parents, others have maintained relatively satisfactory ones. Some experienced relationships burdened by pathology or disrupted by discontinuity. After the family breakup, the child is affected by the change or lack of change in the parents' relationship with one another as well as by the repercussions on his or her relationship with each of them. In some cases we have seen the relationship with one or both parents improve, in others there was a greatly diminished or even no opportunity for relationships with both or either parent. Some felt a marked change, others almost none. I am referring here to the emotional availability of the parents, but we need to keep in mind that the physical presence of one or both parents plays a part as well, curtailed, increased, or unchanged by the custodial parent's working hours, the non-custodial parent's proximity to or distance from the new home, and by great variations in visiting arrangements. Moreover, whereas one child is left with barely one parent, another soon has four with the addition of two stepparents. Brothers and sisters in any number may be gained or lost and, of course, whether or not there are siblings and whether or not the relationship with them is helpful or adds further stress, is an important factor, as is the role of members of the wider family, such as grandparents.

Apart from the complex and varied relationship patterns, there is great diversity in the nature and extent of other changes. J. Wallerstein's (1985a, 1986) findings in following up children of broken homes stress how frequently divorce entails loss of home, school, and friends, how often economic circumstances change for the worse and restrict access even to such services as good schooling, how often children are left overburdened by having to care for themselves or the parent they live with. Yet we have also treated children who did not encounter such hardships and experienced no change in place or style of living, or where divorce settlements brought about improved economic conditions and allowed the custodial mother to devote herself to her children and home.

It is self-evident that all these individually varied circumstances, and the interplay between them, present children with very different psychological tasks, different also at different developmental levels, and make for difficult comparisons. With parental bereavement, there is the central fact of death itself and the irrevocable loss it entails. The bereavement task, of which mourning is a part, effects an intrapsychic adaptation to this fact. We know that a multitude of inner and outer circumstances, preceding, attending, and following a parental bereavement, can facilitate or burden or altogether prevent a child from engaging in or completing this task, but that does not change the fact that there is a specific intrapsychic task. Is there such a central task to cope with in the case of a family breakup, and if so, which psychic mechanisms are used to accomplish it?

THE CHILD'S MENTAL TASK IN COPING WITH THE PARENTS' SEPARATION OR DIVORCE

Most studies and discussions of divorce focus on the loss of a parent and stress the attendant losses of home, friends, and lifestyle. Yet, as has just been described, partial or even improved relationships with each parent can be the outcome of divorce. Our data suggest that the loss of a parent, as well as attendant losses and changes, are very important complications but do not constitute the main issue.

A family breakup signifies the decision by one or both parents that their relationship has failed to such an extent that they no longer can or wish to live together as a couple. I stress the word *decision* because it is a conscious, deliberate act, and I stress the word *failed* because every marriage, legal or common law, implies a promise of ongoing togetherness and an expectation of shared responsibilities, especially when they have created a child or children. Among our cases there was a time of relationship even in those families where the breakup came soon or where the child, raised out of wedlock, was conceived of a temporary liaison. Regardless of the manifest and precipitating causes of the failure, it was always a shared failure, to which both partners' personalities had contributed. Legal proceedings may attribute guilt to only one party, common sense may recognize the need for distancing oneself from an abusive, irresponsible, criminal, or unsafe partner. Yet, however clearly delineated the rights and wrongs appeared to be, psychologically there was always a measure of interaction, with difficulties on both sides. Thus, for our child patients the most crucial, though not often conscious, issues were (1) the parents' inability to create and maintain an ongoing good enough relationship and (2) the imperfection and fallibility of each, exposed in the process.

The first issue, the parents' inability to maintain their relationship, implies that any close relationship can end, that dislike or anger, self-interest or inconstancy, can win out over love, can override the positives and cancel out mutual loyalty, and can interfere with consideration or even allow hurt and abandonment of a loved one. These are the very conflicts of adequate drive fusion and object constancy that every child struggles so to master in himself from infancy on and in different ways at successive developmental levels. They underlie the achievement of oedipal engagement and renunciation, the internalization of adaptive superego and ego identifications, and ultimately, the ability to maintain a marital relationship and to parent. During the difficult years of progression, the child fears abandonment and loss of love as retaliatory threats from his parents and he usually looks to them for reassurance and demonstration that a maturationally higher level of considerate relationships can be achieved and maintained, that the parents will contain and "survive" his own ambivalence, selfishness, and disloyalty, and that he will in time become like them. When the parents fail with each other, there is both the fear that they will also fail in their relationship with him and that he himself will fail. Unfortunately, both fears are often realized. The failure of the parental relationship suggests to the child that his destructiveness has real, as opposed to imagined, power and lends substance to his fears of retaliation. Usually both drives are overstimulated by the failure of the parents' relationship, but it is the preponderance of aggression and the experience that it actually can cause harm which render it especially dangerous. Children deal with this very differently, with varying but always significant effects on many areas of their personality development and functioning. To illustrate just one circumscribed aspect, let me mention the many youngsters who need to deprive themselves of angry fantasying and its use as a safety valve. Whereas the child who can count on the parents' ability to relate to each other and to withstand the onslaught of his rage, can entertain aggressive wishes of hurting or abandoning a parent or of separating them and taking possession of one or the other partner, many children of divorce cannot stop wishing for and imagining a marital reconciliation, which masks their unconscious, unattenuated ambivalence and denies their perception of the parental pathology.

The second issue, the child's conscious or unconscious perception of the parents' imperfection and fallibility, which have caused the breakup, is experienced as a significant narcissistic injury and diminishment of the self. Since, throughout the maturational years, the parent not only provides libidinal supplies but is invested with some of the child's unrenounced early narcissistic perfection, shortcomings in the parent inevitably lower the child's self-esteem. "My Daddy can count to a thousand" and similar boasts reflect the extent to which young children especially, but all children to some extent, lean on the parent's "greatness" to bolster their own adequacy. In the course of growing up, all children have to perceive and come to terms with their parents' inadequacies and weaknesses, but this is usually accomplished piecemeal, allowing for gradual integration, with positives outweighing negatives, with pride and admiration compensating for disappointments. The marital disharmonies which lead to a breakup of the family are qualitatively and quantitatively different, sometimes shattering in their impact, and threaten to tilt the balance toward the negative. This, as well as the anger it arouses, deplete the child's positive self-investment and handicap him in building a balanced realistic appreciation of himself and others. Children deal with this narcissistic injury and loss in different ways, but always with far-reaching effects on their personalities. To illustrate this too in a small way, we may recall the many youngsters who are consciously ashamed of the parents' divorce, avoid mentioning it, and even lie about it, as though it revealed an inadequacy in themselves, or the ones who, by contrast, exhibit it defensively and make light of it, shocking and embarrassing others with their inappropriate revelation and affect.

Both aspects of the breakup—the failure of the parents' relationship and their implied imperfection—thus tend to create an interference in the child's ability to achieve or maintain adequate drive fusion. This interference stems from an imbalance between the drives, with aggression outweighing libido. It also may stem from a prevalence of pregenital components in the parents' relationship with each other, and, more often than not, in their relationship with their child. The attendant libidinal overstimulation, produced, for example, by witnessing the pregenital excitement in overt parental strife, by interacting similarly with them himself, or by the temptations of becoming one parent's partner or confidant, does not helpfully contribute to fusing the drives. The reason for this is that the libido thus generated is experienced as excitement, often overwhelming primitive excitement, rather than as love and affection, which would be modulated by the ego and in this form could better serve to bind and tame the aggression. In "On Fusion, Integration and Feeling Good" (E. Furman, 1985), I described the psychic process of drive fusion, the conditions which facilitate or hinder it, and detailed the effects of relative achievement or failure of drive fusion on the investment and development of self and object representations, on the closely related growth of the integrative function and of the capacity for neutralization of drive energy.[2] Noting that a preponderance of aggression over libido and a preponderance of excitement over ego-attenuated love, interfere with adequate drive fusion and hence with all the related aspects of personality functioning, I listed a number of inner and outer factors which were found to contribute to this unfortunate mental state of affairs and showed how it manifests itself in very different clinical disturbances. Among the contributing

---

[2] If we were to view the effects of drive fusion primarily in terms of self and object representatives in Mahler's terms, we would relate it to achieving or maintaining separation-individuation and object constancy; in Kleinian terms we would relate it to achieving or maintaining the depressive position.

factors were family pathologies which sometimes lead to divorce. In fact, proponents of divorce often point to the child's experiences of ongoing marital difficulties and of troubled parent–child relationships as having a more damaging effect than the disruption through separation and divorce. This is no doubt correct in some instances, but this does not erase the impact of an actual breakup. Also, the breakup is sometimes merely one phase of the parents' problems with relationships and does not put a stop to their interactions nor does it guarantee a more mature relationship between parent and child after the breakup. When the parents' separation brings about a greater or lesser loss of one or both parents, this causes further diminished opportunity for supplies of love, augmenting the unhelpful imbalance of the drives. R. A. Furman and both of us (R. A. Furman, 1986; chapter 13) have described the effects of this subsequent partial or total loss on children's development in greater detail. Here I wish to focus on the impact of the breakup itself and of the difficulties that caused it.

If then, the breakup of the parents' marital relationship and the personality difficulties which led to it tend to cause or augment an interference in the child's drive fusion, his psychic task is clear but difficult. He has to bring about internal circumstances which would facilitate drive fusion, would enable love to bind, tame and neutralize aggression, and would thereby initiate or restore progressive development. In clinical terms this means: (1) The child has to recognize and acknowledge the personality interferences in *both* parents' relationship with one another and with him and to understand and accept them as their troubles. (2) He has to trace these difficulties and their effects in the functioning of his own personality, in the symptoms, defenses, gratifications, identifications, and other forms in which they manifest themselves and to recognize them as interferences. (3) At the same time, and equally important, he has to let himself know and appreciate the positives in his parents' personalities and in himself and in his experiences with them. I might mention that difficult though it is to face the negatives, it is often even harder to acknowledge fully the positives in everyone, yet they are crucial in enabling the child to gain a realistic understanding.

Moreover, they are the very force and tool his personality can use to tame his anger, to better his self and object investments, to forgive as much as is possible to forgive and to resign himself where necessary. From this basis he can then try to limit or overcome his own difficulties and seek and build a more harmonious life for himself with real hope and courage, as opposed to magic fantasy.

Just how difficult this task is depends on many factors within and without, in the past, present, and future yet to come. It does not always necessitate analytic treatment, but even with the help of therapy it is never mastered quickly or completely or for all time. However, insofar as the child succeeds and at whatever stage in his development he may then be, it always brings with it a premature wisdom and this is a gain but also a sad loss. Our patients as well as the accounts of the children of divorce in the lay literature bear witness to this (Krementz, 1984).

THE CASE OF MARIA

Let me briefly illustrate some of these points with clinical material from the analysis of a child of divorce. To highlight the central rather than secondary issues, I decided to describe a girl whose parents cared very much about each other and her, who struggled painfully to repair and rescue their relationship, and tried their best to handle the breakup and its aftermath with thoughtfulness for each other and their child, including opportunities for her ongoing and improved relationships with both of them and without loss of school, friends, or lifestyle.

Maria was an only child in midlatency at the start of her four years of five times weekly analysis. By that time her parents had been separated for a couple of years but still hoped to work out their marriage. Although the mother was living with another man, she described herself as "loving both" and maintained many business and social contacts with her husband. They shared in taking care of Maria, had a weekly at home family dinner, and always acted as partners in matters concerning their child, such as school conferences and performances, birthday and holiday celebrations, and interviews with the therapist. They were attentive and affectionate with each other and agreed in their view of Maria's current and past behavior and of issues that had affected her development, and they were eager to cooperate and help her. Maria had her own room and belongings in each parent's home. She usually spent one or two nights weekly with her father and some weekends and vacation periods, depending on her wishes and their convenience. Like her parents, Maria was good looking, well built, athletically gifted, and of superior intelligence.

She suffered from a pervasive debilitating learning disability, was disorganized and incompetent in caring for herself and her belongings, had a tendency for bodily complaints, and was somewhat accident prone. She did not have friends and felt rejected by peer groups. When a playmate visited or when she was on her own, her usual good manners and impulse control occasionally broke down and there were incidents of considerable damage to home property which Maria disowned, minimized, or explained away. In the evaluation interview with me, she described herself as "weird," a confession she later often denied, and she began her analysis by drawing ever more intricate mazes through which I was to find a way to the central core. This precious, vulnerable place had many meanings at different levels, as did her challenge and fear to have me reach it, but most of all it was her true self, a very needy, dependent self, which longed to be empathically close but had to guard against it fiercely, lest the loved one engulf and annihilate it or be destroyed by her own primitive rage. Yet to think and feel independently or just be herself was also equated with angrily abandoning the loved one and in turn being abandoned and left helpless and overwhelmed. At the phallic–narcissistic level, a similar mutual threat was posed by her destructive envy of the loved one's perfection in bodily and mental attributes, belongings, and ability to attract and command the subservient admiration of others, and by the love object's assumed intolerance of competition and retaliatory devastating humiliation. Success in any undertaking was therefore too dangerous and had to be avoided or undone. We came to know these aspects only gradually, primarily through the transference and could link them to Maria's relationships with her parents even more gradually.

Her wish to be close came via puppets and toy animals who took kind care of one another and were her spokesmen in interacting with me. She was deeply distressed at having lost a set of beloved toy figures at the time of the parents' separation, and asked me to replace some of the individual pieces as birthday and Christmas presents. Later she talked in baby talk and sign language, challenging and testing my ability to "read" her and reach her, and later yet showed an amazing capacity to evoke feelings in me without the use of words, both positive and negative ones. Whenever she could briefly allow sufficient closeness to feel understood or to gain some insight from an interpretation, or when, by contrast, she felt I had failed to meet her need, for example, through a scheduled separation, many days, even weeks would follow when I was disdainfully discarded, threatened with cancelations, or rendered helpless in my efforts to reach her, as she had so often felt and as she had wanted to treat her parents. Much further along, when she once again killed me day after day with silent fury, I said "I think my job now is to prove that I can survive being killed over and over again," to which Maria replied "Exactly." But even to kill was safer than to love and trust.

As long as a mutually nondestructive relationship with closeness yet considerate autonomy was felt to be impossible, what we saw mostly were the mechanisms Maria's personality had derived to preserve the parents, especially mother, and their love. Even legitimate criticisms of or complaints against them were inadmissible, and all ego functions had to be surrendered and instead taken over from the loved one. Depending on which parent she was with or whose interest she felt called to represent, she felt, talked, and perceived the reality as they did, conveying a bizarre picture of changing and often contradictory personalities. In compliance with the parental attitudes, anger was turned against the self or displaced and projected to peers and adults outside the family. Self-gratification at any level was abhorred and breakthroughs denied or condemned. She mothered her mother and shone for her with short-lived athletic triumphs, yet depended on her desperately in the area of learning, the only area where mother responded with doing for Maria. Unable to think, even write, for herself, Maria was coached and tutored, but all to no avail. It was a big step forward when I could show her that her spelling, a series of indecipherable anagrams, was intended to hide rather than communicate what she knew, and later, when she had an anxiety attack during a math test, that she feared putting down the right answer lest it reveal an unwelcome truth.

This truth related not only to Maria's ambivalently conflicted feelings but to her perception of her parents' personality difficulties which were so similar to her own and warded off with the very defenses she had identified with. Their ambivalently dependent relationship, like their relationship with their child, also precluded comfortable closeness, demanded constant mutual rejection and abandonment through physical or emotional unavailability, with excitement and anger breaking through suddenly and violently in bitterly cruel altercations which were then quickly isolated and denied. Although they happened mostly in private, Maria knew of them and unconsciously replicated them with her occasional excited–aggressive bouts with playmates or property destruction, related to her masturbation fantasies. Although she had her own reasons for feeling "weird," ultimately this feeling belonged to her parents whose behavior seemed strange and incomprehensible to her. As long as the positive elements could, at least superficially, contain and maintain the family, Maria's development could progress in spite of some difficulties, but when the conflicts escalated and the mother, in panic and distress, left the home and could not return to it—the start of the parents' separation—Maria suffered a deep shock: the negatives had prevailed, the shared home had ceased to exist. From then on, all her energies went into patching up what relationships remained and avoiding anything that could further jeopardize them. Her already troubled positive and negative oedipal feelings were dealt a further blow when she visited her mother some weeks after the breakup and found her with her male friend. Maria's long-maintained insistence that Daddy was so unreasonable not to accept and like this man as a friend and family member, warded off her own bitterness at mother having turned to another man.

As with other children who have experienced a family breakup, Maria had to first deal with her own pathological, primitively exaggerated ambivalence and become capable of a more mature one-to-one relationship and improved self-investment, before she could reengage herself with the earlier abandoned oedipal situation. Introducing this topic in the form of a lesson on isosceles triangles, she declared herself ready to work out her threesome relationships—a difficult task when, as she once commented, one is really part of a quadrangle. Her earlier defensive wish for her parents' reunion had subsided by this time. When the legal divorce came, she realized that, in spite of the parents' anguish and hurt over it, it was merely another manifestation of their ongoing interactions. Slowly and painfully, she could forgive and resign herself, bring out the best and protest the worst in their relationships with her, and be her own person, doing her own thing. She became an excellent student, could enjoy her successes, and was most thrilled when she realized she could engage in real friendship. Although developmental progression was well under way, we cannot know yet how or to what extent her own adult relationships and parenting will be affected.

SOME FACILITATING AND IMPEDING FACTORS

Maria's personality and circumstances are uniquely individual, but she shares with others the task of coping with the impact of the breakup caused by the heightened ambivalence and all that this entails. How masterable a task it is, depends on many factors of which I shall mention a few.

First there is the nature of the parents' difficulties with each other and the extent to which they encompass also their relationships with the child. Some parents' marital troubles are relatively isolated and allow each to maintain a less conflicted relationship with the child. Some parents can also cooperate with each other as parents vis-à-vis their child, whereas with others the child is an integral part or even focus of their disharmony. Much depends on how long and how intensely the difficulties have gone on during the child's life and thereby contributed to the shaping of his personality. Of equal or even greater importance, however, are the positive factors that have been available. Are there and have there been good enough periods in the parents' life with each other and with the child, and are there and have there been good enough aspects in their personality functioning to balance the difficulties and to enable the child to progress in his development? The greater the child's emotional health and the more mature his own personality are at the time of the breakup, the better his chances of coping. Worst hit are the youngsters who had never sufficiently fused the early pregenital ambivalence, in contrast to those whose achievement in this basic area is merely threatened or secondarily interfered with by the failure of the parents' relationship.

A great deal depends on just how much the parents assist their child with mastery. The younger the child, the more crucial is their help. As with bereavement, it is often said that the parents cannot be expected to focus on the child's needs and feelings at a time when their own distress is so intense and unresolved. Yet, as with bereavement, many parents can rally to the task, can find comfort and satisfaction in doing what makes them feel good about themselves as parents, and can help themselves by helping their child to gain a balanced, realistic view. They can salvage the good and accept, even forgive or resign themselves. Consultations with a child analyst at the time of the breakup and following it, can make a helpful difference. In working with the parent or parents during these periods we have found that, with divorce as opposed to bereavement, it is especially hard for them to recognize and empathize with the child's feelings as these may be so different from the parent's, may face him or her with the guilt of having caused the child's hardship, or with the realization of his or her own, not just the other parent's, personality difficulties. A child may love and long for a parent who is hated as a spouse; he may be sad when the parent feels relieved; he may confront a parent with being selfish or unkind just when the parent is convinced of being morally superior.

Allowing and supporting the child's own feelings goes hand in hand with helping him to maintain a relationship with both parents. A 4-year-old boy in our Hanna Perkins School summed it up. He was talking about an outing with his father, only to be interrupted by some peers' startled comment "But your Mom and Dad are divorced!" to which he replied, "I am not divorced from my Dad, only my Mom is." When parents can be helped to appreciate the importance of the child's continuing relationships with both of them, they can overcome all kinds of practical hurdles. Some have changed jobs to remain in town; some have gone to the trouble and expense of traveling hundreds of miles to make twice monthly or monthly visits; some have sent cards or letters every other day and phoned at prearranged times that suited the *child's* schedule. Parents who found it impossible to plan cooperatively and to help the child integrate the visits by letting each other know what transpired before, during, and after visits, agreed to use a middleman, usually a social worker, whom they called separately and who coordinated visits and passed on the necessary information. In cases where visits with a parent were unsafe for the child, a social worker provided a supervised setting for limited get-togethers. In order to tailor visits to the changing developmental needs of the child, some parents not only sought a child analyst's advice initially, but included in their divorce settlement a provision for repeated consultations at intervals, to assist with suitable changes; e.g. whereas for under-fives frequent short visits work best, latency children can manage overnights and, as they get older, can increasingly enjoy longer vacation stays.

The opportunity for continuing relationships not only diminishes the loss. It affords an ongoing means of gaining a realistic picture of both parents. A parent never ceases to be a part of the growing child's inner world. Absence does not erase this fact and does not stop the influence of the absent parent on the child's personality. Real experiences with a parent, good and bad (though not unsafe or overwhelming ones), help to correct the inevitable distortions wrought by fantasy, memory and misunderstanding due to immaturity and perhaps one-sided accounts. It is only with the help of real contact that a child can, in time, sort out whether or not a relationship is viable. Some of the children we worked with had had no contact with one of their parents for many years and sometimes had barely known them. When these hitherto absent parents then turned up or were sought out, usually at the child's insistence, the new or renewed contact sometimes resulted in a good enough relationship. In other instances it led to the realization that such was impossible. One girl was drawn to her long absent, abusive father by her own pathology and idealization of him and, in puberty, almost opted to live with him when he unexpectedly sued for custody. With the help of carefully managed contacts she could acknowledge the reality, forego the temptation, and resign herself.

The relationships with stepparents and other relatives can never simply serve as substitutes. Their role is most helpful either as additions to an ongoing relationship with the original parents or as a new investment if and when, as in bereavement, the attachment to the original parent has been sufficiently decathected and identifications with him or her are such as to facilitate rather than hinder the capacity to build new relationships. In contrast to bereavement, however, this mental task is not prompted by the parent's actual unavailability but by the child's realistic assessment and inner acceptance of his or her unalterable personality pathology.

SUMMARY

The data gained through long-term analytic work with fifty-five children of parental separation or divorce were reviewed and compared with those of fifty-three children who suffered the loss of a parent through death. Most of these youngsters, aged 2 to 14 years at the start of therapy, were treated at the Child Analytic Clinic of the Cleveland Center for Research in Child Development and/or at the Hanna Perkins Therapeutic School. A few were private patients. The findings showed that the children's personalities and experiences before, during, and after the family breakup differed greatly, yet they all faced a mental task as specific to their situation as mourning is with bereavement. This especially difficult mental task consists of reversing the unfavorable imbalance of the drives which has been demonstrated by the parents through their inability to maintain a good enough relationship and which has been generated in the child by the attendant overstimulation of his aggression and depletion of his libidinal self and object investment. The drive imbalance interferes with the child's ability to achieve or maintain adequate drive fusion, with far-reaching effects on many areas of personality functioning. To bring about improved internal circumstances which would enable love to bind and neutralize aggression, the child's task begins with needing to recognize and acknowledge fully the personality interferences in *both* parents as well as in himself and to balance them against the positives in each and in their experiences with one another. Material from an analytic case was used to illustrate this process. In conclusion, some factors were discussed which have been found to facilitate or impede the children's capacity for mastery.

13
Some Effects of the One-Parent Family on Personality Development

**Erna Furman and
Robert A. Furman, M.D.**

Since the late 1960s, our Cleveland group of child analysts has worked on understanding some of the vicissitudes of the child's development in the one-parent family. Initially our interest was focused on the study of parentally bereaved children and twenty-three such cases were reported in *A Child's Parent Dies* (E. Furman, 1974). Since that time we have treated another thirty children who have lost a parent by death, bringing the total of such cases we have studied now to fifty-three. In addition, we have extended our research to cases in which one parent was absent for other reasons, such as parental separation or divorce, or where children were raised out of wedlock. Forty-nine children comprise this latter group (chapter 12).

As with the previous study of mourning, our data derive from five times weekly analyses of children of all ages (a few

---

We are greatly indebted to our Cleveland colleagues for sharing their material and allowing us to learn from and with them. We do, however, bear sole responsibility for the contents of this chapter.

seen privately, the majority at the Child Analytic Clinic of the Cleveland Center for Research in Child Development) and from two to three years of observation and treatment via the parent at the Hanna Perkins Nursery School and Kindergarten (R. Furman and Katan, 1969). Of the fifty-three bereaved children, twenty were in analysis and thirty-three in treatment via the parent. Of the forty-nine cases from one-parent families without bereavement, twenty-three were in analysis and twenty-six were treated via the parent at Hanna Perkins. In most of the analytic cases in both groups analysis followed prior treatment via the parents.

As with the previous study also, none of these patients came to us because we sought them out or publicized our interest and no family indicated their concern about the effects of the bereavement or absence of one parent as the main reason for referral. They wanted help for their children with a wide variety of symptoms, most of which seemed manifestly unrelated to the one-parent family constellation. In some cases, the parents could more readily recognize the connection. This was especially true with those instances where parental death or divorce happened during the child's treatment and in those where current experiences served to revive the past and occasioned upset or exacerbation of difficulties in the child. However, even in these situations the child's response could be fully understood only through the slow and painstaking therapeutic work which enabled patients, parents, and therapists gradually to unravel the individual underlying causes and shed light on their connections with the manifest pathology.

We have compared the material gained from the therapies of children with similar losses; we have compared cases of bereavement with those whose parents were absent for other reasons; we have compared those who did and did not have access to parent substitutes; and we have compared these individuals and groups of patients with the analytic data of children who grew up with both parents. Throughout we have tried, as best as possible, to separate out the specific effects of growing up in a one-parent home and to distinguish these from difficulties in coping with the events and circumstances which caused the other parent's absence, be it a death to be mourned, a divorce to be mastered, or other cause to be understood and accepted. The great amount of available information has not made our task easier. The more cases we see and the more closely we study them, the more do we appreciate the myriad of diverse factors at work and the complexity of their interaction. It is very difficult to pinpoint a few single determinants even in individual instances. General conclusions inevitably risk oversimplification and distortion. With this caution in mind, we shall nevertheless attempt to describe some areas of personality development which seem particularly difficult for the child in a one-parent family and to delineate some of the factors which appear to contribute to putting him or her at risk. Not all such children are burdened enough to run into problems, and indeed some children who have both parents in the home encounter similar difficulties. The total or partial unavailability of one parent has, however, proven itself to carry a potential danger for every child thus affected and therefore has to be viewed as a significant developmental interference.

Gathering of observations and material has proceeded gradually, and understanding has come piecemeal as one or another clinical aspect forced itself to the fore, sometimes in its striking manifestations in one case, but more often through its subtler but repeated occurrence in many. It is noteworthy, however, that with this, as opposed to other developmental interferences, the behavioral manifestations of difficulties have been such that their profound effect on the total personality functioning is easily overlooked, underestimated, or attributed to other factors. In many instances only the exploration of later pathology shed light on earlier factors and manifestations whose significance we had not appreciated, and prompted us to study them more closely and in greater detail in statu nascendi with younger children. For example, when enormous problems in superego integration surprised us in youngsters who had functioned well within the normal range until then, the analytic understanding of their pathology helped to pinpoint early forerunners in the nature and regulation of self-esteem. At the same time, our understanding was sometimes halted by the fact that the patients' pathology alerted us to general developmental processes which in themselves required further elucidation.

In fact, insofar as we have formulated our findings in writing, most of the papers addressed one or another of these aspects, for example, the transition into latency from the phallic–narcissistic phase (R. A. Furman, 1980); the role of the father's love during the child's phallic–oedipal phase (R. A. Furman, 1986; E. Furman, 1987); normal and pathological aspects of superego integration in early latency (E. Furman, 1980a,b); the role of drive fusion in the oedipal phase (E. Furman, 1983); the relationship between drive fusion, integration, and neutralization in normal and pathological development (E. Furman, 1985); aggressive and homosexual aspects of object removal in adolescence (R. A. Furman, 1988b).

At this time it seems appropriate to bring together the various strands of this research in progress, to begin to see how they interweave to make up the fabric of the growing personality of the child in the one-parent family, and to use the emerging developmental patterns as a base which may facilitate further investigation.

Briefly stated, we find that many youngsters in one-parent families start to show manifestations of difficulty in the very earliest stages of phallic–narcissistic development, that their conflicts in this phase are exaggerated, and that its attendant drive, ego, and relationship characteristics tend to persist. These boys and girls have great difficulty in progressing to the oedipal phase proper or in achieving oedipal phase dominance. This affects the nature of their superego formation and its integration, as well as their ego identifications during latency, and later presents them with special difficulties in resolving the developmental tasks of adolescence.

In discussing some aspects of each of these maturational phases in greater detail, the clinical manifestations will be described, causative factors highlighted, and chances of helpful intervention indicated.

THE PHALLIC–NARCISSISTIC PHASE

This phase, described by Edgcumbe and Burgner (1975), spans the developmental period between the earlier toddlerhood and the later oedipal phase proper, and shows some overlap with both. The phallic–narcissistic phase, with its still primarily dyadic relationships, is the earliest phase during which difficulties related to the one-parent family constellation manifest themselves. It is also the phase during which these early troubles are most easily overlooked, in part because they appear phase-appropriate. Most prominent is a lowered self-esteem which affects many areas of functioning. It may show in exaggerated concern about bodily intactness and adequacy as well as about mental competence, especially in comparison with peers. At entry to nursery school, and sometimes already in the toddler group, many of these children are so convinced that everyone else is bigger and better that they either shrink in fear from interaction, imitate the activities of others, or defensively boast and belittle their fellows. They are reluctant, however, to compete for real, do not offer their own ideas or do not follow through on them, expend little effort on tasks or easily abandon started projects, and when they do accomplish something, it gives them little pleasure. Indeed, they rarely feel good in themselves. They tend to keep busy with a restricted range of familiar materials and activities, to persist with what they feel they are already acceptably good at, and to avoid new challenges. Often they refuse suggestions with an "Oh, I want to do something else," or "I just want to play now," but their play also lacks zest and creativity. Role-play, especially in the housekeeping corner, is limited, and, even when they do participate, they do not seem to know how to interact, conveying the feeling that they do what they have seen or been told but not what they have experienced and felt. For example, one 3-year-old boy, fatherless since birth, liked to be the daddy, put on a big hat, carried a briefcase with lots of papers to his "office"—as indeed his grandfather did—but going to the office and then returning was the only thing he could do. Neither his grandparents' home life nor his mother's boyfriend's visits in his home had enlarged his concept of a man's role and function in the family. He did not know how to spend the early morning with his pretend family or have dinner with them, how to go on an outing—all the things his playmates took for granted as part of their game. What was striking, however, with him as with many others, was not just that he did not know, but that in this as in all other situations he was extremely touchy about not knowing.

Indeed, the tendency to have one's feelings hurt too easily is another very marked characteristic. Not only is the least criticism, admonition, or reprimand felt as major injuries, but slight or rejection is readily misperceived even in unrelated and unintentional behavior. For example, a remark directed to someone else is taken personally, an accidental brush by a passing child is mistaken for an attack, not being noticed right away on entering the room is viewed as a deliberate snub. Some children deal with their extreme vulnerability by avoiding situations in which they might expose themselves. Some turn the tables defensively and become standoffish to the point of rudeness, or become brusque and insensitive to the feelings of others. Steven, who had lost his father through suicide when he was barely 3 and whose treatment was detailed earlier (E. Furman, 1981c), actually did not greet people because he thought they did not want to have anything to do with him.

A number of youngsters respond to real or imagined hurts to their feelings with quick flares of exaggerated anger, anger untempered and untamed by caring consideration, anger which does not allow them to feel regret or to forgive easily. These angry upsets, though not necessarily part of an overall excessive manifest aggression, highlight the major third area of observable difficulty, namely an inability to cope with ambivalence and a reluctance to invest in loving relationships with peers and adults outside the family. Of course, not all children show all these behaviors or to the same extent. Nevertheless, close observation usually reveals direct or defensive signs of them in most areas and it is their concomitance, rather than single occurrence, which seems significant.

It is also striking that, with most of these children, these difficulties do not show themselves in the home, especially not with the parent, or at least much less so. One reason for this is that the child uses the loved adults in the family for narcissistic supplies, even to the extent of overestimation, and adapts his or her behavior so as to elicit the most positive response from them. Whatever especially appeals to the parent is what the child says, wears, and does. With some this may be an emphasis on their good looks or athletic prowess, with others it is an excited sensual interaction, or a special form of aggression, and still others work, play, and pursue neutral activities with the parent with a concentration, perseverance, and even enjoyment which altogether fails them when they are on their own. The parent's appreciation (and the teacher's, if they can engage her to fill the same role) is used to an excessive extent to compensate for the hidden lack of self-worth. Often it is only with entry to nursery school that the difficulties surface. This is a surprise and hurt to the parents as they observe their child's response to the separation, difficulty in functioning on his own, distress as others fail to admire what the parent admired, and frequent complaints about not liking or being liked at school. To some extent all children experience a diminishment in self-esteem and an increase in phallic anxieties on entry to nursery school because all of them age-appropriately rely on parental narcissistic supplies (E. Furman, 1969b). It is an important part of their adjustment process to transfer that parental love into self-love or, as one little girl put it to her mother, "When I am at school I love myself a little more because then you are not there to love me." For the one-parent child, however, this process is especially difficult. Also, all children act in such a way as to elicit parental appreciation, especially during the phallic phase when they wish to impress the parents and when being admired constitutes such an important gratification in their relationships. The one-parent child's wish to please the parent is thus easily seen as a part of his or her phallic dyadic relationship. What differentiates it, however, in these youngsters is the pressing need to maintain this relationship, sometimes to the point of surrendering their own aspirations, the inability to draw on their own resources, and the difficulty in extending the relationship to others. They either do not trust that anybody other than the parent could admire them, or they do not trust themselves to be able to meet other people's different expectations.

What these nursery school observations in fact reveal is that the child's functioning is not merely affected by phase-appropriate phallic concerns, but rather that the conflicts of this phase are so hard to cope with because they touch on and exacerbate a diminished libidinal investment of self and others. This libidinal investment proves inadequate to regulate self-esteem, to invest in new objects for their own sake and without threat to the existing relationships, to bind and attenuate the excessive aggression, and to thus free energy for integration and neutralization (E. Furman, 1985). Although we see all this in children who live with both parents and suffered different interferences, and although even the children from one-parent families have had other experiences which contributed to their troubles, their therapeutic material shows time and again how diminished and wounded they feel by not having a complete family and by missing out, partly or wholly, on the opportunity to love and be loved by both parents. This finding emerged earlier and was reported in connection with bereaved children (E. Furman, 1974). It applies just as much, if not more, to children of divorce or separated parents for, although their parent may remain partly available, his or her absence from the home was consciously willed and hence is more readily felt as a rejection. Moreover, the break in the parents' relationship with each other is a formidable reminder that love really can disappear and mutual anger or dislike really can overtake it. This is something young children struggle so to master in their own personalities and usually rely on the parents' help and example to accomplish in time.

The parent's absence causes not only libidinal depletion and hurt, but anger: at the remaining parent and at the absent parent, anger that is very difficult to express and to master because it threatens to overwhelm the inner loving ties and to bring about disastrous consequences in the external world. It is hard indeed to recognize and voice the full extent of one's destructive wishes to the sole available parent one needs so much or to the wholly or partly unavailable one who cannot be reached and whose return may be jeopardized. This is especially so when lasting separation and loss of object have really happened and therefore constitute a real threat. When both parents are in the home, the child has more opportunity for love and loving, less arousal of aggression, and can more readily distinguish imaginary from real consequences of aggression. Thus, especially prone to an unfavorable imbalance of the drives and especially handicapped in tolerating and verbalizing anger, many of these youngsters face serious problems with ambivalence. Their primitive unattenuated aggression tends to invade their self-investment as well as their relationships, surfacing in projections with fears of retaliation, in displacements from the parents to peers and adults outside the family, and later, as we shall see, in primitive instinctual identifications. Since the difficulty with drive fusion also affects integration and the capacity for neutralization, these children's ego energy becomes only partly deinstinctualized and their functions tend to lag in achieving secondary autonomy. As reported earlier (E. Furman, 1974), sometimes the loss of the parent during the first two years even results in inadequate initial investment of developing functions which creates a lasting weakness and susceptibility to later interference.

As soon as we learned that these difficulties did not subside with maturation but actually interfered with it, we began to study what helped some children to experience a lesser measure of trouble and how we could intervene to ameliorate the more serious conditions. Obviously, access to skilled observations in a sound preschool setting is most helpful to evaluation (E. Furman, 1978), especially when the nursery, like our Hanna Perkins School, includes opportunities for analysts to observe and to work with the parents as part of the program. Even if the child is taken into analysis, it is, at this stage, mainly the parents who need to be helped to be in tune with the child so that they can fulfill their important role of what A. Freud, as quoted by Rosenfeld and Sprince (1965), called the mediator between their child's id and ego. The parent's task here consists of assisting the child's ego in containing and integrating feelings and in mastering the stress of the external reality. Children were greatly helped when they could understand and cope with the cause and circumstances of one parent's absence, however painful or problematic, and when they could be assured that the fate of the parent or of the parental relationship was not caused by them and would not be repeated with them. One boy announced with relief, "My Mommy is divorced from my Daddy but I will never be divorced from my Daddy."

It also helped when the child could be supported in forming a realistic and detailed inner representation of the absent parent, in contrast to having to rely on a fantasied and therefore mainly instinctual image. In the case of death, this included memories, photos, material possessions, and above all the surviving loved one's descriptions of the personality and activities of the deceased. In the case of divorce, it implied regular contact with and parental functioning by the absent parent, in keeping with the child's needs rather than the parents' convenience. Of course, each parent's attitude to the partner as well as the nature of the relationship with the child are most important, a point discussed also by Neubauer (1960). Just as important is the parent's help with feelings. The partial or total absence of a parent creates an inevitable void which the child recognizes and feels, usually from toddlerhood on, even if he or she has never lived with both parents. It is a void that cannot be filled by the remaining parent trying to be both mother and father, nor can it be sufficiently filled by substitutes. It helps most when this void and the many feelings about it are acknowledged with the child, when sympathy is extended, and discussion and expression of feelings are encouraged and accepted. Then, at least, the parent's unavailability does not become an insurmountable wall in the existing relationship and the child can put to better use what the parent has to offer.

THE OEDIPAL PHASE

In "Some Vicissitudes of the Transition into Latency" (R. A. Furman, 1980) some of the clinical findings were described which led to the conclusion that children may "move into latency from many points along a continuum from the phallic–narcissistic phase through the oedipal phase" or, put differently, that "an almost infinite variety of combination of various aspects of the phallic–narcissistic and oedipal phases . . . can be operative at the time of transition into latency" (p. 38). Children who maintain a predominantly phallic–narcissistic position may show some true oedipal feelings and conflict but of very limited duration and intensity. In contrast to true oedipal phase dominance, their relationships are dyadic rather than triadic, lacking in thoughtfulness and consideration for the loved one, and focused on the aggressive envy and resentment of the other parent as an intruder whose primitive retaliation is feared. The emphasis is on acquiring bodily attributes rather than on engaging in mutually giving love. The primitive aggression toward the intruder, projected and feared, differs from the painful inner conflict the truly oedipal child experiences in being angry with a loved rival. In these instances, the oedipal disappointment is experienced as an unforgivable narcissistic blow and the attendant ego and superego identifications bear the marks of inadequate drive fusion and insufficiently neutral ego participation. Whereas during the phallic–oedipal period these differences may be overlooked, the later consequences in early latency are often so striking that we soon learned to pay closer attention to the developments which immediately preceded them.

Phallic–narcissistic predominance may be related to several factors, among them identification with phallic–narcissistic parents, prephallic and phallic stresses, as well as innate disposition. However, we found it to be such a frequent occurrence among boys and girls in one-parent families, regardless of the parent's sex, that we could only conclude that the total or intermittent absence of the other parent played a significant part. Particularly important is the absence of an ongoing marital relationship between mother and father in the child's home life. In this connection it was of interest that, in discussing this issue with unselected classes of high-school students, who, after giving it careful thought, arrived at this conclusion: For the healthiest and happiest resolution of early childhood there should be a family unit that consists of mother, father, and child. Uncles and aunts, grandparents, boy- and girl friends of the parents, all can help, and something is better than nothing, but it is just different from the child's mother and father being married and all living together (Maynard, 1985; R. A. Furman, 1986).

There are, nevertheless, children who achieve sufficient oedipal dominance to assure healthy phase resolution, even though they live with but one parent. This happened with some of our bereaved children who delayed decathexis in mourning and could fully utilize their rich memories of the deceased parent, or who, after the completion of mourning, could build new relationships with stepparents. In some instances belated but intense unfolding of oedipal relationships took place when an absent parent was restored. Some children could also make sufficient use of very intermittent contacts or of parent substitutes. Many youngsters, however, failed to progress toward oedipal development although parents or substitutes were partially available, and could not even catch up when, for example, through remarriage, they lived with a couple. Such was the case with the girl of divorced parents, reported by Neubauer (1960). The difficulty, in these cases, lies in the child's personality, especially in the primitive unattenuated ambivalence embedded in the prephallic and phallic object relationships and self-investment, and intensified by the libidinal deprivation of missing out on the relationship with the unavailable parent during the phallic phase.

We consider these children to be at risk because their conflicts, fixations, and pathological formations endanger the resolution of the Oedipus complex and we class them in a diagnostic category specifically so designated (E. Daunton, 1969). Our experience suggests that analysis and sometimes even treatment via the parent can help such children resolve their difficulties. With improved drive fusion, their object relationships become less ambivalent and conflict-laden, and their self-investment more positive and harmonious. They also take concomitant progressive steps in other ego manifestations, in the areas of integration and frustration tolerance, in the functions of reality testing, secondary process thinking, and verbal mastery, in their ability to pursue and enjoy neutral, noninstinctual activities and to develop sublimations. They are able to experience a wider range of affects which are more subtle and modulated and can feel good (E. Furman, 1985). These youngsters can then achieve oedipal personality development and utilize their memories of the absent parent, or even very limited contacts with a parent or parent substitute, to form meaningful oedipal relationships. A case vignette, some aspects of which were also described earlier (E. Furman, 1983), may help to clarify and illustrate these points.

CASE EXAMPLE 1

Evelyn entered Hanna Perkins school in her fifth year and began her analysis a few months later, following preparatory work via her mother. She was physically well developed and of superior intelligence, gifted and precocious in some of her ego functions and activities. Her large, expressive brown eyes and animated features mirrored an everchanging inner turmoil of moods. The driven quality of her insistent talking and restless, rather jerky, motility impressed and dominated her surroundings. Despite her good capabilities, she could not concentrate and learn, in part because she could not tolerate the slightest imperfection in herself or the greater knowledge of adults or peers. Her self-initiated projects, imaginative and of grand verbal design, were invariably abandoned as soon as her actual skills and perseverance proved inadequate to accomplish the fantasied task. Although Evelyn crumpled up her drawings, demolished her block buildings, mistreated and lost her possessions, and dishevelled her hair and clothes, she was unaware of her deep self-hatred and never acknowledged that anything was wrong. Instead, she was quick to pick out others' weaknesses or shortcomings and criticized them mercilessly. When the teachers offered a suggestion or tried to reassure her about a little mistake, she turned on them viciously and blamed them for interfering and spoiling her efforts.

Evelyn's relationships were stormy but invested with depth and zest which endeared her to most adults. She could be genuinely loving and affectionately demonstrative with her mother and other women, as well as helpful and protective with younger children, including her little brother. The next moment, however, she would become angry, mean, and spiteful, burst into temper tantrums, and, especially with other children, was not only verbally but also physically abusive. Sometimes these changes followed a minor frustration, or when the other person's refusal to comply with Evelyn's wishes interfered with her need to be fully in control of them; at other times her switch of mood seemed prompted only from within. Evelyn's love and hate were not always genuine. Excessive shows of devotion could thinly disguise mounting inner aggression, and provocative meanness could serve to solicit anger and punishment from others for sins they, and even she, often did not know about. Her extreme, unmitigated ambivalence also played a part in her severe separation fear (she was frantic for mother's safety and felt deeply rejected by her absences), and in her constant complaints of not being liked. She would go out of her way to be nasty to newcomers, expecting them to find her unacceptable.

Her relationships with men and boys were quite inappropriate. She sought out men, even when she hardly knew them, absorbed their attention with brash excited talk and bodily seductiveness, and given the least encouragement, she hung and climbed on them, kissed them, provoked them to tussle with her or swing her around, and begged them to live in her home and be her daddy. With boys, her mixed feelings, her fear of not being liked, and her sadomasochistic sexual fantasies were evident as she complained of their meanness, provoked their attack, and masochistically exaggerated her suffering.

In contrast to her bright, precocious demeanor, Evelyn's self-care was infantile and symptom-ridden. She had a severe eating disturbance, sleep difficulties, occasionally soiled and wet herself, dawdled over dressing, did not bathe independently, cared poorly for her toys and possessions, and could not tolerate being on her own. Her analysis revealed quickly that this often highly competent little girl's personality structure was very vulnerable and subject to disintegration. When I would speak to her, within a couple of sentences, she would cry out "Stop, stop" and cover her bowed head with her arms. We came to understand that, if she could not control my words, they represented an intolerable intrusion, overwhelmed her ego functions, and split up her body image. She called these episodes her "muddled thinking" and described how, at these times, her hands, feet, and other body parts did things she didn't even want to do.

Evelyn came by her strengths and weaknesses honestly. She was the wanted child of an intelligent middle-class couple who loved her, not wisely but too well. From the start, the parents' handling alternated between intrusive sensuous overstimulation and emotional withdrawal or absences. Well intentioned, they made her a part of their own primitive, fiercely loving relationship and overwhelmed her as a witness and as a partner. During Evelyn's toddlerhood, they welcomed and extolled her precocious intellectual and verbal development, but abused her with harsh physical punishment and exposed her to repeated sexual perversions with an adolescent boy. The mother's difficult pregnancy and birth of the younger brother contributed to the deterioration of the marriage. Physical violence between the parents intensified, leading to a partial separation when Evelyn was 2½. The father was murdered at his place of work when Evelyn was about 3½.. During the hectic chaos of the next year, the idealized image of the father became a near-concrete presence for her distraught mother, and Evelyn received little help in understanding and containing the confusing circumstances surrounding the father's death itself. Evelyn often introduced herself to people by shocking them with: "My daddy is dead. He was shot and killed."

Like her mother, Evelyn was eager for help and hoped to gain mastery of her inner distress through treatment. The first months of analysis were largely devoted to a repetitive shared game in which an intact puppet family of four got up, had breakfast, and drove off to school and work. We also played card games in which it was very important for Evelyn to win and not to possess black cards, spades and clubs. In time we understood that the family's contented mornings masked the agony of her own mornings, spent in compulsive phallic and anal masturbation. Unable to get ready, she usually provoked an altercation with her mother who retaliated with frustrated yelling and hitting. The black cards, we learned, signaled the danger of the black queen who stood for the "witchy" mutual "killing feelings" between mother and child and were encapsulated in her guilt- and shame-ridden sadistic masturbation fantasies. The analytic work focused on the question to which Evelyn devoted most of her unconscious, and later conscious, mental efforts: "How can one love a person?" How could she make sure that her intense but fragile love would not be swept away by her boundless hatred, and kill her mother? And how could she be sure that this would not also happen to her mother's love for her, the mother who was her only remaining parent but whose aggression was so dangerous?

We worked on Evelyn's past and current developmental conflicts and real experiences which had so greatly exacerbated her anger and convinced her of its danger. At times she was helped by gaining insight, by linking her anger to its true content and mastering it verbally. Many times, however, her angry thoughts and wishes threatened to engulf her and she could not draw on her positive feelings to fuse and attenuate them. It then helped to remind her that she also loved mommy, or the therapist, wanted to keep her, appreciated her care, and enjoyed their good times. As Evelyn's personality achieved better integration of her aggressive impulses, she developed acute anxieties and phobias in lieu of the earlier sadistic outbursts. Evelyn was delighted when she managed to complete a nice Mother's Day present, but she decided to give it several days early lest "my meanness ruins it by Sunday."

Evelyn's love for herself was similarly precarious. With analytic work, her investment of herself, as of her loved ones, became more stable and effective and she began to view herself more kindly. Prior to her birthday party she told me: "I know what you'll wish me most: that I'll be able to like myself because then I'll be nice to my guests." She could not enjoy learning and working as she could not forgive herself for her mistakes and forgive others for their superiority. She was calmer, warmer, and functioned in a more integrated manner.

Her relationship with men and boys took a new turn. The oedipal theme of "Can one love two people?" became the focus of the analysis. Evelyn's excited provocative approach to males and her desperate demand for a father primarily contained her need of their penis. She even tried to produce one for herself with her masturbation. It would not only satisfy her phallic wishes but protect her from her aggression toward her mother and change her into an acceptable love object, like her brother, father, and mother's boyfriends. Now these same males became people she loved and longed for. She became friendly with mother's boyfriend, gave presents to her teenage half-brother, and was especially warmly enamored of a classmate. For the first time she brought her real unhappy memories of her father. He had hit her, exposed himself, fought with mother, and disregarded her pleas to stop. Perhaps he had not loved her. Then one day she brought to her session a toy she had found in a forgotten basement corner, a toy her father had expertly crafted for her. We talked about how much love and care must have gone into making it and she recalled good times of playing and learning her ABCs with him. The toy became newly precious. This helped her to integrate her image of her father and to fuse her feelings for him. She asked for his picture to keep in her room. He would not have been an ideal daddy but nice enough. She also thought she had wanted to live with him, had wanted mother to die instead of him, and had suspected her of killing him.

The therapist's husband became an important love object. Evelyn had known him even before her analysis from his weekly observation visits in her classroom. She had always tried to seduce and control him as she did with all males, and, at the start of treatment, had tended to follow up these encounters by provoking me to punish her for wanting to take him away from me. In time she adapted to the routine of his visits, her attitude softened, and she was often warm and charming with him. She was also less concerned with my response until we learned that the beloved classmate was a displacement for my husband whom she longed for as the most desirable daddy. To her happy surprise, one day she met Dr. Furman in my home as she was leaving her session. That night she had a nightmare which we understood in terms of her oedipal aggression to me. She was deeply chagrined and said, "But I like you too and I don't really want you to die." The following week she baked cookies, brought two for Dr. Furman, but, after some conflict, decided that I should keep one and give him the other.

Although her earlier defenses and conflicts were often still in evidence, Evelyn's personality strides included a marked affective change. She could sustain rich loving warmth as well as true sadness, could feel scared and helpless but also kind and concerned. Soon we began to see the beginnings of oedipal resignation. Evelyn was now about 6½.. On one of his visiting days, Dr. Furman briefly returned to her classroom later in the day, and Evelyn, like many of her peers, begged him to admire yet another something she had accomplished. He told her he really did not have time but reminded her that he had looked at some of her other work earlier. Much to his surprise she replied nicely, "I know you did. Thank you." When we discussed this even in her analysis and I wondered what had made it possible for her to accept the disappointment so well, Evelyn said: "I have come to feel that something is better than nothing." Another day she commented that the flowers in my office were wilting. What would I do with them? I told her I would dig them into a flower bed so that, as they turn into earth, they would enrich the soil and help new flowers to grow better. This led to renewed discussions of death, and, for the first time ever, Evelyn could integrate the concrete aspects of her father's death without terror or excitement. A week later, she talked about her father with sadness. She then said quietly, "But he also lives on with the things I do, that he did with me, and liked, and did for me." After a pause she added, "And my children will do the things I like when they grow up and after I am dead, and so it will go on always."

This condensed and selective account may raise more questions than it answers and may not adequately illustrate the point that oedipal development depends on a necessary degree of drive fusion and its concomitant ego manifestations. We do not know to what extent the therapist's husband represented a real or transferred love object for Evelyn, how much the analytic work or the therapist's real relationship with her helped her toward better integration, or how much difficulty she would have encountered in establishing oedipal ties if both parents had continued to be available to her. However, the same theme has emerged prominently in several other cases. Some of these were treatments via the parent where the transference played no part but where the children could utilize minimally available parent-figures after they had been helped. In other cases, children could not progress to a viable oedipal phase, even though they lived with both parents, until they achieved drive fusion, integration, and resolution of earlier conflicts.

The oedipal experience in these cases does not insure untroubled further development but it mitigates later difficulties and makes them more accessible to therapy. We therefore conclude, with Evelyn, that something is better than nothing.

SUPEREGO FORMATION AND THE LATENCY PERIOD

In contrast to some of the subtler manifestations of difficulty during the phallic–narcissistic and oedipal phases, early latency pathology is often ushered in with a bang. The case of Steven (E. Furman, 1981c) described how this seemingly well-progressing boy with appropriate preoedipal reaction formations and impulse control suddenly turned into a most provocative, unmanageable behavior problem on entering our Hanna Perkins Kindergarten after the summer vacation. As he put it, "There are no rules for me!" Prompted by the understanding of his symptom as well as by the observations and material gained from therapeutic work with our many other patients in this developmental phase, we learned that all youngsters experience difficulty in integrating their newly harsh superego; that all use the defense of externalization of superego to some extent to ward off the intense anxiety generated by the unfamiliar structural conflict; and that all experience a regressive exacerbation of phallic–narcissistic concerns (E. Furman, 1980a,b). However, the most marked pathological exaggeration of difficulties in the new phase was experienced by children from one-parent families, like Steven, and others who for various reasons formed their superego when phallic–narcissistic personality characteristics predominated and when progressive drive fusion was impeded by an excess of aggression over libido. Also, their symptoms did not subside with maturation and required therapeutic help, whereas the children within the normal range could, merely with sound educational support, achieve superego integration and use their conscience to consolidate a latency adjustment.

With some of the youngsters, as with Steven, the new symptom showed mainly in unruly behavior, giving the impression that they not only had not developed a conscience but had lost all previously acquired inner controls. With others it manifested itself in severe temper outbursts, which often started out with teasing provocative interplays but ultimately crested in frenzied screaming and attacking of others and self as well as destruction of materials. Some even ran into the street traffic or dashed onto precipitous ledges threatening to kill themselves before they finally crumpled into a fetal position, overwhelmed, helpless, whimpering, and in need of comfort. We learned that the initial stage of provocative misbehavior served to externalize the unbearable threat of the punishing superego introject, entrusting the much kinder caring adults with the role of controlling and punishing their transgressions. The later stage of feeling that they had to hurt, even kill themselves, and collapsing overwhelmed, represented the failure of the earlier defense and the ensuing anxiety attack, experienced when the internal superego retribution seemed imminent. Neither permissiveness nor punitiveness helps. The attending parents or teachers are left in no doubt as to the child's harrowing anxiety because he or she does, to an extent, spread and/or externalize it to them, and, although tempted to act on this anxiety, they assist the stricken child best by protecting him from harm, by pointing out that the turmoil stems from within, and soothing sympathetically when it subsides.

Some children with similar inner conflicts do not succumb to such anxiety attacks and even their misbehavior is less clearly geared to eliciting external punishment. They appear as though they had not formed a superego at all and are easily misdiagnosed as arrested at the phallic or prephallic levels. However, observations and treatment data gained from work with them during the preceding period clearly show that superego formation was beginning, and, although their defenses are so strong and effective, it often surfaces in isolated anxieties, especially in night fears and bad dreams.

It is striking with these children, whose superego gives them so much trouble, that its threatening manifestations and the transition into latency come much more quickly and suddenly, even at a relatively earlier age than the more normal onset, which tends to take place later, gradually, and in a "two steps forward, one step backward" progression. In the pathological instances, it is not uncommon to see a child transformed during a summer vacation or even within a week or two. This suddenness, along with the extreme harshness and unintegratability of the superego, provide clues to the nature and causes of the difficulty. Instead of piecemeal acceptance of an oedipal resignation and preservation of the aim-inhibited aspects of the positive relationships with both parents, the more primitive personality of the phallic–narcissistic position with its unfused instinctual impulses, narcissistic vulnerability, and insufficient capacity for integration and neutralization, responds to the obstacles to oedipal fulfillment with hurt, fury, and fear.

The parental images, distorted by projected aggression and unmitigated by loving consideration, are primitively introjected and cannot be assimilated by the personality. At best, such introjects burden children with greatly troubled consciences, causing them chronic discontent with themselves and tending to make them appear rather nasty and selfish in relation to others. Children of one-parent families are, of course, not helped by their diminished opportunities for loving interactions and for comparing their distorted image of the parent with his or her real behavior. However, the forces which shape the inner image, especially the imbalance of the drives, predominate even over the actual experiences with the available parent. The tendency to set up harshly instinctual introjects has been noted by several authors who studied children of one-parent families, among them M. Meiss (1952), A. Reich (1954), and P. Neubauer (1960). It was also described in *A Child's Parent Dies* (E. Furman, 1974).

As mentioned earlier, therapeutic intervention at a younger age does not prevent this difficulty with superego formation, even when the child could be helped to achieve a good measure of oedipal dominance, but it does appear to make it less severe and more amenable to treatment. With children who are not yet in therapy, the mere dramatic nature of their symptomatology serves as an impetus for analysis, but even the more muted manifestations of superego pathology are valid indications for treatment, especially as they usually coexist with difficulties in ego identifications and availability of neutral energy for latency pursuits.

Latency is the time of consolidation and modification of ego identifications with the parents, a process not unlike that which progresses in the integration and maturation of the conscience. By the term *ego identifications* we refer to various character traits that a child will acquire to assist him in mastery of his latency developmental tasks. These tasks are primarily concerned with learning how to get along and function with his peer group, both at school and at play, and with the learning or educational tasks set before him at school. In these areas we hope to see children able to control their instinctual side, assisted by their conscience, so that they can be firmly protective of their bodies, their rights, and their needs. We hope they will be able to be kind and considerate of others, abide frustration, and accept delays in gratification; able to persevere with tasks; be inquisitive, alert, and discriminatory; to have fun and enjoy themselves as they learn about the world outside of home and family.

The more children enter latency from the phallic–narcissistic position and the less favorable their drive balance, the more their motivation is derived from instinctual fears, the more primitive and hard to modify will be the identifications they make in this process. By contrast, the more the move into latency results from phallic–oedipal conflicts of resolving the aggression to beloved parents, the more neutral and modifiable will be the emerging identifications (R. A. Furman, 1980). An example of the more primitive type of ego identification in action may be helpful here.

CASE EXAMPLE 2

Not too long ago, in working with a midlatency boy, the analyst became concerned with the boy's constant neglect and dismissal of his homework, his inability each night to apply himself to some relatively simple tasks. Unfortunately, in one sense, this boy was bright enough to get good grades with even the most perfunctory approach to his assignments. If the analyst was after him enough, to please him or to silence the complaints, the boy would have periods of application to the tasks at hand. But there was no gratification for him at these times, nothing that rewarded him so that he wanted to persist in these efforts. It was no use pointing out the reality of the need to learn to enjoy studying while it was still easy, as a preparation for the increasingly difficult academic tasks that awaited him down the road. The boy felt he would come to these in time; right now he wanted nothing to interfere with his just having fun, such as in watching television. When the boy was approached about how he felt about himself, whether he was aware of his lack of persistence and task application, his lack of standards for himself, his faulty reality perception, there was no distress whatsoever.

When the analyst asked how the boy's father dealt with his work, his father being a most successful and enterprising businessman, the boy replied, "I do just like him!" It turned out that all the boy saw of his father at home, and that had never been very often as the father traditionally worked long hours, was his father at play, partying, drinking, taking it easy. The boy had long since made this early ego identification with his father, an immature and unmodifiable one. The boy was now old enough to know, and it had been discussed often enough at home, how hard and successfully the father worked at his job. There was much that was admirable in the father that the boy could inquire after, seek out, learn about, and emulate, but he did not.

Unfortunately this was a distant father, one actually little involved with his son and unable to demonstrate in activities with him the attributes that made the father so financially successful. Instead, what he demonstrated in his interaction with his son was either his temper, when it seemed the boy misbehaved, or else his rather excited ways of relaxing.

One can describe the mechanism of acquisition of this boy's identification with his father in a number of ways. Annie Reich (1954) described early narcissistic identification with early glorified pictures of the parents, identifications put in place to overcome the hurts or narcissistic wounds endured, such as feeling ignored or uncared for by a parent. These very early, distorted identifications are difficult to integrate, to assimilate, to use to enhance one's own character because they are so unrealistic. Even when partly recognized as unrealistic, they are clung to. Another way of looking at this problem is to focus on the primitive, unfused, unneutralized energy that fuels the identificatory process and makes it so hard for the ego to modify and integrate the identifications which, through the instinctual energy involved, are much more under the control of the id. One could also focus on the fact that some children often have stayed much too long involved, fixated at the phallic–narcissistic phase for any of a number of possible reasons, simply leaving too little time for involvement with phallic–oedipal conflicts before the curtain of repression descends and latency arrives (R. A. Furman, 1980). Edith Jacobson (1954) pointed to yet another factor of unresolved ambivalence when she described two variants of mourning and its accompanying identifications. In the melancholic type of resolution there is an ego identification with the lost loved one, an introject upon which the superego vents its aggression, as Freud described so long ago (1917). In health, we are familiar with the identification with the lost loved one that leads to modification of the ego, taking on ego-syntonic constructive aspects of the deceased. Identification is operative in each instance, but in healthy mourning, ambivalence is mastered leading to an adaptive resolution. This is lacking in the melancholic.

All children make the early, more primitive identifications. One factor that can lead to their modification over time is the presence of the reality of the parent, available with his or her more neutral ways of relating that offer the child the constant opportunity to correct and modify his earlier impressions and identifications. These are difficult to modify later in analysis and take a great deal of work, work that is successful in part because the parents are both realistically available, able to modify instinctual ways of interacting, if such be needed.

In following up our cases at the Hanna Perkins Therapeutic Nursery School and Kindergarten (R. A. Furman and A. Katan, 1969), we were struck with how well the gains acquired in treatment by way of the parent had persisted with our successful cases. At first we thought this was due either to the nature of the child's conflicts or to the basic soundness of the treatment approach. In time we became aware of yet another factor, the parents' maturation during the prelatency years of work that enabled them to bring to the children in their latency a relatively stress-free period in which to consolidate their gains, make further modifications in their identifications, both ego and superego. Parents successful in the work are relieved and impressed with what they have accomplished, learn to listen to and respect their child, and let things be talked out when necessary. These are some of the prerequisites of a constructive latency.

Two contrasting examples of problem management in latency may be helpful here. In one instance, a child became aware of a parent's dishonesty over minor financial matters, a most unfortunate neurotic symptom with which the child began to identify. The parent could recognize what was occurring and discussed the problem fully with the child, acknowledging his own problem, the distress it brought him, and expressing his wish that the child would not have the same unfortunate difficulty. That child's problem subsided entirely. In another instance, one parent of a child in analysis had difficulty with alcohol which the entire family totally denied, despite the child's witnessing many episodes of drunken, out-of-control behavior. The parent was quite unable to acknowledge the problem, much less discuss it with the child, and this contribution to the child's lack of control could never be mastered in the analysis.

Latency is a time when deficient or unhelpful ego identifications can come to the fore and can be observed if they are not denied—the example given earlier of the difficulty with homework being a case in point. Even if their roots lie much earlier, sometimes much can be done if they can be addressed, their origin accepted and discussed. This work can be difficult for single parents, however. In cases of bereavement an idealization of the lost parent may be difficult for a surviving parent to avoid or to help a child put right. In cases of separation or divorce or a child raised out of wedlock, it can be difficult for the responsible parent to discuss the absent parent without rancor. These difficulties, however, are not insuperable; they can be and frequently are overcome.

ADOLESCENCE

The psychological processes active during adolescence are as intricate and complex as they are important and crucial. Perhaps only the period of the resolution of the oedipal phase is as important for future mental health. One aspect of adolescence, of course, involves a recrudescence of the forces operative at the end of the phallic–oedipal phase. Each therapist will have his own most favored or useful way of conceptualizing what occurs during adolescence, and it should not be surprising if child analysts from Cleveland lean heavily on Anny Katan's formulation (1937).

In her paper that introduced the concept of object removal, Katan started with the return of the oedipal strivings in adolescence, noting that the personality had but two options available in managing these to avoid incest: defenses against the drives or a change in object for the drives. Although asceticism is often a temporary phenomenon of this developmental period, health requires that one must fail in the struggle against the drives. Attention then focuses on a change in the object of the drives, the process of object removal. This has two components: a removal of the libidinal investment in the internal representative of the infantile object; a displacement of a particular and unique kind of energy freed from the old object to enable its reinvestment in a new object outside the family. This combination of decathexis and displacement serves well for the positive oedipal strivings, the libidinal attachment to the parent of the opposite sex. It has further been proposed (R. A. Furman, 1988b) that decathexis operates with the negative oedipal libidinal or homosexual strivings and with the aggressive urges accompanying the libidinal ones, but displacement of these would lead to a homosexual object choice and uncontrolled aggression. Although both are seen often as temporary phenomena, they do not represent adaptive resolution. The suggestion has been made, the hypothesis offered, that following decathexis, in lieu of displacement, the homosexual and aggressive strivings are contained or managed by a combination of identification and the processes inherent in neutralization and sublimation.

This thinking helps us to understand the great flood of instinct with which the adolescent is faced as well as the painful loneliness of this period, the result of withdrawal of the instinctual investment in the internal representatives of the parents. This thinking emphasizes the role of the ego in the developmental conflicts of this phase in managing the identifications as well as the economic considerations inherent in drive fusion, neutralization, and sublimation. Also to the fore come the neutralized, reality-based relationships with the parents, since withdrawal of the instinctual investment in the early objects will be able to proceed in proportion as the other aspects of investments remain. Without them it can feel to the adolescent that the withdrawal of the instinctual investment has in effect destroyed the inner representation of the parent.

If the developmental tasks of adolescence are viewed in this fashion, it becomes easier to understand how marginal adjustments in latency no longer suffice and how these adjustments fall apart and fail in adolescence. This is particularly true of the difficulties encountered by the child of the single-parent home that have been addressed in this paper. To the extent identificatory processes are modeled on the early, instinctualized identifications of the phallic–narcissistic phase, it will be difficult and unhelpful to utilize them in adolescence. To the extent that the processes of fusion of aggression, neutralization, and sublimation have been inadequate in the past, they will have difficulty with assisting the adolescent in mastery. To the extent that the ego has had a deficit of integrative capacity and neutralized energy available for its tasks, there will now be problems. It is almost as if the developmental requirements of successful adolescent development were peculiarly designed to expose the difficulties inherent in a basically phallic–narcissistic personality orientation.

With other phases the attempt has been made to emphasize what still can be done to deal with arrests or regressions that go back to the phallic–narcissistic level. In adolescence it is much more necessary to say that prevention is the most important approach to these problems because they often present enormous difficulties even in a treatment setting. Adolescents stand the best chance of dealing with their developmental conflicts when their positive investments in themselves and others are already healthily in place. Their attempts at this time to receive such loving investment from without, almost regardless of source, too often seem regressive in nature and, to the extent such loving is an attempt to fill an old void, will have to be rejected as infantilizing and antidevelopmental. It is not that adolescents do not require an inordinate amount of patient loving, which of course they do. It is just that the time is past when such loving can be reparative. They very much need stable objects for identification at this time, crucially so, although there are times when these are superficially rejected. Adolescents are very attuned to the problems inherent in parental exhortation to do as I say, not as I do. At this point they are very much more apt to do as the parents have done.

In conclusion, we wish to underline what has been implicit throughout this chapter, that the effects of the one-parent family on the child's personality development are potentially most serious when they impinge upon him or her during the earliest years of life and when he has few, if any, experiences of a positive relationship with both parents. However, total or partial loss of a viable relationship with either parent at later stages threatens to revive early fixation points in the prephallic and phallic–narcissistic phases because the narcissistic hurts and intensified aggression cause regression.

14
On Motherhood

I shall now focus on an aspect of female psychology that has been sidestepped, more often than not, in analytic contributions to this topic, namely the fact that the potential for being a mother and its realization, or lack thereof, forms the genetic core of womanhood and plays a crucial role in the development of boys and girls from the very start. The widespread neglect of the central role of motherhood, exemplified, for example, by Tyson's (1994) review of contemporary contributions to female psychology, is in striking contrast to our clinical experience. It is clear from a clinical viewpoint that the female and male body ego develop by differentiation from that of a mother (not just a woman). Girls and boys perceive their mother as a mother first and only later as a woman. Their mother (in her mothering rather than womanly function) is their first object of identification; little girls want to be a "Mommy" long before they want to be a "lady" and refer to their doll as their "baby" long before it is given a special name. Last and not least, the conscious and unconscious feelings and concerns about being or not being a mother (and what kind of a mother) remain a crucial part of being a woman throughout every woman's, and possibly every man's, life.

In keeping with this neglect, much of the controversy about sexual phallic monism has focused on establishing a concept of bedrock femininity characterized by a sense of bodily wholeness from the start and reenforced by identification with the mother's female genitals, without reference to motherhood. The emphasis, instead, has been on showing that little girls do not define themselves as lacking or inferior, but actually feel safer and more comfortable with their female genitals than boys do with their exposed, vulnerable penis. Summarizing contemporary views, Tyson (1994) points out that establishing core gender identity is easier for the girl by virtue of her anatomy as well as through identification with her mother. The girl's "genitals and associated diffuse, whole body sensations are experienced as an integral and protected . . . part of her body from the beginning. . . . Therefore, defining a sense of body integrity is normally a smoother process for the girl" (p. 452). At the same time, identification with her mother provides "an experiential sense of being female, like mother, with female genitals" (p. 454). With motherhood left out, these considerations remain limited to boy–girl comparisons and the related phallic–narcissistic question of who is "better" or "better off."

It is noteworthy that the many analytic contributions that focus on the basic role of motherhood and the "inner space" as part of it, remain as isolated and neglected as the topic itself, especially in the United States. Among these are contributions by Horney (1926, 1932), Erikson (1956, 1964), Kestenberg (1956a, 1968), Chasseguet-Smirgel (1976), T.-B. Hägglund et al. (1978), T.-B. Hägglund and Pika (1980), V. Hägglund (1981), and Torsti (1993). In her 1976 paper, Chasseguet-Smirgel suggests that sexual phallic monism wards off the boy's double narcissistic wounds sustained in the relationship with the mother; his initial helplessness and dependency on her, and his oedipal disappointment and sexual inadequacy with her later. She finds that a powerful, envied, and terrifying maternal imago lies behind the defensive scorn of female inferiority. I do not dispute this insightful observation, but I think it does not explain everything.

Since boys *and* girls, men *and* women, find it so difficult to accept that the "psychological striving for motherhood is the core of femininity" (V. Hägglund, 1981, p. 143) and are so ready to exclude it from its role in male and female gender development, motherhood must imply additional deep-seated early concerns. Over many years I have struggled to learn about these concerns and formulated some of my findings (E. Furman, chapter 4, 1984, 1992a, 1993a, chapter 6). I shall now retrace my steps briefly in the hope of clarifying these inherently difficult issues, and using them to answer two questions: (1) Why is motherhood so often sidestepped and misunderstood, and (2) why is womanhood so often viewed as deficient or inferior, so much so that its wholeness and adequacy are defensively underlined?

THE CHILD AS PART OF THE MOTHER'S BODY EGO

In 1969 I described the parents' special investment in their child as a hallmark of their entry into the phase of parenthood. In contrast to the investment of all other object relations, that of the parents in their child is characterized by a narcissistic cathexis, the child as a part of the self, which to start with, far outweighs the concomitant object cathexis, the child as a loved person. As the child grows, there is a relative shift in the balance between these two kinds of investment, but the narcissistic one is never fully replaced and always remains a significant factor, qualitatively and quantitatively different from narcissistic elements in other relationships. I noted at the same time that, just as the parental investment of the child differs from other object relations, so the maternal investment differs significantly from the paternal one. Both parents include the child in their own mental self, but only the mother invests him also as a part of her bodily self (i.e., he is included in the boundaries of her body ego). The physiological and biological givens of pregnancy parallel and facilitate this latter process but they do not guarantee it. Some biological mothers fail to integrate their baby into their body ego or achieve it only partially; some adoptive mothers, though by no means all succeed in this respect (chapter 2).

Although, at the time, I did not appreciate the full implications of the mother's bodily investment in her child, it proved to be a crucial and most helpful concept to me in understanding motherhood and is pertinent to the present discussion.

MOTHERS' RESPONSES TO THE DEATH OF THEIR BABY

My first dramatic encounter with the manifestations of the maternal bodily investment came through my work with perinatal loss, mothers who lost a newborn or very young baby through death (chapter 3). Along with their conscious and very understandable feelings of distress, sadness, anger, guilt, despair, and unconscious defenses against them, they complained of symptoms which disturbed them but which they in no way associated with their loss or, at best, vaguely related to the aftermath of a difficult pregnancy or delivery. Most often they experienced abdominal sensations which felt to them either like a growing cancerous tumor or like a strange "hole," "like something's all wrong with my insides," "some awful illness." Quite often too, they described radiating aches in their arms, a strange heaviness and difficulty in lifting or extending them. Occasionally, they attributed the disconcerting experience of "something all wrong" to their minds, fearing they were falling apart mentally and going crazy, and sometimes they could neither localize nor find words for their worry. Since others seemed not to take their complaints seriously, did not even want to hear about them, or told them to "pull yourself together," they felt even worse. Despite the intense anxiety, some of these mothers did not seek medical help and those who did were not reassured by the negative findings.

They were, however, greatly helped by two interventions: (1) My putting into words for them that the baby had been an integral, most important part of their body; that its removal from their inside (the hole) and lack of restitution by being also unavailable on the outside (the arms intended to hold him) were therefore experienced as an amputation of a vital body part or as the loss of a vital function, such as vision. They were feeling crippled and undone and, as with a real amputation or loss of function, would take a long time to adapt to the loss and repair their sense of bodily and mental wholeness without the baby. And because this experience was different and separate from the baby as a loved person it represented, instead, a major injury to their bodily integrity, it was something that, like the sight of cripples, disturbed others and made it hard for them to empathize or even listen to their distress. (2) A concerted effort on the part of hospital staff as well as in working with the bereaved parents to afford them postnatal contact with the baby, even the dead baby, and to enlist their active role in arranging a funeral and burial or cremation. This facilitated the process of the mother transferring her cathexis of the inside baby to the outside baby and provided some opportunity for object cathexis. The more object cathexis, the greater the opportunity to mourn the child as a separate loved one—a difficult task in itself, but much easier for others to support than coming to terms with a shattered body ego (chapter 3).

MOTHERS' RESPONSES TO THE DEVELOPMENTAL LOSS OF THEIR CHILD

Subsequently, I could increasingly compare my child analytic findings with data from my work with mothers of infants and toddlers. I came to realize that the deeply shattering breach to the integrity of the maternal body ego accompanies not only the total loss of the child through death, but each developmental step in his personality growth and resulting increase in self-sufficiency (E. Furman, chapter 4, 1984, 1992a, 1993a, chapter 6).

The "ordinary devoted mother" of the living growing child usually uses immediate and effective defenses against the threat of these primitive anxieties. During babyhood, turning passive into active is most commonly used. I have described some of the many instances when the mother shifts the "trauma" of weaning from herself to her baby; she responds to his signs of readiness for self-feeding and rejection of the breast by leaving him first—by going to work, going on a trip, going out one night in such a way that he wakes up to an unexpected sitter; that is, leaving him just enough to convey the terror of abandonment (chapter 4). These ways of leaving him first around the time of weaning often mark the start of the many sleep disturbances during the latter part of the first year.

These sleep disturbances, however, result as often from another maternal defense, namely transferring her hold on the child's body from nursing to sleeping. While letting go of the former, mothers tighten the reins on the latter as they unwittingly interfere with the child's "not needing" them during his night or nap time (chapter 4). Indeed, changing the form or area of owning the child's body is as common a defense as leaving him first. For example, spoonfeeding or rigid control of the types and amounts of food offered easily nullify the child's potential independence resulting from weaning; similarly, mother's ownership of nursing (what goes in) is often transferred to elimination (what comes out) which tends to be rationalized as related to the changes in digesting new foods.

During the toddler phase, the child's second and third years, mothers face the most concentrated task of changing the balance of their investment in the child, from predominantly narcissistic to object-oriented, in keeping with the child's personality growth (chapter 5). For mother and toddler this process focuses on the transfer of bodily ownership from her to him. She, who heretofore gauged and met all his needs, is expected to yield to his demand for bodily self-care and ownership, for it is mainly through the bit-by-bit process of owning, gauging, and ministering to his own bodily needs that the child differentiates himself from his mother and defines his body ego. This includes protesting pain, learning to avoid common dangers, washing, dressing and undressing, gauging hunger and self-feeding, gauging elimination and keeping clean, recognizing fatigue, and putting himself to sleep.

I have described the arduous steps by which mother and child negotiate the transfer of bodily ownership—doing for, doing with, standing by to admire, doing for oneself—and I have described how extraordinarily difficult it is for mothers to do their part (Furman, 1992a, 1993a). They repeatedly ignore or deny the child's signals of readiness, they prolong the first two steps, and with the third step of standing by to admire, tend to turn away, feeling no longer "needed." In doing so they have passed on the skill, the knowhow of self-care, but reneged on graciously handing over the gratification they experienced in performing it. By keeping that for themselves, they deprive their child of the most valuable part of owning his body. Once again, they leave him before he can leave them. The mothers' denials, delays, and reluctance are all the more striking when contrasted with their frequently expressed wishes for the child to do for himself, complaints about the tiring job of doing for him, even pride in his achievements of self-care, and often lavish support of the child's nonbodily skills, such as his motor activities, speech, block-building, or interest in puzzles. The same child whose small muscle dexterity is praised and admired may be deemed quite incapable of learning to wipe his behind.

Some mothers avoid being "left" by taking active control of their toddler's steps toward bodily self-care. Instead of heeding and responding to his signals of readiness and self-initiative, they are intent on teaching him each skill, and insist on his doing his "chores" when they consider it the right time, which means, their time. In doing so, they both push him away and retain ownership of his body because the process proceeds at their behest, while the child feels the threat of abandonment and needs to satisfy mother rather than himself by performing for her.

All these maternal defenses protect her from the threat of losing the part of her body ego that is invested in her child. Unfortunately, they also constitute considerable interference in the child's ability to differentiate and integrate his own body ego and to invest it and his caring for it in an optimally pleasurable, gratifying way.

Many mothers are well aware of the wrench caused by the child's becoming his own person, be it his weaning, dressing himself, entry to nursery school, leaving for summer camp or college, getting married. They feel and verbalize their pain and sadness and, since they are also happy with and proud of his achievements, experience it as a bittersweet time that still allows them to support rather than impede his growth. Yet their awareness, though helpful to them and their child, derives from the more mature parts of their personalities. The primitive anxieties about bodily loss and disintegration surface in the form of sudden unwarranted panic states about losing something, which they in no way connect to the current situation of loss of the child. Let me add a couple of examples to several cited previously (chapter 6).

Example A

Following my presentation of this topic to an analytic group, an experienced analyst confided this episode: That very morning she had looked in vain for the sweater she was now wearing. As she rummaged through her drawers a panic seized her, quite disproportionate to the value of the sweater. She feared she had lost it for good. It finally occurred to her that her married daughter and grandchild had left that morning after a nice visit, and she became convinced that her daughter, who liked the sweater, had taken it with her. She found herself quite angry at her adult child, then opened once again the drawer where the sweater was supposed to be—and there it was. She could not think how she had overlooked it, but she realized now that its presumed disappearance stood for the more profound loss of her daughter.

Example B

The mother of a 2-year-old arrived for our appointment late and distraught. She had been "out of it" during the last four days because she had lost her wallet. She was without cash, credit cards, driver's license. She had searched everything in vain and spent her time telephoning around to stop misuse of the lost documents. She felt she was going crazy, could not function, and she also felt guilty for not being available to her little girl. As she retraced the events, it turned out that the night before the disappearance of the wallet the child had, at her own request, slept in a big bed for the first time, did so with pleasure, and wanted the crib removed. Mother had been pleased and appreciative of her daughter's developmental step but had reneged on removing the crib "in case she changed her mind."

Since the various effects of developmental loss on this mother had been a topic of our work in the past, I wondered with her whether perhaps, in addition to her positive feelings about her child's progress, there were also feelings of losing something very basic to her own self, so basic that it felt like she could not function without it. She connected the losses at once and cried out, "Oh, my goodness, the wallet!" On returning home she called me, greatly relieved. She had found the wallet. It was where she had looked for it before.

Instances of pseudoloss are more or less effective ego measures to bind the emerging primitive experiences occasioned by body-ego loss of the child. We are alerted to them by the primitive panic the mother experiences temporarily, and often by the accompanying anger at the child who, one way or another, is unjustly blamed for the loss or unwittingly "punished" for it, such as by mother's emotional withdrawal. It is only when mother and child reach an impasse during the transfer process, or when the child reacts with symptomatic behaviors that upset the mother enough to request help, that the ensuing therapeutic work reveals a glimpse of the forces that underlie mother's manifest idiosyncracies.

Example C

One mother came for help with her 18-month-old's persistent sleep disturbance which manifested itself in not going to sleep, waking repeatedly, and getting up very early. It "ruined" mother's life and she was also concerned for him, fearing she was doing something wrong. She was not concerned about his still frequent nursing, lack of self-feeding, and showing no initiative in other areas of bodily self-care. We came to understand that his sleep trouble related on the one hand to his total dependence on her ministrations, without any means of self-comfort (thumb-sucking, transitional object, or soft toy); on the other hand, it related to her many irregular absences during the day as well as emotional withdrawals when she was physically present. With closer observation we learned that her absences often appeared to be prompted by her son's even minor steps toward independence.

When his sleep trouble improved with the help of her increased insight and changes in handling, it suddenly got worse again. It turned out she had just begun an exercise program in the early mornings which made it necessary for the father to attend to the boy on his waking up. She felt she had to exercise "to get myself in shape and put my body together"—a rather common maternal response to the loss of the child as part of her body. With further insight into their mutual conflict about bodily ownership and delineation of body boundaries, she stopped the exercises, remained available in the morning, and his sleep again improved.

Then the following episode took place which frightened mother and child: She had always carried him downstairs, considering his learning to negotiate the stairs too unsafe. He had wanted to walk on his own on several occasions, but she reneged. That morning she again carried him downstairs, stumbled under the weight, and both fell headlong, sustaining minor injuries. She found herself in a rage and lashed out at him with, "See what you've done! You are much too big and heavy to be carried. From now on you will just have to get yourself downstairs on your own." She was chagrined and puzzled about her outburst and later apologized to him. She could begin to recognize that her need to thwart his "leaving" her and to push him away instead of supporting his independent steps warded off her sense of panic and rage at being "cut off."

She was not an abusive mother. Her anger was usually in good control, and she wished for and appreciated her child's achievements in many areas. His bodily independence, however, constituted such a threat to her bodily integrity that her experience of it overtook the more mature aspects of her personality and allowed primitive panic and rage to surface.

THE NATURE OF THE MATERNAL, FEMALE BODY EGO AND SOME CONSEQUENCES

Some mothers can never allow their child to delineate and own his body ego for fear of what it would do to themselves and what they would do to him. Some can, with much effort, take the necessary steps if they are helped to gain sufficient insight into the nature of their predicament, and if this work takes place in the context of a containing, supportive relationship. With less vulnerable mothers, such support does not need to be available through a therapist but can come through the relationship with an emotionally available husband, grandmother, or close friend (chapter 6).

The mother's psychic state at the time of these shattering experiences of bodily loss resembles those of an older infant or young toddler during the period of initial differentiation from the mother when his primitive, incomplete body ego is overwhelmed from within or without, or when the still essential parts of his mother's ego have disappeared, such as through her physical or emotional unavailability. He can only reconstitute his body ego by being bodily contained within the mother's, such as through her empathic holding and soothing of him. The extent to which the early states of bodily disintegration were effectively contained and repaired will determine how quickly and well he will later be able to use his own more mature personality parts to protect himself from such overwhelming, or to contain and repair them when they occur.

I have come to understand that the maternal body ego, and therefore motherhood itself, is characterized by never fully delineating itself. The female body ego is flexible, adapted to include a baby within its boundaries not only during pregnancy in its inside space, but also after birth when the child is physically outside the mother. This so essential extension of the mother's body ego to her child (how else could she care for him round the clock, often sacrificing satisfaction of her own bodily needs?) does, however, need to be renounced bit by bit and handed over to the child when he wants it as his own. Having thus far underlined the stressful and distressing aspects of the maternal body ego, let me emphasize that its flexibility and ease of encompassing the internal and external child are also a source of enormous bodily and mental gratification. It would not be so hard to give up something if it had not been so exquisitely and basically satisfying.

Graciously to surrender and even support and enjoy his taking away, as it were, now an arm, now a leg, now a need or function, renders her bodily integrity extremely vulnerable. No wonder mothers want to hold onto these outside parts of themselves or at least control the timing and form of the bodily transfer. No wonder they feel shaken to the core at times when they are not ready for it and are taken by surprise (chapter 6).

Many mothers experience difficulty in including the baby within their body ego when it grows inside them. Glenn's (1993) description of his pregnant patient's bodily sensations could be regarded as exemplifying this. Many avoid getting pregnant or carrying through a pregnancy because the attendant changes in their body ego are too threatening to their sense of bodily wholeness. Many experience great difficulty in letting the inside baby go (which contributes to prolonged labor). Many more find it difficult to effect the body ego changes by which the bodily, self-invested inside baby becomes the bodily self-invested outside baby. This contributes to mothers' postnatal depressive or paranoidlike anxieties and is, in part, related to postpartum psychosis.

The lifelong process of "being there to be left" is, however, the hardest and most threatening aspect of motherhood (chapter 4). It never ends. It is repeated with each child. When one speaks of it with mothers they feel deeply understood and tend to respond with tears—not with words because these experiences predate words, predate symbolic representation, predate sexual gender experience in the usual sense of the term.

The maternal capacity to include the inside and outside child within her body boundaries and also to respond to his need for release by allowing him to own this most treasured part of herself, constitutes the mixed blessing of motherhood—its primitive gratifications and dangers. As boys and girls, men and women, we all once were, and to a variable extent remain, a part of our mothers. Our earliest bodily unit with and differentiation from her leave us with a sense of the power and vulnerability of her flexible, undelineated body ego. This engenders awe, envy, terror, and all the defenses against them. It is a part of the way our own body ego is formed and maintained and serves as the matrix for sex-specific gender development (chapter 8).

DELINEATING AND INVESTING ONE'S OWN BODY EGO

Since the early seminal contributions by Winnicott (1941) and Hoffer (1949, 1950), there have been many studies of the ways infants and toddlers use their sensations and perceptions to form their own body ego, to delineate it as an increasingly complete entity, including the genitals and their sexual function, and to invest it narcissistically. Much less has been said and understood about how protracted and difficult this process of integration is and how much it depends on the role of the mother. During infancy and toddlerhood the child's progress toward owning and investing his own circumscribed body ego depends crucially on the mother's capacity to facilitate, or at least to tolerate, this development. It proceeds most markedly through their interactions around needs and the related impulses during the transition from mother's care to self-care.

The mother's vulnerability and difficulty in surrendering her narcissistic investment of the child's body and retracting the boundaries of her body ego accordingly have already been described. The healthy child's striving for autonomy is usually zestful (he has more to gain than to lose), but for him, too, there are satisfactions in owning mother's body and being owned by her. Being one's own separate person means relinquishing her omnipotence, having to make do with one's limited capabilities, and bearing the frustrations of working toward mastery. Just as the mother never fully withdraws her cathexis of the child's body, so the child too retains a measure of his early bodily unit with the mother.

SOME DIFFERENCES BETWEEN BOYS' AND GIRLS' BODY EGO

In keeping with the different biological roles of men and women, boys' and girls' body egos develop along different lines. Among the several authors who have, as mentioned, studied the girl's recognition and investment of her inside genital organs, destined to become child bearing, Kestenberg (1956b) views the girl toddler's early doll play as an externalization of her internal sensations and means of mastery as well as a preparation for motherhood.

My observations of toddlers and data available through treatment via the parent and the analyses of girls confirm Kestenberg's findings, and provide some additional material (chapter 8; Furman, 1992a, 1993a, chapter 6). Just prior to and often overlapping with the adoption of the baby doll, toddler girls tend to adopt a container—a bag, purse, little box—which they treasure and fill with precious items. Mothers vary in supporting this activity. Sometimes they give their little daughter an old purse of their own to use; sometimes they provide special items to put into it to keep. Insofar as they are comfortable with their own motherly body, they at least regard the child's behavior with bemused appreciation. I have come to view this developmental step as a sign of the inside space being integrated into the growing body ego and serving as a precursor to the doll play—the transition from the inside baby to the outside baby. Sometimes this transition is made quite explicit; for example, when the treasured container is filled with a little figure or soft toy. Sometimes all containers have to be filled with a potential baby, such as when little Mary inspected her childless aunt's pretty bowl on the coffee table and then, just before leaving, placed a little teddy in it, molding it into the concave space.

I describe elsewhere (chapters 6 and 8) how the baby doll and the maternal caring activities performed with it become such an invested part of the girl's body ego that she spontaneously remembers it, talks about it, worries about it when they are separated, and rushes to embrace it on their reunion, such as on returning home after a walk without the doll.

In other words, in normal body ego development, given mother's facilitation and absence of bodily overwhelming (illness, abuse, medical–surgical treatments), the girl toddler's body-ego integration allows for the potential of including an inside and outside baby, retains flexible boundaries, and tolerates, by virtue of same, a measure of bodily interdependence with her mother. Her maternal development is part and parcel of her gender identity. As little Mary, by then a bit older, put it one day, seemingly out of the blue, "Mommy, when you have your next baby, will you please give it to me." Mary had not been in the company of babies, and her parents intended her to remain the youngest. Winnicott (1964) describes the maternal capacity for changeable boundaries as woman always being also someone else, with mother, grandmother, and little girl interchangeable within her, whereas man is all unto himself.

The boy's body-ego integration and related narcissistic distribution is indeed quite different. He too grows out of the joint mother–child bodily matrix, reflected perhaps in "feeding" his penis and owning mother's breast or elimination. He too includes items outside his body as part of himself as he carries around a briefcase or tool box, becomes absorbed in big machines and how they work, or feeds his soft toys. But his precious items do not go into treasured boxes, they go into his pockets. As he assumes ownership of his bodily functions and their care, including his penis, he encloses them within the clearly delineated boundaries of his body ego. This is often reflected in his play (so different from the girl's) which focuses on creating a circumscribed space, such as the circular or oval train track or block-built corral for the toy animals. I view this as a sign of body-ego integration, comparable to the girl's treasured box.

With the boy, as with the girl, a measure of mutual bodily investment remains part of him and of the mother–child relationship. Insofar as his body-ego outlines achieve sufficient stability and narcissistic self-investment, these remnants will serve him adaptively—to be attracted to potential mothers, to allow temporary loss of ego boundaries with them in sexual intercourse, and to value, empathize with, and appreciate their mothering. But when the mother's facilitation and the child's self-delineation are not sufficiently successful, the remnants of the primary bodily unit with its unstable boundaries of encompassing the mother and being encompased by her may become a lasting threat to the integrity of their basic body ego—a dread of mothers and of mothering. Such dread, primitive as it is for both sexes, is, of course, warded off by an array of defenses. This becomes incorporated in later characterological or symptomatic attitudes to mothers and women, including avoidance, denigration, idealization, and phallic monism. It affects later conflicts and compromise formations. It also plays a marked part in anorexia and bulemia and contributes to homosexual orientation in men and women. Regardless of its effect on sex- and gender-related personality aspects, the early phase of struggling to achieve a stably invested body ego is, for all of us, a source of potential creativity in many spheres.

THE ROLE OF THE FATHER

Boys especially, but girls too, are greatly helped with the differentiation and boundaries of their body ego by being able to relate with their father. Among the many benefits of the father–toddler relationship, I want to underline a specific one, pertinent to this context. It is the fact that the father's body ego is clearly and stably delineated, however much he may want to include the child as a bodily part of himself and be motherly in this sense, and however much the child is tempted to effect such a bodily unit with him. It is a big help to sense that fathers are and remain physically separate, can therefore support the child's separateness and can, at the same time, relate with and tolerate mother's relative lack of separateness. I am speaking, of course, of the role of the father in addition to the mother and do not wish to imply that body-ego formation is facilitated by not experiencing a bodily unit with the mother to start with (Furman, 1992a, 1993a).

SOME IMPLICATIONS FOR LATER DEVELOPMENT

As with all areas of personality, the development of sexual gender is made up of a series of interrelated steps. The earliest strata described above are as significant in affecting the subsequent ones as the latter are in modifying and integrating the preceding ones. To understand the relative contribution of each we have to be in feeling touch with all. Our difficulties in recognizing and appreciating the role of the bodily mother–child matrix and its effect on body-ego and gender development are, inevitably, handicapped by the fact that these experiences are preverbal and preconceptual and arouse very primitive annihilation anxieties. It may therefore be easier for us to identify women by their lack of a penis or to prove that women do not lack anything, and to disregard the role of motherhood. Yet these views may owe their intensity and persistence to the fact that *women do lack something, namely, clearly delineated, stable body-ego boundaries.*

Lack of a penis brings the threat of castration fear. Lack of body-ego boundaries brings the much more overwhelming, primitive threat of annihilation anxiety. This danger, to an extent, is part of motherhood. It is a very immediate threat to all men and women who encountered difficulty in differentiating and investing their body ego. The greater the threat, the stronger are women's defenses against owning and using their maternal body ego and men's against empathizing with and appreciating mothers and their mothering (chapter 6). Inevitably, this threat also contributes to difficulty in resolving later developmental conflicts and shapes the resulting compromise formations. Colleagues who analyze adults have personally shared such findings and found it helpful to trace and interpret the early origins of these pathologies. I hope they will, in time, publish their material and that others will contribute to the further elucidation of the links between the investment and differentiation of the basic body ego and later disturbances.

Afterword

For all the lip service we pay to an idealized picture of motherhood, in our daily lives motherhood is grossly underrated—the job that requires no skill and no pay, can be done by anyone but isn't really a job at all. Men and women often think of "at home" mothers as taking a holiday and being unproductive. Yet, all working mothers know that no workplace is as relentlessly demanding and frustrating as ongoing care of child and home—unbearable, except that, at least at times, it brings the richest and deepest moments of satisfaction.

Motherhood is indeed a deeply disconcerting part of our emotional lives—tempting, threatening, enviable, abhorrent, gratifying, exasperating—everywhere, always. It helps to recognize it for what it is, in all its richly textured uncontained complexity. In his brief essay on "The Mother's Contribution to Society" Winnicott (1957b) expressed a feeling I profoundly share: When even a single man or woman can acknowledge, accept and lend support to all that being and having a mother entails, it helps to make our families, societies, world a safer, kinder place to live in. Perhaps this book will do its bit along this way.

Erna Furman

References

Annual School Center Award (1991), *Child Analysis,* 2:2–3.
——— (1992), *Child Analysis,* 3:2–3.
Bain, A. J. K., & Barnett, L. E. (1980), *The Design of a Day Care System in a Nursery Setting for Children Under Five.* London: Tavistock Institute of Human Relations.
Benedek, T. (1959), Parenthood as a developmental phase: A contribution to the libido theory. *J. Amer. Psychoanal. Assn.,* 7:389–417.
Chasseguet-Smirgel, J. (1976), Freud and female sexuality. *Internat. J. Psycho-Anal.,* 57:275–286.
Daunton, E. (1969), Diagnosis. In: *The Therapeutic Nursery School,* ed. R. A. Furman & A. Katan. New York: International Universities Press, pp. 204–214.
Edgecumbe, R., & Burgner, M. (1975), The phallic–narcissistic phase: A differentiation between preoedipal and oedipal aspects of phallic development. *The Psychoanalytic Study of the Child,* 30:161–180. New Haven, CT: Yale University Press.
Erikson, E. H. (1956), The problem of ego identity. *J. Amer. Psychoanal. Assn.,* 4:56–121.
——— (1964), Womanhood and the inner space. In: *Identity, Youth and Crisis.* New York: W. W. Norton, 1968, pp. 261–294.
Fiedler, E. S. (1974), Danny. In: *A Child's Parent Dies,* ed. E. Furman. New Haven, CT: Yale University Press, pp. 198–218.
Freud, A. (1935–1982), Katan Correspondence. The Katan Archives. The Cleveland Center for Research in Child Development, 2084, Cornell Road, Cleveland, Ohio 44106.
——— (1953), Some remarks on infant observation. *The Psychoanalytic Study of the Child,* 8:9–19. New York: International Universities Press.

———— (1964), Comments on psychic trauma. In: *The Writings of Anna Freud,* 5:221–241. New York: International Universities Press.
———— (1967), About losing and being lost. *The Psychoanalytic Study of the Child,* 22:9–19. New York: International Universities Press.
———— Burlingham, D. (1943), *War and Children.* New York: International Universities Press.
———— ———— (1944), Infants without families. In: *The Writings of Anna Freud,* 3:541–664. New York: International Universities Press, 1973.
Freud, S. (1917), Mourning and melancholia. *Standard Edition,* 14:237–258. London: Hogarth Press, 1957.
———— (1916–1917), Introductory Lectures on Psycho-Analysis. *Standard Edition,* 15 & 16. London: Hogarth Press, 1961.
———— (1920), Beyond the Pleasure Principle. *Standard Edition,* 18:1–64. London: Hogarth Press, 1955.
Furman, E. (1956), An ego disturbance in a young child. *The Psychoanalytic Study of the Child,* 11:312–335. New York: International Universities Press.
———— (1957), Treatment of under-fives by way of the parent. *The Psychoanalytic Study of the Child,* 12:250–262. New York: International Universities Press.
———— (1966), Parenthood as a developmental phase. Presented at the first scientific meeting of the Association for Child Psychoanalysis, Topeka, Kansas.
———— (1967), The latency child as an active participant in the analytic work. In: *The Child Analyst at Work,* ed. E. Geleerd. New York: International Universities Press, pp. 142–184.
———— (1969a), Treatment via the mother. In: *The Therapeutic Nursery School,* ed. R. A. Furman & A. Katan. New York: International Universities Press, pp. 64–123.
———— (1969b), Observations on entry to nursery school. *Bull. Phila. Assn. Psychoanal.,* 19(3):133–152.
———— (1974), *A Child's Parent Dies.* New Haven, CT: Yale University Press.
———— (1977a), The roles of parents and teachers in the life of the young child. In: *What Nursery School Teachers Ask Us About.* Madison, CT: International Universities Press, 1986, pp. 3–20.
———— (1977b), Readiness for kindergarten. In: *What Nursery School Teachers Ask Us About.* Madison, CT: International Universities Press, 1986, pp. 207–234.

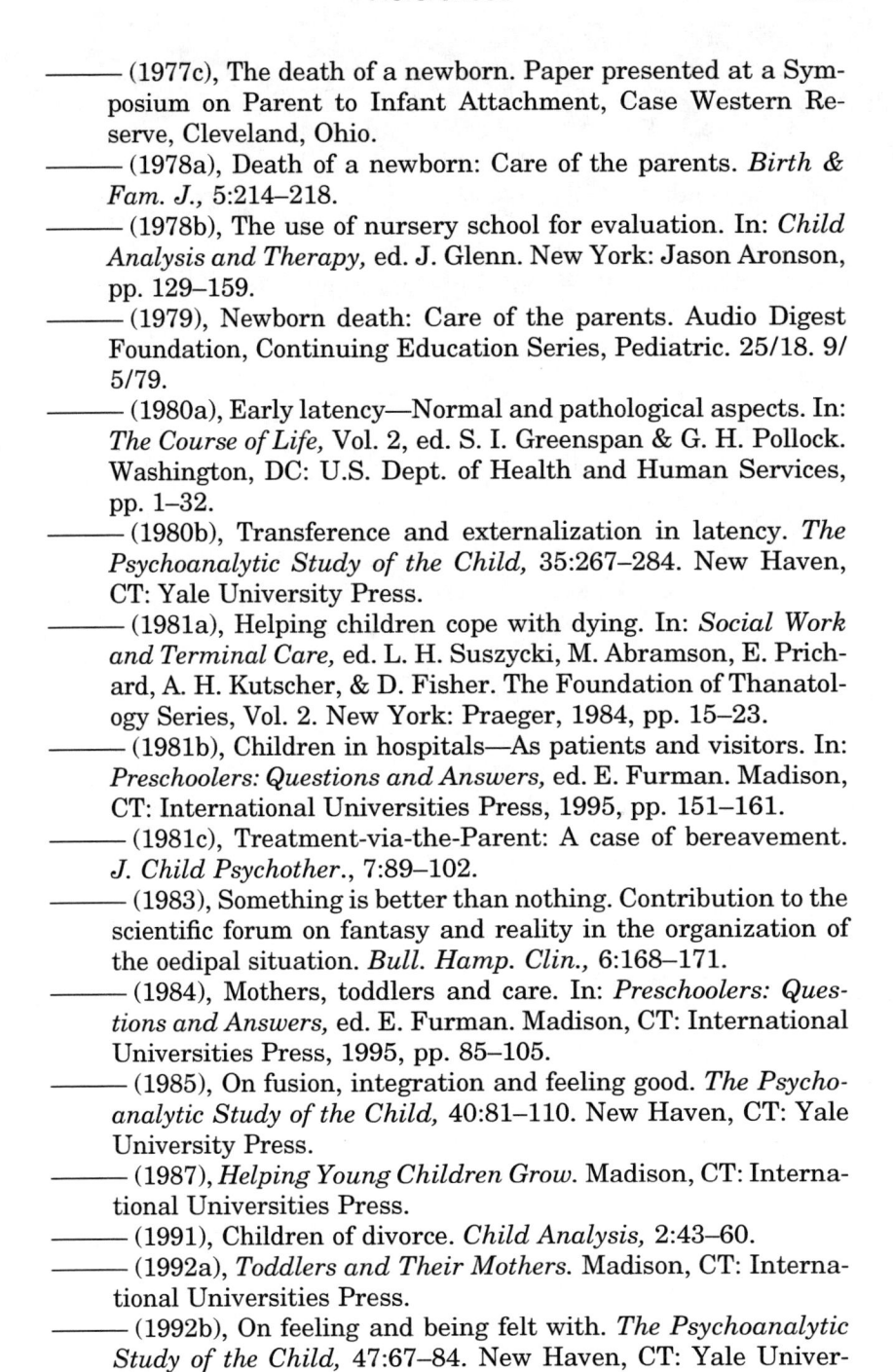

——— (1977c), The death of a newborn. Paper presented at a Symposium on Parent to Infant Attachment, Case Western Reserve, Cleveland, Ohio.

——— (1978a), Death of a newborn: Care of the parents. *Birth & Fam. J.,* 5:214–218.

——— (1978b), The use of nursery school for evaluation. In: *Child Analysis and Therapy,* ed. J. Glenn. New York: Jason Aronson, pp. 129–159.

——— (1979), Newborn death: Care of the parents. Audio Digest Foundation, Continuing Education Series, Pediatric. 25/18. 9/5/79.

——— (1980a), Early latency—Normal and pathological aspects. In: *The Course of Life,* Vol. 2, ed. S. I. Greenspan & G. H. Pollock. Washington, DC: U.S. Dept. of Health and Human Services, pp. 1–32.

——— (1980b), Transference and externalization in latency. *The Psychoanalytic Study of the Child,* 35:267–284. New Haven, CT: Yale University Press.

——— (1981a), Helping children cope with dying. In: *Social Work and Terminal Care,* ed. L. H. Suszycki, M. Abramson, E. Prichard, A. H. Kutscher, & D. Fisher. The Foundation of Thanatology Series, Vol. 2. New York: Praeger, 1984, pp. 15–23.

——— (1981b), Children in hospitals—As patients and visitors. In: *Preschoolers: Questions and Answers,* ed. E. Furman. Madison, CT: International Universities Press, 1995, pp. 151–161.

——— (1981c), Treatment-via-the-Parent: A case of bereavement. *J. Child Psychother.,* 7:89–102.

——— (1983), Something is better than nothing. Contribution to the scientific forum on fantasy and reality in the organization of the oedipal situation. *Bull. Hamp. Clin.,* 6:168–171.

——— (1984), Mothers, toddlers and care. In: *Preschoolers: Questions and Answers,* ed. E. Furman. Madison, CT: International Universities Press, 1995, pp. 85–105.

——— (1985), On fusion, integration and feeling good. *The Psychoanalytic Study of the Child,* 40:81–110. New Haven, CT: Yale University Press.

——— (1987), *Helping Young Children Grow.* Madison, CT: International Universities Press.

——— (1991), Children of divorce. *Child Analysis,* 2:43–60.

——— (1992a), *Toddlers and Their Mothers.* Madison, CT: International Universities Press.

——— (1992b), On feeling and being felt with. *The Psychoanalytic Study of the Child,* 47:67–84. New Haven, CT: Yale University Press.

——— (1992c), What is depression in childhood? *Child Analysis,* 3:101–123.
——— (1992d), Working with and through the parents in child therapy. *Child Analysis,* 6:21–42, 1995.
——— (1993a), *Toddlers and Their Mothers: Abridged Version for Parents and Educators.* Madison, CT: International Universities Press.
——— (1993b), Helping with prevention and treatment of sexual abuse. *Child Analysis,* 4:113–129.
——— (1995), Sexual abuse: Experiences with prevention, detection and treatment. In: *Preschoolers: Questions and Answers,* ed. E. Furman. Madison, CT: International Universities Press, pp. 163–178.
——— (1996), Parenting the hospitalized child. *Child Analysis,* 7:88–112.
Furman, R. A. (1966), Experiences in nursery school consultations. In: *Ideas That Work with Young Children,* ed. K. Baker. Washington, DC: National Association for the Education of Young Children, 1972, pp. 225–236.
——— (1971), Helping children cope with stress. In: *Preschoolers: Questions and Answers,* ed. E. Furman. Madison, CT: International Universities Press, 1995, pp. 51–64.
——— (1980), Some vicissitudes of the transition into latency. In: *The Course of Life,* Vol. 2, ed. S. I. Greenspan & G. H. Pollock. Madison, CT: International Universities Press, 1991, pp. 205–219.
——— (1984a), The father–child relationship. Pamphlet Series of the Cleveland Center for Research in Child Development, 2084 Cornell Road, Cleveland, Ohio 44106.
——— (1984b), On toilet mastery. *Child Analysis,* 2:98–110, 1991.
——— (1986), The father–child relationship. In: *What Nursery School Teachers Ask Us About.* Madison, CT: International Universities Press, pp. 21–34.
——— (1988a), On preparation: "New" perspectives. In: *Preschoolers: Questions and Answers,* ed. E. Furman. Madison, CT: International Universities Press, 1995, pp. 37–50.
——— (1988b), Object removal revisited. *Internat. Rev. Psycho-Anal.,* 15:165–176.
——— Furman, E. (1984), Intermittent decathexis: A type of parental dysfunction. *Internat. J. Psycho-Anal.,* 65:423–433.
——— Katan, A., Eds. (1969), *The Therapeutic Nursery School.* New York: International Universities Press.
Galenson, E., & Roiphe, H. (1971), The impact of early sexual discovery on mood, defensive organization and symbolization. *The*

Psychoanalytic Study of the Child, 26:196–216. New York: Quadrangle Books.

——— ——— (1974), The emergence of genital awareness during the second year of life. In: *Sex Differences in Behavior,* ed. R. C. Friedman, R. M. Richart, & R. L. Van de Wiele. New York: John Wiley, pp. 223–231.

——— ——— (1980), The preoedipal development of the boy. *J. Amer. Psychoanal. Assn.,* 28:805–827.

Gauderer, M. W. L., Long, J. L., & Eastwood, D. W. (1989), Is there a place for parents in the operating room? *J. Pediatr. Surg.,* 24:705–707.

Glenn, J. (1993), Developmental transformation: The Isakower phenomenon as an example. *J. Amer. Psychoanal. Assn.,* 41:1113–1134.

Goldman, M. W. (1974), Addie. In: *A Child's Parent Dies,* ed. E. Furman. New Haven, CT: Yale University Press, pp. 140–148.

Greenson, R. R. (1949), The psychology of apathy. *Psychoanal. Quart.,* 18:290–302.

Hägglund, T.-B., Hägglund, V., & Ikonen, P. (1978), Some viewpoints on woman's inner space. *Scand. Psychoanal. Rev.,* 1:65–77.

——— Pika, H. (1980), The inner space of the body imago. *Psychoanal. Quart.,* 49:256–283.

Hägglund, V. (1981), Feminine sexuality and its development. *Scand. Psychoanal. Rev.,* 4:127–150.

Hall, R. (1991), Working with parents. In: *Preschoolers: Questions and Answers,* ed. E. Furman. Madison, CT: International Universities Press, 1995, pp. 65–77.

Hanson, C., & Strawser, (1993), Family presence during cardiopulmonary resuscitation: Foote Hospital emergency department's nine-year perspective. *J. Emerg. Nurs.,* 18(2):104–106.

Harrison, H. (1993), The principles for family-centered neonatal care. *Pediatrics,* 82(5):643–650.

Hoffer, W. (1949), Mouth, hand and ego integration. *The Psychoanalytic Study of the Child,* 3/4:49–56. New York: International Universities Press.

——— (1950), Development of the body ego. *The Psychoanalytic Study of the Child,* 5:18–24. New York: International Universities Press.

——— (1952), The mutual influences in the development of ego and id: Earliest stages. *The Psychoanalytic Study of the Child,* 7:31–41. New York: International Universities Press.

Horney, K. (1926), The flight from womanhood: The masculinity complex in women as viewed by men and women. *Internat. J. Psycho-Anal.,* 7:324–339.
——— (1932), The dread of woman. Observations on a specific difference in the dread felt by men and by women respectively for the opposite sex. *Internat. J. Psycho-Anal.,* 13:348–368.
Jacobson, E. (1954), Contribution to the metapsychology of psychotic identifications. *J. Amer. Psychoanal. Assn.,* 2:239–262.
Katan, A. (1937), The role of "displacement" in agoraphobia. *Internat. J. Psycho-Anal.,* 32:1–10, 1951.
——— (1960), Distortions of the phallic phase. *The Psychoanalytic Study of the Child,* 15:208–214. New York: International Universities Press.
——— (1973), Children who were raped. *The Psychoanalytic Study of the Child,* 28:208–224. New York: International Universities Press.
Kestenberg, J. (1956a), On the development of maternal feelings in early childhood: Observations and reflections. *The Psychoanalytic Study of the Child,* 7:31–41. New York: International Universities Press.
——— (1956b), Vicissitudes of female sexuality. *J. Amer. Psychoanal. Assn.,* 4:453–476.
——— (1956c), On the development of maternal feelings in early childhood: Observations and reflections. *The Psychoanalytic Study of the Child,* 11:257–291.
——— (1968), Outside and inside, male and female. In: *Children and Parents.* New York: Jason Aronson, 1975, pp. 101–154.
Klaus, M. H., & Kendell, J. H. (1976), *Maternal-Infant Bonding.* St. Louis: C. V. Mosby.
Klein, M. (1934), A contribution to the psychogenesis of manic-depressive states. *Internat. J. Psycho-Anal.,* 16:145–174.
——— (1940), Mourning and its relation to manic-depressive states. *Internat. J. Psycho-Anal.,* 21:125–153.
——— (1957), *Envy and Gratitude.* London: Tavistock.
Krementz, J. (1984), *How It Feels When Parents Divorce.* New York: Alfred A. Knopf.
Mahler, M. S. (1963), Thoughts about development and individuation. *The Psychoanalytic Study of the Child,* 18:307–324. New York: International Universities Press.
——— (1972), On the first three subphases of the separation-individuation process. *Internat. J. Psycho-Anal.,* 53:333–338.
——— Pine, F., & Bergman, A. (1975), *The Psychological Birth of the Human Infant.* New York: Basic Books.

References

Mause, L. de. (1974), The evolution of childhood. In: *The History of Childhood,* ed. L. de Mause. London: Souvenir Press, 1980, pp. 1–73.

Maynard, R. C. (1985), Young people seek family-core values. *The Plain Dealer,* July 11, p. 23A.

Meiss, M. (1952), The oedipal problem of a fatherless child. *The Psychoanalytic Study of the Child,* 7:216–229. New York: International Universities Press.

Neubauer, P. B. (1960), The one-parent child and his oedipal development. *The Psychoanalytic Study of the Child,* 15:286–309. New York: International Universities Press.

Niklas, S. (1993), Making a difference for the dying child. Paper presented at the Twenty-Five Years of Child Life at Rainbow Babies and Children's Symposium, October, Cleveland, Ohio.

Panel (1984). Trauma revisited. Association for Child Psychoanalysis. London.

Provence, S., Naylor, A., & Patterson, J. (1977), *The Challenge of Daycare.* New Haven, CT: Yale University Press.

Reich, A. (1954), Early identifications as archaic elements in the superego. *J. Amer. Psychoanal. Assn.,* 2:218–310.

Rosenfeld, S. K., & Sprince, M. P. (1965), Some thoughts on the technical handling of borderline children. *The Psychoanalytic Study of the Child,* 20:495–517. New York: International Universities Press.

Schiff, E. J. (1974), Jim. In: *A Child's Parent Dies,* ed. E. Furman. New Haven, CT: Yale University Press, pp. 88–95.

Spitz, R. A. (1945), Hospitalism: An inquiry into the genesis of psychiatric conditions in early childhood. I. *The Psychoanalytic Study of the Child,* 1:53–74. New York: International Universities Press.

——— (1946), Anaclitic depression: An inquiry into the genesis of psychiatric conditions in early childhood. II. *The Psychoanalytic Study of the Child,* 2:313–342. New York: International Universities Press.

Spock, B. (1963), Striving for autonomy and regressive relationships. *The Psychoanalytic Study of the Child,* 18:361–364. New York: International Universities Press.

Tate, T. W., & Ammerman, D. L., Eds. (1979), *The Chesapeake in the Seventeenth Century—Essays on Anglo-American Society and Politics.* Chapel Hill, NC: University of North Carolina Press.

Thomas, R. D. (1977), *The Man Who Would Be Perfect.* Philadelphia: University of Pennsylvania Press.

Tolstoy, L. (1876), *Anna Karenina,* tr. J. Carmichael. New York: Bantam, 1960.
Torsti, M. (1993), The feminine self and body image. *Scand. Psychoanal. Rev.,* 16:47–62.
Tustin, F. (1973), *Autism and Childhood Psychosis.* New York: Jason Aronson.
Tyson, P. (1994), Bedrock and beyond: An examination of the clinical utility of contemporary theories of female psychology. *J. Amer. Psychoanal. Assn.,* 42:447–467.
Wallerstein, J. S. (1985a), The overburdened child: Some long-term consequences of divorce. *Social Work,* 30(2):116–123.
——— (1985b), Children of divorce: Preliminary report of a ten-year follow-up of older children and adolescents. *J. Amer. Acad. Child Psychiatry,* 24(5):545–553.
——— (1986), Women after divorce: Preliminary report from a ten-year follow-up. *Amer. J. Orthopsychiatry,* 56:65–77.
Weil, J. (1989a), *Instinctual Stimulation of Children: From Common Practice to Child Abuse,* Vol. 1. *Clinical Findings.* Madison, CT: International Universities Press.
——— (1989b), *Instinctual Stimulation of Children: From Common Practice to Child Abuse,* Vol. 2. *Clinical Cases.* Madison, CT: International Universities Press.
White, D. W. (1978), *The First Three Years of Life.* New York: Avon Books.
Winnicott, D. W. (1941), The observation of infants in a set situation. In: *Through Paediatrics to Psycho-Analysis.* New York: Basic Books, 1958, pp. 52–69.
——— (1949), *The Ordinary Devoted Mother and Her Baby: Nine Broadcast Talks.* London: Brock.
——— (1953), Transitional objects and transitional phenomena. In: *Playing and Reality.* New York: Basic Books, 1971, pp. 1–25
——— (1954), The depressive position in normal emotional development. In: *Through Paediatrics to Psycho-Analysis.* New York: Basic Books, pp. 262–277.
——— (1957a), *Mother and Child.* New York: Basic Books.
——— (1957b), The mother's contribution to society. In: *The Child and the Family.* London: Tavistock.
——— (1958), The capacity to be alone. In: *The Maturational Processes and the Facilitating Environment.* New York: International Universities Press, pp. 29–36.
——— (1960a), The theory of the parent–infant relationship. In: *The Maturational Processes and the Facilitating Environment.* New York: International Universities Press, pp. 37–55.

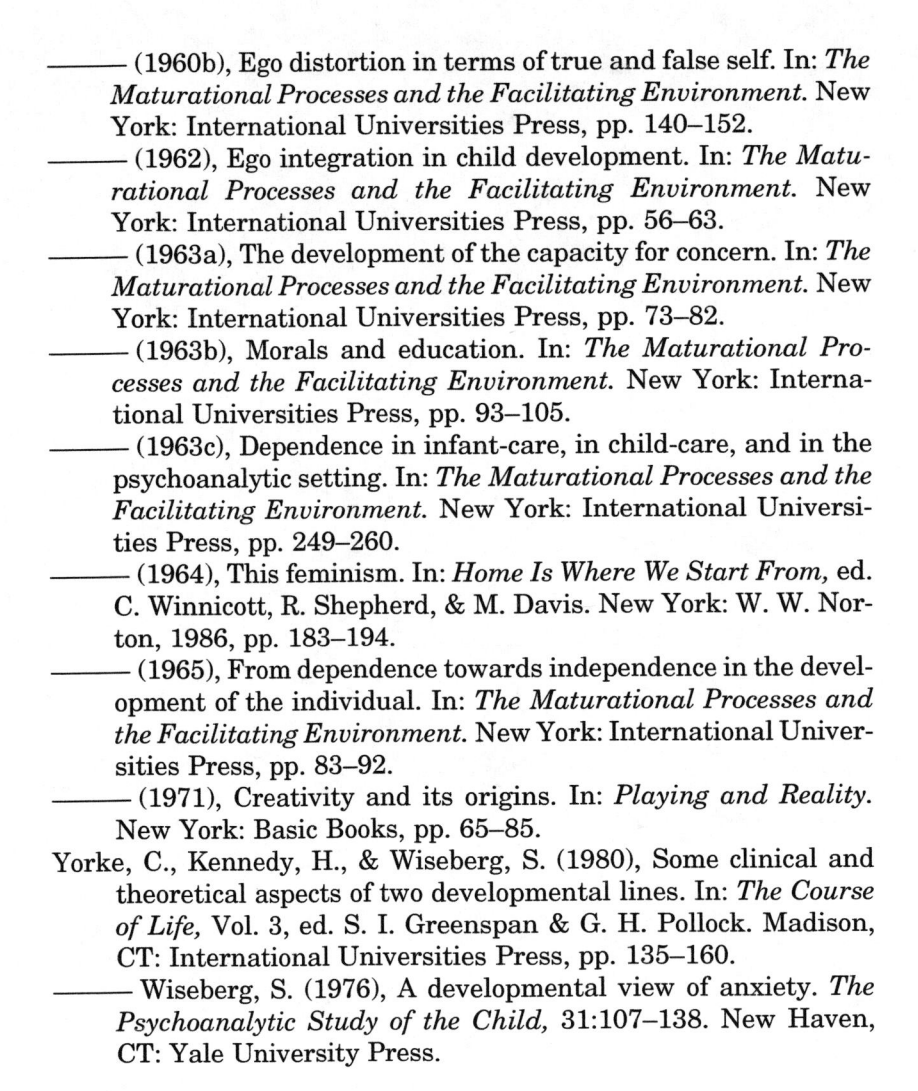

——— (1960b), Ego distortion in terms of true and false self. In: *The Maturational Processes and the Facilitating Environment.* New York: International Universities Press, pp. 140–152.

——— (1962), Ego integration in child development. In: *The Maturational Processes and the Facilitating Environment.* New York: International Universities Press, pp. 56–63.

——— (1963a), The development of the capacity for concern. In: *The Maturational Processes and the Facilitating Environment.* New York: International Universities Press, pp. 73–82.

——— (1963b), Morals and education. In: *The Maturational Processes and the Facilitating Environment.* New York: International Universities Press, pp. 93–105.

——— (1963c), Dependence in infant-care, in child-care, and in the psychoanalytic setting. In: *The Maturational Processes and the Facilitating Environment.* New York: International Universities Press, pp. 249–260.

——— (1964), This feminism. In: *Home Is Where We Start From,* ed. C. Winnicott, R. Shepherd, & M. Davis. New York: W. W. Norton, 1986, pp. 183–194.

——— (1965), From dependence towards independence in the development of the individual. In: *The Maturational Processes and the Facilitating Environment.* New York: International Universities Press, pp. 83–92.

——— (1971), Creativity and its origins. In: *Playing and Reality.* New York: Basic Books, pp. 65–85.

Yorke, C., Kennedy, H., & Wiseberg, S. (1980), Some clinical and theoretical aspects of two developmental lines. In: *The Course of Life,* Vol. 3, ed. S. I. Greenspan & G. H. Pollock. Madison, CT: International Universities Press, pp. 135–160.

——— Wiseberg, S. (1976), A developmental view of anxiety. *The Psychoanalytic Study of the Child,* 31:107–138. New Haven, CT: Yale University Press.

Name Index

Ammerman, D. L., 112

Bain, A. J. K., 113
Barkey, M., 154n
Barnett, L. E., 113
Benedek, T., 21n
Bergman, A., 43
Bline, D., 154n
Bowers, M., 154n
Burgner, M., 176–177
Burlingham, D., 113

Chassequet-Smirgel, J., 202

Daunton, E., 21, 184

Eastwood, D. W., 145
Edgcumbe, R., 176–177
Erikson, E. H., 202

Fiedler, E. S., 131
Freud, A., 39, 69–70, 113, 124, 125, 126, 135, 150, 181
Freud, S., 124, 125, 126–127, 129, 135, 196
Furman, E., vii, x, 20, 21, 22–28, 30, 32, 40, 51, 52, 71, 72, 74, 75, 76–77, 79–80, 90, 93–95, 98, 105, 114, 123, 130, 137, 138, 141–142, 147–148, 149, 150, 152, 155, 162, 173, 176, 178, 179, 180, 181, 184, 191, 193, 202, 205, 213–214, 216, 125–126
Furman, R. A., vii, 22, 40, 50n, 51, 71, 72, 90, 93n, 142, 149, 155–156, 163, 174, 176, 182, 183, 194, 196, 198

Galenson, E., 93n
Gauderer, M. W. L., 145
Glenn, J., 212
Goldman, W., 155
Greenson, R. R., 125

Hägglund, T.-B., 81, 96, 202
Hägglund, V., 81, 96, 202
Hall, R., 149
Hanson, C., 146
Harrison, H., 146
Hoffer, W., 75, 86, 90–91, 212–213
Horney, K., 202

Ikonen, P., 96

Jacobson, E., 196

Katan, A., vii, 22, 40, 71, 72, 94, 128, 137, 156, 157, 174, 196, 198
Kennedy, H., 125, 126–127
Kennell, J. H., 29–31, 105.
Kestenberg, J., 80–81, 96, 202, 213–214
Klaus, M. H., 29 31, 105

231

Klein, M., 43
Krementz, J., 164

Long, J. L., 145

Mahler, M. S., 43, 162n
Mause, L. de, 99
Maynard, R. C., 183
Meiss, M., 193

Naylor, A., 113
Neubauer, P. B., 182, 184, 193
Niklas, S., 152–153, 154n

Patterson, J., 113
Pika, H., 81, 202
Pine, F., 43
Provence, S., 113

Reich, A., 193, 195
Roiphe, H., 93n
Rosenfeld, S. K., 181

Schiff, E. J., 134
Silver, 97
Smith,B., 154n
Spitz, R. A., 150
Spock, B., 44
Sprince, M. P., 181
Strawser, 146

Tate, T. W.,. 112
Thomas, R. D., 112
Tolstoy, L., vii, 1–20, 157
Torsti, M., 96, 202
Tyson, P., 201–202

Wallerstein, J., 158
Weil, J., 92
White, D. W., 113
Winnicott, D. W., 11, 32, 40n, 43, 72, 81, 100, 124, 127, 212–213, 214–215, 219
Wiseberg, S., 125, 126–127

Yorke, C., 125, 126–127

Subject Index

Abandonment
　with child's independence, 43–44
　fear of, 205
　narcissistic vulnerability and, 73–74
Accident proneness, 131
Adaptive narcissistic involvement, 79–91
Adolescence
　developmental tasks of, 198–199
　maturational phase of, 23
　in one-parent family, 197–200
　psychological processes during, 197–198
Aggression
　imbalance of libido with, 162–163, 171–172
　mastery over, 187–188
　of mother toward child, 73–74
　with mother's sense of disintegration, 75–76
　in object removal in adolescence, 176
　unfused, 132–133
Aggression-neutralization-sublimation fusion, 199
Aggressive strivings, containing and managing, 198–199
Ambivalence
　extreme and unmitigated, 185–186
　melancholic mourning and, 196
　in one-parent family, 180–181
　unattenuated in one-parent family, 184
Amputation, coping with, 34–36
Amputees, outsiders' reaction to, 36
Anger, over parents' divorce, 163–164
Anna Karenina, vii
　Anna and her son in, 2–5
　Anna's investment in newborn daughter in, 6–8
　Anna's loss of son in, 11–12
　birth and death in, 18–20
　divorce in, 157–158
　Dolly and her children in, 5–6
　hostility in, 15–18
　Kitty as mother in, 10–11
　lover versus son in, 8–10
　meaning of children in, 12–15
　three mothers in, 1
Annihilation anxiety, 127, 135–136
　recurrent, 136–137
　situation-specific, 128
Anxiety
　mother's defenses against, 72–73
　in trauma, 126–127
Apathy, with trauma, 125
Autonomy, child's striving for, 213
Auxiliary ego, 131
　availability of, 135–136
　functioning of, 139

233

in recuperation from trauma,
    136–137
Being there to be left, 39–50, 212
Bereaved children
    study of, 173
    trauma in, 130–134
Bereavement
    with divorce, 159–164
    mother-infant relationship and,
        30–38
Binding process, 126
Blindness, coping with, 34–35
Bodily investment, in child, 203
Bodily loss
    mother's experience of, 211
    primitive anxieties about, 207
Bodily mastery
    lack of self-worth in, 59–60
    shared steps in achieving, 55–61
Bodily maternal investment, ix
Bodily narcissistic cathexis, 75
Bodily ownership, negotiating
    transfer of, 206–210
Bodily self, including child in, 79–80
Bodily self-care
    mastery of, 52–55
    in personality development,
        51–52
Body ego, 52–53. *See also* Female
    body ego; Male body ego
    boys' versus girls', 213–216
    child as part of, 203
    child's independence as threat to,
        86–87
    delineating and investing in,
        212–213
    delineating boundaries of,
        216–217
    early development of, 89–91
    factors facilitating integration of,
        91–93
    father's role in, 216
    gender identity and formation of,
        94
    integration of, 90–91, 214–215
    maternal, female, 210–212

narcissistic vulnerability and,
    83–84
parts of, 85–86
unstable, 79–80
vulnerability of in toddlers, 96–98
Boundaries
    changeable, 214–215
    difficulty delineating, 84–87
    early steps in delineating, 90–91
    father's role in, 216
    fluidity of in toddlers, 96–97
    insecure, 20
Boys' body ego, 213–216
Breast-feeding, problems weaning
    from, 44–47

Caregivers
    adapting care of toddlers to avoid
        developmental damage,
        117–120
    attitude of, 109–111
    in home, 149
    mother-toddler relationship and,
        117–120
    during separation from mother,
        108
Caring relationships, early care in
    ability to maintain, 116
Castration fear, 217
    in trauma, 134
Child
    disinvesting in, 73–74
    of divorce, 155–172
    grieving loss of parents, 173
    investment in, 26–27
    love of, 18–20
    meaning of in *Anna Karenina*,
        12–15
    mothers' response to
        developmental loss of,
        205–210
    as part of mother's body ego, 203
    response to death of newborn
        sibling, 37–38
    treatment via parent of, 156–157
Child Life workers, xi, 139
    consulting with, 141–154

Subject Index

hostile reactions to parents, 147–148
learning parents' role in hospital, 142–147
motivations of, 148–150
professional task of, 141–142
"protecting" parents, 142–145
self-assessment of, 152–154
Childbirth-death connection, 18–19
Childcare, x
Cleveland Center for Research in Child Development (CCRCD), viii
Child Analytic Clinic of, 171–172, 173–174
data on children of divorce, 155–156
Cleveland Day Nursery Association, 115
Containers, girls' interest in, 95–96
Coping mechanisms, for loss of narcissistic investment, 72–73
Core gender identity, 201–202

Day-care centers
studies of, 113–116
during World War I, 113
Death, acceptance of, 32
Decathexis, 198
Defenses
against loss, 72–73
in mourning process, 33
Defensive identification, 60
Denial, 33
in loss of part of self, 35
Depersonalization, with trauma, 125
Detachment
in infant death, 33
with loss of part of self, 35
Development
mother's narcissistic involvement and, 79–81
in one-parent family, 173–200
posttraumatic manifestations and, 137–138

Developmental interferences
with mother's anxiety, 72
from stressful separations, 111–116
Developmental loss, mothers' responses to, 205–210
Developmental phase, parenthood as, 21–28
Developmental tasks
mother's difficulty with mothering and, 120–121
of parenthood, vii–viii, 21–28
toddler care and, 117–120
of toddler phase, 101–104
Disintegration
primitive aggression with sense of, 75–76
primitive anxieties about, 207
Disinvestments, 73–74
Divorce, xi. *See also* One-parent family
in *Anna Karenina,* 157–158
children of, 155–172
child's continued relationship with parents after, 170–171
child's mental task in coping with, 159–164
data on, 155–159
nature and extent of changes with, 158–159
therapy for loss in, 174–175
"Doing for oneself" stage, 55, 59–60
"Doing for" stage, 55
"Doing with" stage, 55, 58–59
Doll play, in female body ego, 213–214
Dressing, 103
Drive defusion, 128–129
with trauma, 137–138
Drive fusion, 129
achieving and maintaining of, 172
divorce interfering with, 162–163
in normal versus pathological development, 176
in oedipal development, 176, 190
primitive degree of, 130

restoring internal circumstances to facilitate, 163–164
Dyadic relationships
  phallic, 179
  in phallic-narcissistic phase, 177

Edith Jackson Creche, 113
Ego
  integration of, 86
  partial mastery of, 70–71
Ego functions, of child, 62–63
Ego identification, 60
  consolidation and modification of, 193–194
  deficient, 197
  with lost parent, 196
Ego states, primitive, 75–79
Emotional withdrawal, 186–187
Emptiness, with infant loss, 35
Excretory functions, child's ownership and mastery of, 91–93

Failure-to-thrive infants, 29
Family
  child coping with breakup of, 159–164
  pathologies of leading to divorce, 162–163
Father
  empathy with mother, 32
  involvement with Child Life worker and hospitalized child, 144–145
  love of during phallic-oedipal phase, 176
  narcissistic cathexis of, 76–77
  relationship that resists mutual engulfing, 91–92
  role of, 216
Father-child relationship, 31–32
Female body ego
  integration of, 214–215
  nature and consequences of, 210–212
Female psychology, motherhood in, 201

Foster Parents Association, 113
Frustration tolerance, 103–104, 184

Gender
  development of, 216–217
  early development of, 89–98
  factors facilitating, 91–93
  sources of, 89
Gender identity, early steps in, 94–98
Genital organs, integration of, 94–98
Girls' body ego, 213–216
Going-on-being, interruption of, 127, 131
Good enough parenting, 152–153
Grandmothering, vii
Growing up
  developmental losses with, 51
  mother letting to and, 39–50
Guilt, healthy, 25–26

Hampstead nurseries, 113
Hanna-Perkins Center, 92–93
  Toddler-Mother Group of, 114–115
  work of, viii–ix
Hanna Perkins School
  helping mothers, 39–40
  treatment of children through parents, 21–22
  weekly interviews at, 131–132
Hanna Perkins Therapeutic School, viii, 72, 84–85
  data on children of divorce, 155–156
  divorce studies of, 171–172
  parent participation in, viii
Hanna Perkins Toddler Group, 51
Helplessness, mastering, 37
Holding environment, 124–125, 131
Home Start Project, 115
Homosexual strivings
  in object removal in adolescence, 176
  negative, 198
Hospital, parents' role in, 142–147

Subject Index

Hospitalized child, x–xi
  best parent for, 147–150
  parenting of, 141–154
  physical and emotional distance from, 30
  stress of having, 151–152
Hurt feelings, in one-parent family, 178
Hyperactivity
  castration fears and, 134
  heedless, 131

Identification, partial, 28
Independence, 39–40
Infant death, 29
  causative factors in, 29–30
  mother's response to, 204–205
Inner representation, of absent parent, 182
Inner space, 202
Instinctual energy, in early narcissistic identification of parent, 195–196
Integration
  impairment of, 128–129
  in normal versus pathological development, 176
  in oedipal development, 190
  trauma-related impairment, 137–138
Internalization, 55

Kibbutzim, effects on children, 113

Latency period
  consolidation and modification of parental identification during, 193–194
  in one-parent family, 191–197
  pathology in, 191–197
  prerequisites to constructive resolution of, 196–197
  problem management in, 197
  sudden transition into, 176, 192–193
Learning disability, parental separation and, 164–168

Libidinal energy, binding of, 129
Libidinal investment, inadequate, 179–181
Libido, imbalance of aggression with, 162–163, 171–172
Limbs, coping with loss of, 34–36
Losing things, panic over, 67–71
Loss
  child therapies for, 173–175
  mother's defenses against, 72–73
  of parent, 123–139
Love
  external sources of, 14–16
  loss of inner and outer supplies of, 4–5
Love object, acceptable, 188–189, 190
Lover, versus son in *Anna Karenina*, 4, 8–10

Male body ego
  early steps in forming, 94
  integration of, 215
Mastery
  of bodily self-care, 52–55
  in children of divorce, 169, 172
  over ambivalence and aggression, 186–188
  stages toward, 55
  wish for, 102–103
Maturational forces
  of parenthood, 22–28
  personality inhibiting, 23
"Me do," 53–54, 56
  mother's recognition of, 57–58
Melancholic mourning, 196
Metapsychology, of loss of child, 74–75
Mother
  ability to reintegrate self, 70–71
  ability to stay "in tune," 56–58
  aggression toward child, 73–74
  in *Anna Karenina*, 1–20
  auxiliary ego of, 136–137
  being there to be left, 39–50, 212
  in charge during separations, 109
  child as part of body ego of, 203

clinging to children, 41–42
defenses against loss, 72–73
difficulty of being left, 41–42
guilt and personal responsibility in, 25–26
ignoring child's ego functions, 62–63
ignoring child's tolerance for stimuli, 65
investment in newborn by, 6–8
maturing as, 28
meaning of to toddlers, 100–101
narcissistic cathexis of, 60–61
narcissistic investment of, 58–59
phase-inappropriate narcissistic investment of 61–66
primitive ego state of, 75–79
primitive panic in, 208–209
response to child's developmental loss, 205–210
response to death of baby, 204–205
sense of responsibility of, 61–62
separation from child, 11–12
special narcissistic vulnerability, 73–74
stable investment in child, 106
toddler's new relationship with, 103–104
transition from caregiver to, 119
Mother-child matrix
bodily, 216–217
father's investment in, 32
narcissistic omnipotence of, 97–98
Mother-child relationship
difficulties of, 21–22
difficulty with personality boundaries in, 84–87
interruptions of, 99
investment of, 26–27
milestones in, ix
mutual bodily investment in, 215–216
mutually object-oriented investment in, 52–55
during pregnancy, 31
prestructural personality core in, 78–79

self-care and, 51–66
self-love and gratification from 5–6
stages in, 55–61
substitute mother and, 110–111
unresolved ambivalence in, 48
Mother-infant bonding, 105–106
Mother-infant relationship, bereavement and, 30–38
Mother-son relationship
in *Anna Karenina,* 2–5
lover and, 4, 8–10
Mother-toddler relationship
factors affecting during separations, 107–111
physical togetherness of, 105–106
separations adversely affecting, 111–116
Motherhood, 201–203
central role of, 201
developmental tasks of, 21–28
flexibility and character structure in, 24–25
flexible concept of, 27–28
healthy, 10–11
infantile fantasies of, 27–28
primitive basis of, xii
psychological striving for, 202–203
Mothering
difficulty with, 120–121
early aspects of, 67–81
hallmark of, 106
interferences in, 29–30
in recuperation from trauma, 136
Motor control, enjoyment of, 101–102
Mourning, 32–34
in children, 173
as internal mental process, 34
metapsychological aspects of, 74–75
stages of, 33
types of, 196
Mutual engulfing, father-child relationship that resists, 91–92

Subject Index

Narcissistic cathexis, of father, 76–77
Narcissistic depletion, 20
Narcissistic equilibrium, 86
Narcissistic identification, early, 195–196
Narcissistic injury, 92–93
  to children of divorce, 161–162
  with child's independence, 76
  glorified picture of parents and, 195–196
  versus guilt and responsibility, 26
Narcissistic investment, 52–53, 58–59
  child's self-esteem and, 60–61
  differences in boys' and girls', 80–81
  mother's difficulty in surrendering, 213
  phase-inappropriate, 61–66
Narcissistic involvement
  developmental and adaptive aspects of, 79–81
  metapsychological aspects of, 74–75
  mother's defenses against loss of, 72–73
  panic with loss of, 67–71
  primitive ego states and, 75–79
Narcissistic vulnerability
  mother's body-ego and, 83–84
  special, 73–74
Neurosis, in parenthood, 23
Neutralization
  containing homosexual and aggressive strivings, 198–199
  in normal versus pathological development, 176
Newborn, mother's investment in, 6–8
Newborn death, ix, 29–38
  assistance to parents for, 36–38
  understanding causes of, 36–37
Nursery school, child's entry into, 39–43

Object investment, 44

transforming narcissistic investment into, 91
Object libidinal cathexes, 26–27
Object libidinal relationship, in mourning process, 75
Object-oriented investment, in mother-child relationship, 52–55
Object removal, 39–40
Object representations, tenuous, 77–78
Obsessional neurosis, 47–48
Oedipal libidinal strivings, negative, 198
Oedipal phase, in one-parent family, 182–184
Oedipal resignation, 189–190
Oedipal situation, abandoned, 167
Oedipus complex, difficulty resolving in one-parent family, 184
One-parent family, xi
  adolescence in, 197–200
  case examples of developmental problems in, 185–191, 194–197
  oedipal phase in, 182–184
  personality development and, 173–200
  phallic-narcissistic phase in, 176–191
  phallic-narcissistic predominance in, 182–183
  superego formation and latency period in, 191–197
Overstimulation, 186–187
  protection from, 92–93

Paralysis, coping with, 34–35
Parent-child relationships
  Child Life Worker interfering with, 148–150
  discontinuity of, 158
  with divorce, xi
  nature of, 31–32
  separation in due to hospitalization, x–xi

Parent death, x
  mourning of, 173
  trauma of, 123–139
  traumatic versus stressful, 124–125
Parental identification, consolidation and modification of, 193–194
Parental images, primitive introjection of, 193
Parental investment, 51
  in hospitalized child, 151–154
Parental separation
  case study of child in, 164–168
  child's mental task in coping with, 159–164
Parenthood
  developmental tasks of, vii–viii, 21–28
  experience for men versus women, 24–25
  inner struggles of, 23–24
Parenting. *See also* Mothering
  earliest stages of, 29–30
  of hospitalized child, 141–154
Parents. *See also* Father; Mother
  assistance for death of newborns, 36–38
  Child Life worker competing with, 148–150
  child's perception of imperfection of, 161–162
  continued relationship with after divorce, 170–171
  coping with death of newborn, 29–38
  death of *See* Parent death
  denial of problems of, 197
  dishonesty of, 197
  early narcissistic identification with, 195–196
  inability to maintain relationship, 160–161
  inner representation of when absent, 182
  internalization of image of, 89
  marital troubles of, 168–169
  narcissistic supplies from, 178–179
  overstimulation and emotional withdrawal from, 186–187
  respected and self-respecting, 152
  role of in hospital, 142–147
Personality boundaries, difficulty delineating, 84–87
Personality development
  bodily self-care in, 51–52
  damage to with separation, 114
  factors in for toddler, 104–106
  in one-parent family, xi, 173–200
Personality growth, mothers' aggression and, 74
Phallic fears, in one-parent family, 179
Phallic-genital impulses, 89
Phallic-narcissistic personality
  difficulties of, 199
  in superego formation, 191–194
Phallic-narcissistic position
  factors in predominance of, 183
  oedipal feelings in, 182–183
  in one-parent family, 176–182
  primitive personality of, 192–193
Phallic-narcissistic woman, 18
Phallic-oedipal phase, father's love during, 176
Phallic-sadistic excitement, uncontrollable, 93
Phallic-sexual excitement, premature and excessive stimulation of, 92–93
Phallic sexual impulses, 89
Physical togetherness, 105–106
Play, toddler's interest in, 103
Posttraumatic recuperative process, 139
Posttraumatic states, 125–126
  developmental factors in, 137–138
Pregenital ambivalence
  insufficiently fused, 169
  overcoming, 167–168
Pregnancy
  investment in newborn during, 6–8

Subject Index

mother-infant relationship during, 31
Premature infants, treatment of, 29
Primitive ego states, mother's, 75–79
Provocative misbehavior, 191–192
Pseudoloss, 208–209

Rainbow Babies and Children's Hospital, 29–30
 parental presence at, 145–146
Reaction formation, in toilet training, 90
Recovery, process of, 126–130
Rejection, mother's experience of with child's independence, 43–44
Reparation process, 125
Repetition
 passive-into-active, 132, 133, 136
 types of, 126
Repetition compulsion, 129–130
Responsibility, sense of, 25–26
Role-play, in phallic-narcissistic phase in one-parent family, 177

Sadomasochistic sexual fantasies, 186, 187
Sadomasochistic sexualization, 136
Self, coping with loss of part of, 34–36
Self-care
 mother-child relationship and, 51–66
 wish for, 102–103
Self-control, in toddler, 103–104
Self-esteem
 early care in development of, 116
 joy in bodily mastery and, 59–61
 loss of, 35
 lowered in one-parent family, 177–178, 179–181
 mastery of bodily self-care and, 52–55
 reaffirming after death of newborn, 37–38

Self-hatred, unconscious, 185
Self-investment, in baby, 211–212
Self-love
 dependent on external supplies, 14–15
 inadequate, 20
Self-object differentiation, 44
Separation, x
 caretaker attitude during, 109–110
 child's mastery of, 39–40
 child's mental task in coping with, 159–164
 due to death of parent, x
 due to divorce, xi
 due to illness of parent, x–xi
 frequency and timing of, 107
 maintaining mother-toddler relationship during, 107–111
 masterable stresses of, 111–112
 of mother and son, 11–12
 mother remaining in charge during, 109
 need for physical closeness and, 2–4
 overtaxing mother and toddler tolerance, 111–116
 problems with, 44–50
 shared preparation for, 108
 sharing mutual feelings to bridge, 104–105
Sexual gender, development of, 216–217
Sexual phallic monism, 201–202
Sexualization, of traumatic event, 129–130
Signal anxiety, 133
 failure of, 126–127
 progress toward, 136–137
"Standing by to admire" stage, 55, 56, 58–59
Stepparents
 building relationships with, 184
 relationships with, 171
Stimulation, protection from excess of, 92–93

Sublimation, 184
  containing homosexual and aggressive strivings, 198–199
Substitute mothering, 99
  mother-child relationship and, 110–111
Superego
  harsh, unintegratable, 192–193
  normal and pathlogical aspects of integrating, 176
  in one-parent family, 191–197
  with predominant phallic narcissistic personality characteristics, 191–194

Temper outbursts, 191–192
The Therapeutic Nursery School, vii–viii, 22
Thumb-sucking, 100
Toddler
  adapting care for, 116–120
  behavioral hallmarks of, 100
  boundary fluidity in, 96–97
  definition of, 99–100
  factors in personality development of, 104–106
  individual personalities of, 62–66
  lack of interest in self-care, 64
  mother and, 100–101
  protection from excess stimulation of, 92–93
  tolerance for stimuli of, 65
Toddler phase, developmental tasks of, 101–104

Toilet mastery
  in gender identity, 94–95
  mother's control of, 90
  preoccupation with, 95–96
Transference
  phenomena of, 126
  trauma reexperienced in, 137
Transitional object, 100
Trauma
  definition of, 123–126
  impaired integration and drive defusion with, 128–129
  in parentally bereaved children, 130–134
  recovery from, 126–130, 138
  reparation process for, 135–136
  treatment for, 138–139
  walled off, 137
Traumatic event, sexualization of, 129–130
Traumatic overwhelming, 127–128
Triadic relationship, father's role in, 91–92

Uncooperativeness, 56
Unruly behavior, 191–192
Unthinkable anxiety, 127

Vegetative excitement, 125, 131

Weaning, 39–50
  of mother from infant, 49–50
  potential trauma of, 43–44
  trauma of, 205
Well-being, in toddler's personality development, 104–105